DEMOCRACY IN SMALL GROUPS

DEMOCRACY IN SMALL GROUPS

Participation, Decision Making, and Communication

John Gastil

New Society Publishers
Philadelphia, PA   Gabriola Island, BC

Inquiries regarding requests to reprint all or part of *Democracy in Small Groups* should be addressed to:
    New Society Publishers
    4527 Springfield Avenue
    Philadelphia, PA 19143

ISBN USA 0-86571-273-5 Hardcover
ISBN USA 0-86571-274-3 Paperback
ISBN CAN 1-55092-216-5 Hardcover
ISBN CAN 1-55092-217-3 Paperback

Printed in the United States of America on partially recycled paper by Capital City Press of Montpelier, Vermont.

Cover art by Karen Kerney.
Cover design by Nancy Adams.
Book design by Martin Kelley.

To order directly from the publisher, add $2.50 to the price for the first copy, 75¢ each additional. Send check or money order to:
    New Society Publishers
    4527 Springfield Avenue
    Philadelphia, PA 19143
In Canada, contact:
    New Society Publishers/New Catalyst
    PO Box 189
    Gabriola Island, BC VOR 1XO

New Society Publishers is a project of the New Society Educational Foundation, a nonprofit, tax-exempt, public foundation in the United States, and of the Catalyst Education Society, a nonprofit society in Canada. Opinions expressed in this book do not necessarily represent positions of the New Society Educational Foundation, nor the Catalyst Education Society.

CONTENTS

ACKNOWLEDGMENTS

> The word democracy has been ... used and betrayed by state, party, sect, and interest. Yet it still has honest lovers, who detect in it something that has mysteriously remained immaculate and true.
>
> —Charles Lummis

I GRATEFULLY ACKNOWLEDGE all those honest lovers of democracy who have helped make this book possible. I begin by thanking those who taught me about politics and communication at Swarthmore College and the University of Wisconsin-Madison. For helping me develop my initial ideas on democratic deliberation, I thank the students in my small group communication courses, the Kettering Foundation staff, Todd Wynward, Perry Deess, Lea Haravon, Harry Boyte, Richard Merelman, and C. David Mortensen.

Fortunately this book bears little resemblance to my original manuscript. For their encouragement and suggestions, I thank Murray Edelman, Raymond Gastil, Len Krimerman, Jane Mansbridge, Roger Smith, and Phil Weiser. Readers should personally thank Barbara Hirshkowitz of New Society Publishers, because she has done everything in her power to make this book both intelligent and intelligible. Following protocol, I absolve reviewers of responsibility for the heresies and omissions in this book.

My parents, however, are complicit in this project. I thank them for dragging me to Quaker Meeting (before I was old enough to stay home), exposing me to politics at an early and impressionable age, and inspiring me to follow my dreams. Although they surely think I've gone too far, I couldn't have gotten where I am without them.

Most of all, I thank the current and former staff of Mifflin Street Community Co-op. They courageously revealed the inner life of their workplace and gave freely of their time, filling out questionnaires, participating in lengthy interviews, and making themselves available for endless questioning by the author. When they agreed to let video cameras into their meeting room, they insisted that I pursue publication. Without their gentle prodding, this book would not have been written.

John Gastil
Madison, Wisconsin
February 1993

PUBLISHER'S NOTE

WHAT PRECISELY IS democracy? For those of us who grew up in the United States of America democracy is the foundation of our politics and culture, an assumption so deep and pervasive that we are caught up short when asked to articulate its most basic principles. Apart from voting, the most easily labeled democratic practice, when do we use democracy? Exactly who and what is involved in practicing basic democratic rights?

I never really thought much about these questions and when presented with editing this book *Democracy in Small Groups* realized I could not answer questions about democracy in any coherent way. John Gastil did us the favor of deconstructing the term and terminology of democracy. He then reconstructed a clear and useful set of definitions and practices than any person or group can easily use. Best of all, he found living examples to illustrate his points and make vivid the force of democracy in action.

We all use democracy in our daily lives whatever our level of understanding. Both consciously and unconsciously, with skill or haltingly, people in groups everywhere employ democratic process. Yet we often find ourselves in frustrating situations where democratic practice is assumed to be at work but isn't working. What this book gives us, by its rigorous articulation and extended examples, is the chance to understand democracy better and to use it more fully. The reader of *Democracy in Small Groups* will find not only answers but also solutions to key problems and obstacles that block the democratic process.

John Gastil has gone beyond small groups to look at what happens with democratic processes at the micro and macro levels. The possibilities are provocative and endless—from two-person conversation to the U.N. General Assembly. The exercises given in each section are especially useful for anyone who is willing and ready to begin their search for a more democratic existence.

The benefits of democratic practice are myriad. Our country will be better served and our lives more fully shared by understanding and using what lies at the very heart of our society. For these reasons New Society Publishers is proud to present *Democracy in Small Groups: Participation, Decision Making and Communication.* I hope you both enjoy and employ the practices you find here—and let us know how it goes. Let the experiment continue.

Barbara Hirshkowitz
for New Society Publishers
June 1993

PART 1

UNDERSTANDING SMALL GROUP DEMOCRACY

INTRODUCTION

Rhonda has taught sixth grade at Eucalyptus Elementary School for ten years. She almost quit teaching when discipline problems became intolerable, but when she allowed the kids to create some of their own class activities, they became more involved and attentive. Now Rhonda holds weekly planning meetings in each of her classes. Assembled as small groups, the students make collective decisions about class projects, playtime, and which books Rhonda reads to them.

Tony wanted to get more involved in his community, so he worked as a volunteer with the Jefferson Neighborhood Council. After a year, he joined the planning board that oversaw all of the council's activities. The board met monthly and used a streamlined adaptation of Robert's Rules of Order to move briskly through numerous minor and major decisions. Tony found the meetings fast paced and rigidly moderated. Like other volunteers, he began to see the board members as distant and unreachable. After three months on the board, he quit and stopped working with the council.

Lisa and Alejandro were determined to raise their children differently from the way they had been raised. They tried to create an open, egalitarian family atmosphere for their three adopted daughters. The family jointly decided upon chore assignments and family outings, using consensus during spontaneous family meetings. The daughters became adept at arguing and, to a lesser extent, listening. When the children demanded influence over decisions about allowances, Lisa and Alejandro refused to negotiate. The children tried a short-lived strike, but the issue was eventually forgotten and tensions diffused.

THESE SCENARIOS OFFER a glimpse of the promise and problems of small group democracy. When a decision is made that involves more than one person, the decision can often be made through a democratic procedure. Whether the setting is a classroom, a community group, a family, or a senate chamber, group decision making can proceed according to democratic or undemocratic principles.

3

This book is written for those who want a better understanding of what makes a small group democratic. People usually use the word *democratic* when critiquing or praising large-scale political systems, and scholars and activists have discussed at length the meaning of large-scale democracy. Unfortunately the meaning of democracy in small groups has not been explored. Since it is difficult to bake a pie without a list of ingredients, let alone a recipe, the absence of a definition of small group democracy may partly explain why apple pie emerges from the family oven more often than democracy.

This book is also for those who want to know how to start a small democratic group or make their current groups more democratic. There will never be a cookbook for democracy, because humans and their social appetites are ever changing. Nonetheless, I think I can provide a few cooking tips. Almost everyone has encountered some of the most common group problems. Exceedingly long meetings, for example, are a ubiquitous phenomenon, and they can obstruct the democratic process in many ways. Groups that wish to proceed democratically must also find ways to adapt their procedures to compensate for large memberships, time pressures, and external power constraints.

But there is more to cooking than reading a recipe. Like anything else, democracy takes practice. By drawing on the experiences of existing groups, this book provides ideas and suggestions for those who wish to apply the principles of democracy to their social and political groups, their personal lives, and their world.

The Meaning of Democracy

In "On Participation," Hanna Pitkin and Sara Shumer explain the importance of reexamining the meaning of democracy:

> At first glance, democracy may seem a battle long won, but that is only because we pay lip service to the term without thinking about its meaning, let alone trying to live by its implications. The idea of democracy is the cutting edge of radical criticism, the best inspiration for change toward a more humane world, the revolutionary idea of our time.[1]

As people demand more power over their lives in the name of democracy, they radicalize the definition of democracy. In this way, democracy's meaning has evolved over the centuries, and the term has become applicable to what were once considered apolitical spheres of our lives. People now speak of democratic business meetings, democratic schools, democratic clubs and organizations, democratic families, and even democratic personal relationships.

Every time the definition of democracy evolves, the questions posed by Pitkin and Shumer return. What does democracy mean? How can we live by its implications? These questions are crucial. As Gregory Calvert, former national secretary of Students for a Democratic Society, argues, democratic movements are greatly constrained if they lack a clear definition of democracy.[2]

To understand the full meaning of democracy, one must seek a broader and richer definition than can be found in a dictionary or in existing governments. Democracy embodies powerful philosophical principles that have never been fully realized on large social scales. As Charles Lummis writes, democracy "describes an ideal, not a method of achieving it. It is not an ... historically existing institution, but a historical project."[3]

Democracy connotes wide-ranging liberty, including the freedom to decide one's own course in life and the right to play an equal role in forging a common destiny. Democracy means social and civil equality and a rejection of discrimination and prejudice. Democracy embraces the notion of pluralism and cultural diversity. It welcomes a wide range of perspectives and lifestyles, moving different social groups toward peaceful coexistence or respectful integration. Democracy represents the ideal of a cohesive community of people living and working together and finding fair, nonviolent ways to reconcile conflicts. In sum, democracy embodies all three elements of the famous French Revolutionary slogan, "Liberté, égalité, fraternité."[4]

Working from these principles, we can envision the contours of large-scale democratic utopias. But what would a small democratic *group* look like? How would pluralism and freedom of speech manifest themselves in smaller social groups? Should all groups strive to be democratic? These are the questions with which this book begins.

Democracy in Small Groups

All of us have taken part in small group discussions. Our small group experiences might range from joining friendly gatherings to attending meetings in business, civic, and recreational groups and organizations. We may not be experts, but we all know something about the pitfalls and potential of small group decision making.

We also have our own ideas about the democratic process. Through formal and informal education, we have learned something about both democratic ideals and the behavior of governments that call themselves democratic. For many of us democracy has come to mean elections, parliamentary debates, voting, lobbying, and the like. For others, democracy may mean open discussion, the search for common ground, and egalitarian decision making.

Despite this general knowledge, not all of us have participated in highly democratic groups. Finding information about such groups is difficult, because writings on small groups rarely discuss democracy, per se, at length. The phrase *small group democracy* is not in common use, so it is necessary to begin with a brief definition of this central term.

A *small group* consists of more than two people who have a perception of common goals, a network of communication, some interdependence, some shared norms, and a sense of wholeness.[5] The smallness of a group depends upon both absolute numbers and the intimacy of the membership. Imagine a group as a cluster of people in two-dimensional space: the more people the group has, the larger it becomes; however, the closer the members are to one another, the smaller the group becomes. For convenience's sake, we can think of small groups as having some cohesiveness and fewer than, say, thirty members.[6]

A small group is democratic if it has equally distributed decision-making power, an inclusive membership committed to democracy, healthy relationships among its members, and a democratic method of deliberation. Group deliberation is democratic if group members have equal and adequate opportunities to speak, neither withhold information nor verbally manipulate one another, and are able and willing to listen.

The Time and Place for Democracy

Given this basic definition, should all groups strive to be democratic? If not, when and where can groups use a democratic process? In answering these questions, previous authors have identified a number of key considerations.[7] In Figure 1.1 these are represented as the branches of a decision tree. This tree shows the questions that one asks when deciding whether to solve a problem democratically.

Starting at the trunk of the decision tree, one first assesses the problem. If it involves only one person, an autonomous decision can be reached. While one might wish to consult others, a group decision-making process is unnecessary.

If the problem involves merely implementing or working out the details of a previous decision, an executive (or judicial) decision-making process is in order. When a group decides to buy a computer, the membership would not ordinarily reach a fully detailed agreement and then solemnly march out the door to buy the computer. Instead, the group is more likely to authorize the finance committee to select the computer model and accessories (a matter of detail) and give the treasurer responsibility for handling any problems that arise in making the purchase (a matter of implementation).

If the problem is of no concern to group members, an executive or delegated decision might be in order. Thus a member of a worker-owned

Figure 1.1 Decision Tree for Small Group Democracy

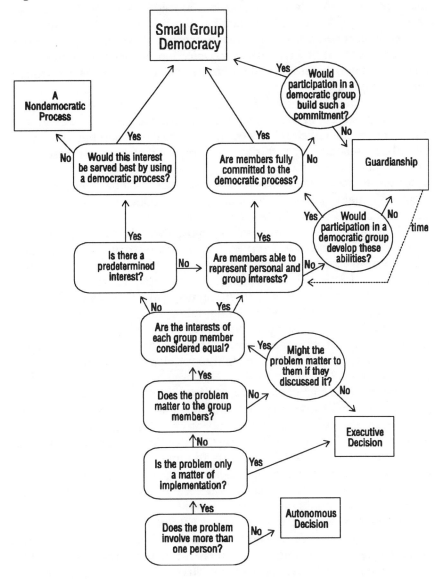

supplier, because the members have expressed no interest in who sells them wood, so long as it is inexpensive.

But note the question in the first oval: might the problem matter to group members if they discussed it? This question raises the possibility that the members would care about a problem if they had the information or insight required to understand it. This question (like the other two questions in ovals) views the decision-making process as a means for changing the character of the membership. It recognizes the dynamic quality of the discussion process. In the case of the aforementioned lumber purchase, workers might wish to boycott the visiting supplier if they learned through discussion that the supplier was nonunion or responsible for clear-cutting.[8]

If the problem is a serious matter to the group as a whole, the decision tree then poses the most difficult question: are the interests of all group members considered equal? This is not a factual question but a moral or ethical one. A *no* answer to this question implies that, for some reason, the interests of an individual or a subgroup have priority over the interests of other group members. A *yes* means that each member's interests are weighed equally in making a decision. Who decides the answer to this question? That is the crux of many a conflict.

Following the imagery of classical philosopher John Locke, if I were to pick my share of acorns and apples, a group of passersby could claim that I should form a group with them and collectively decide what to do with the food I had gathered. But I could reply that I have the right to do what I please with my food, since I gathered it using my own labor.[9]

One might sympathize with the humble gatherer, but in the modern marketplace, matters are more complicated. Does a factory worker have the right to play a role in management or earn a share of company profits? Do community members have a right to regulate local businesses or tax property owners?[10]

Aside from economic matters, are the interests of a spouse or partner given equal weight when the other is contemplating a career change? Are the disapproving views of my neighbors to be weighed equally with my own preferences when I wish to play my Electric Light Orchestra record on a Saturday afternoon? The criteria for answering these questions of inclusiveness are suggested in chapter 2. For present purposes, it is enough to recognize the difficulty of determining when the interests of different people should receive equal weight.[11]

If the interests of group members are considered unequal, an individual (or subgroup) with exclusive authority might still yield decision-making power to the group, simply because there is no predetermined interest or objective. When the individual *does* have an objective, one simply employs the decision-making process that best realizes it. Thus a hypothetical author with a preexisting goal (i.e., making a forthcoming book as good as possible) might choose to forgo a fully democratic review process, believing that such a process would not result in the best possible book. By contrast, an orchard manager might decide that her self-interested goal (profits and high-quality produce) is best served by empowering the orchard workers to make collective decisions about their working hours and conditions.[12]

When the interests of all group members are considered equal, different steps may be needed to ensure that equality. If group members are not the best representatives of their own interests or are incapable of effectively participating in democratic deliberation, guardianship may be the best form of decision making.[13] The term *guardian* is more commonly used in the case of minors or mentally incapacitated individuals—people who require an adult to take responsibility for seeing that their best interests are served.[14] But groups of competent adults can also select provisional guardianship. For example, the members of a political action committee might consider each other's interests as equal, yet choose to let a skilled and experienced member make the decisions about an upcoming press conference. This member becomes the group's guardian with respect to the conference.

More generally, groups usually have goals besides democracy, such as being productive at some group task. If a group holds a goal above that of democracy, it might choose to appoint a group member or hire a nonmember to make a particular decision on its behalf. In effect, the members decide that a provisional guardian will better serve their interests than they would if they acted as a democratic group.[15] Thus a cooperative housing board might send a co-op dispute into binding arbitration under the assumption that the use of a neutral third party will result in a sound decision and avoid the frustration and division that could accompany any further group deliberation on the matter.

In Figure 1.1 note the dashed arrow on the decision tree that moves away from guardianship. This line suggests that with the passage of time, the characteristics of the membership must be reexamined. Ideally a system of guardianship develops the skills and character of its members. This idea underlies the authority of teachers and mentors, many of whom strive to make their students or apprentices fully capable and independent.

In addition, groups must consider whether members assumed incapable of democratic deliberation might become sufficiently skilled through participation in the democratic process.[16] A child unfamiliar with group deliberation might be restless and confused at first but become adept over time.

If some group members do not value democracy, they might willfully or carelessly subvert the democratic process. As with deliberative skills, democratic values might emerge through participation, but it is necessary to gauge whether they would develop in time before the process was subverted. If the danger of subversion is high, guardianship might be appropriate. With this concern in mind, a community improvement board might ask that new board members serve as advisers or observers for their first two meetings, becoming full members only after developing an appreciation for the board's democratic process.

If these questions lead to the conclusion that small group democracy is appropriate, the last consideration is whether there is adequate time for deliberation. If an approaching deadline requires an immediate decision, the group can quickly vote, but this is far from optimal (see chapter 6). If time permits deliberation, then the group can go through a fully democratic process, eventually arriving at a decision.

The decision tree suggests that while some situations do not lend themselves to the democratic process, a broad range of situations do. Consider the three groups mentioned at the beginning of this chapter. Each one has decisions that can be made through a democratic process.

The sixth grade class learned a great deal by making some of its decisions democratically. At the same time, no matter how sophisticated a class of sixth graders became at using the democratic process, they would not be given authority over many other school issues, such as staff hiring and student expulsions. In such cases school decision structures amount to guardianship, because it is presumed that the children are not best at representing their own interests, let alone those of the staff and community.

In the second example, the Jefferson Neighborhood Council is ignoring or shielding itself from volunteer and community input. Presuming the volunteers are competent and capable of democratic participation, there is no reason for the council to prevent them from speaking their minds. Unless the council becomes more receptive, the volunteers might prefer moving to a direct system of decision making, eliminating the representative council altogether.

Finally, the parents of the three daughters have found that many family decisions are best made democratically. The parents forgo democracy only when the interests of each family member are not of equal consideration (e.g., Lisa deciding largely by herself what career she will pursue) or when they believe the children are not best equipped to represent themselves. In this family, as in other groups, democracy is often the most appropriate method of reaching a decision.

I am willing to speculate that if small group democracy were better understood and appreciated, more groups would attempt to make decisions democratically. The publication of this book is an attempt to test the wisdom of this speculation.

Notes

Portions of this chapter are reprinted with the permission of Plenum Publications from John Gastil, "A Definition and Illustration of Democratic Leadership," *Human Relations,* in press.

1. Hanna F. Pitkin and Sara M. Shumer, "On Participation," *democracy* 2 (1982): 43.

2. In *Democracy from the Heart: Spiritual Values, Decentralism, and Democratic Idealism in the Movement of the 1960s* (Eugene, Ore.: Communitas Press, 1991), Gregory N. Calvert makes this argument with regard to the New Left of the 1960s. Similarly, John Burnheim, in *Is Democracy Possible? The Alternative to Electoral Politics* (Berkeley: University of California Press, 1985), argues that "the lack of any clear and plausible view of how a socialist society might work is ... the main obstacle to significant radical activity" (p. 12). He states that Marxists in particular have been hamstrung by their failure to articulate an adequate theory of democracy (pp. 189–190).

3. Charles Douglas Lummis, "The Radicalism of Democracy," *democracy* 2 (1992): 9–10. In arguing that no national political system should be called a democracy, I am following Robert A. Dahl's usage of the term in *Democracy and Its Critics* (New Haven, Conn.: Yale University Press, 1989). Dahl created the neologism *polyarchy* to describe certain forms of representative government. Democracy remains a noble ideal that ought to be pursued, but large-scale systems can only approach it, never fully reaching it. On the danger of labeling an existing system a democracy, see chapter 2, n. 3, below.

When generally defined, *democracy* is broad enough "to allow ample scope for the more elaborated and specific definitions" (Anthony Arblaster, *Democracy* [Open University Press: Milton Keynes, 1987], 8), such as the one I propose for small group democracy. For attempts to cluster different definitions used by politicians, activists, and scholars into different types of democracy, see Benjamin Barber, *Strong Democracy* (Berkeley: University of California Press, 1984); David Held, *Models of Democracy* (Oxford: Polity Press, 1986); C. B. Macpherson, *The Life and Times of Liberal Democracy* (Oxford: Oxford University Press, 1977); Jane J. Mansbridge, *Beyond Adversary Democracy* (Chicago: University of Chicago Press, 1983). For surveys of definitions currently in use, see Raymond D. Gastil, "Varieties of Democracy" (paper presented at the United States Agency for International Development's Perspectives on Democracy Conference, Nepal, India, 1992); Alex Inkeles, ed., *On Measuring Democracy* (New Brunswick, N.J.: Transaction Press, 1991), part I. For a critical history of the term in Western political theory see John Hoffman, *Marxism, Revolution, and Democracy* (Amsterdam: B. R. Gruner Publishing, 1983), chap. 3.

Given these diffuse meanings, one might argue that the term ought to be scrapped altogether. In response I take the position of Samuel Bowles and Herbert Gintis, who also choose to work with the term. Their choice to do so "reflects a recognition of both the hegemony of liberal democratic discourse as the virtually exclusive medium of political communication in advanced capitalist nations and the profoundly contradictory, malleable, and potentially radical nature of this discourse": *Democracy and Capitalism: Property, Community, and the Contradictions of Modern Social Thought* (New York: Basic Books, 1986), 209.

4. As just one example, Mahatma Gandhi connected democracy with many other moral principles, prominently including nonviolence. See the discussions by S. M. Tewari and G. Ramachandran in Krishna Kumar, ed., *Democracy and Nonviolence* (New Delhi: Gandhi Peace Foundation, 1968).

One might claim that such a broad use of the term *democracy* simply ties it to everything good. However, democracy and the ideas historically associated with it have always had their critics in the Western world. What is taken for granted today was unpopular or highly controversial in previous years. See Michael Levin, *The Spectre of Democracy: The Rise of Modern Democracy as Seen by Its Critics* (New York: New York University Press, 1992).

In any case, many authors have argued that a fully adequate definition of democracy has an ethical dimension. On the relationship between empirical and moral definitions see Dahl, *Democracy and Its Critics*, 6–8; on the inseparability of democracy and ethics see Claes G. Ryn, *Democracy and the Ethical Life: A Philosophy of Politics and Community*, 2d ed. (Washington, D.C.: Catholic University of America Press, 1990), esp. chap. 1.

5. This definition is based upon that of Arthur D. Jensen and Joseph C. Chilberg, *Small Group Communication* (Belmont, Calif.: Wadsworth, 1991), 8–16. Instead of discussing the full range of group activities, this book focuses on group meetings. In *The Meeting: Gatherings in Organizations and Communities* (New York: Plenum, 1989), 7, anthropologist Helen Schwartzman provides an excellent definition of what constitutes a meeting. In her view, it is "a communicative event involving three or more people who agree to assemble for a purpose ostensibly related to the functioning of an organization or group.... A meeting is characterized by multiparty talk that is episodic in nature, and participants either develop or use specific conventions (e.g., *Robert's Rules of Order*) for regulating talk."

6. Hereafter I use the terms *group* and *small group* interchangeably. Kirkpatrick Sale, in *Human Scale* (New York: G. P. Putnam's Sons, 1980), suggests that the ideal size for small face-to-face groups is somewhere between seven and twenty people, but there can be no simple delineation between small and large groups. Moreover, other factors—such as cohesiveness and familiarity—enter into how large people consider their group.

7. For a more detailed discussion see John Gastil, "A Definition and Illustration of Democratic Leadership," *Human Relations* (in press). Sources for the decision tree include Dahl, *Democracy and Its Critics*, 85, 97–98, 100; Franklyn S. Haiman, *Group Leadership and Democratic Action* (Boston: Houghton-Mifflin, 1951); Ronald A. Heifetz and Riley M. Sinder, "Political Leadership: Managing the Public's Problem Solving," in Robert Reich, ed., *The Power of Public Ideas* (Cambridge, Mass.: Ballinger, 1987), 179–203; Norman R. F. Maier, *Principles of Human Relations* (New York: John Wiley & Sons, 1952); Marshall Sashkin, "Participative Management Is an Ethical Imperative," *Organizational Dynamics* 12, no. 4 (1984): 5–22; Victor H. Vroom and Arthur G. Jago, *The New Leadership* (Englewood Cliffs, N.J.: Prentice Hall, 1988).

8. The question in the oval parallels an ongoing philosophical debate about whether public policy should respond to people's raw preferences or their informed judgments. This is a classic problem in Western political theory. For example, Mill forced utilitarians to grapple with the question of "lower" and "higher" pleasures. See John S. Mill, *Utilitarianism and Other Writings* (New York: Meridian, 1962). In recent years numerous philosophers have sided with the view that a person's existing preferences must be distinguished from what might be called potential preferences, enlightened judgments, or fundamental interests. See Benjamin Barber, "Opinion Polls: Public Judgment or Private Prejudice," *The Responsive Community* 2, no. 2, (1992): 4-6; Bowles and Gintis, *Democracy and Capitalism*, chap. 5; Michael Briand, "Value, Policy, and the Indispensability of Politics" (Kettering Foundation, Dayton, Ohio, 1991, manuscript); Bernard Manin, "On Legitimacy and Political Deliberation," trans. Elly Stein and Jane Mansbridge, *Political Theory* 15 (1987): 338–68; Claus Offe and Ulrich K. Preuss, "Democratic Institutions and Moral Resources," in David Held, ed., *Political Theory Today* (Stanford, Calif.: Stanford University Press, 1991), 143–71; Daniel Yankelovich, *Coming to Public Judgment* (New York: Syracuse University Press, 1991).

9. See John Locke, *Two Treatises of Government* (Cambridge: Cambridge University Press, 1960), Second Treatise, chap. 5.

10. As one prominent example, there is much debate about the existence of an ethical imperative for democracy in the workplace. See Peter Bachrach and Aryeh Botwinick, *Power and Empowerment: A Radical Theory of Participatory Democracy* (Philadelphia: Temple University Press, 1992); Robert N. Bellah et al., *The Good Society* (New York: Alfred A. Knopf, 1991); Carole Pateman, *Participation and Democratic Theory* (Cambridge: Cambridge University Press, 1970); Sashkin, "Participative Management." For a series of individual case studies and an excellent list of resources and writings, see Len Krimerman and Frank Lindenfeld, *When Workers Decide: Workplace Democracy Takes Root in North America* (Philadelphia: New Society Publishers, 1991). On the ethics of democracy and the economy, see Bowles and Gintis, *Democracy and Capitalism*; Joshua Cohen and Joel Rogers, *On Democracy* (New York: Penguin Books, 1983); Barry Schwartz, *The Battle for Human Nature* (New York: W. W. Norton, 1986).

11. The musical example is inspired by Robert Nozick's idiosyncratic hypothetical examples in *Anarchy, State, and Utopia* (New York: Basic Books, 1974). Among other things, his work addresses consent and obligation, two issues related to inclusiveness.

12. The experimental literature on the relative "productivity" of democratic groups has focused on the effects of member participation and democratic leadership styles. For reviews, see Bernard M. Bass, *Bass & Stogdill's Handbook of Leadership* (New York: Free Press, 1990); John Gastil, "A Meta-analytic Review of the Productivity and Satisfaction of Democratic and Autocratic Leadership," *Small Group Research* (in press); Katherine I. Miller and Peter R. Monge, "Participation, Satisfaction, and Productivity: A Meta-analytic Review," *Academy of Management Journal* 29 (1986): 727–53; George Strauss, "Worker Participation in Management: An International Perspective," *Research in Organizational Behavior* 4 (1982): 173–265; John Simmons and William Mares, *Working Together* (New York: Alfred A. Knopf, 1983).

More generally, recent research has dispelled the "camel committees" myth that individuals are usually better than groups at making efficient, high-quality decisions. One particularly rigorous study on this question found that groups outperformed the most proficient individual group member 97 percent of the time: Larry K. Michaelsen, Warren E. Watson, and Robert H. Black, "A Realistic Test of Individual Versus Group Consensus Decision Making," *Journal of Applied Psychology* 74 (1989): 834–9. See also Vroom and Jago, *The New Leadership*; Richard H. G. Field, Peter C. Read, and Jordan J. Louviere, "The Effect of Situation Attributes on Decision Method Choice in the Vroom-Jago Model of Participation in Decision Making," *Leadership Quarterly* 1 (1990): 165–76; Warren Watson, Larry K. Michaelsen, and Walt Sharp, "Member Competence, Group Interaction, and Group Decision Making: A Longitudinal Study," *Journal of Applied Psychology* 76 (1991): 803–9.

13. For an excellent critique of guardianship see Dahl, *Democracy and Its Critics*. A proponent of guardianship may argue that although group members are capable of representing themselves, a democratic process may not give *equal* consideration to each member's interests. Dahl argues, however, that it is necessary to "demonstrate that the democratic process fails to give equal consideration to the interests of some who are subject to its laws; that the quasi guardians will do so; and that the injury inflicted on the right to equal consideration outweighs the injury done to the right of a people to govern itself" (p. 192).

14. Some of the dangers of legal guardianship for persons deemed incompetent are discussed by Madelyn A. Iris, "Threats to Autonomy in Guardianship Decision Making," *Generations* 14 (1990): 39–41.

15. Groups in such situations can still choose to retain *ultimate* authority, weakening the position of the guardian.

16. Many democratic theorists and activists have stressed this point. As John Dewey argued, "The foundation of democracy is faith in the capacities of human nature; faith in human intelligence, and in the power of pooled and cooperative experience. It is not belief that these things are complete, but that if given a show they will grow and be able to generate progressively the knowledge and wisdom needed to guide collective action": quoted in David Fott, "John Dewey and the Philosophical Foundations of Democracy," *Social Science Journal* 28 (1991): 33. On the educational effects of participation, see Mark Warren, "Democratic Theory and Self-Transformation," *American Political Science Review* 86 (1992): 8–23.

2

SMALL GROUP DEMOCRACY

> In the small group ... is where we shall find the inner meaning of democracy, its heart and core.[1]
>
> —Mary Parker Follett

IN THE EARLY part of this century, Mary Parker Follett called for studying democracy in small groups—the "heart and core" of democracy. Since that time activists, philosophers, social critics, and political scientists have discussed the subject. Their writings, though brief and only partial, provide a starting point. These works, combined with the vast literature on large-scale democracy, provide pieces of fabric that can be trimmed into patches and sewn together, making a quilt that displays the essential features of a small democratic group.[2]

I begin by introducing the concept of a *demos*, a useful shorthand term for a body of people who govern themselves democratically. The demos is usually a large social group, such as a nation or state, but it can also refer to smaller democratic groups. I define small group democracy by specifying the features of an *ideal* demos. The ideal is unattainable, but it is something that a group can strive toward. A group will never become fully democratic, but one can describe it in terms of its distance from the ideal.[3]

Table 2.1 outlines the definition of small group democracy that I propose. Democratic groups exhibit certain forms of power, inclusiveness, commitment, relationships, and deliberation. A group is democratic to the degree it shows these characteristics. In what follows, I clarify the meaning of each of these features.

15

Table 2.1   A Definition of Small Group Democracy

I. Group power
    A. Group sovereignty
    B. Equal distribution of ultimate authority
II. Inclusiveness
III. Commitment to the democratic process
IV. Relationships
    A. Acknowledgment of individuality
    B. Affirmation of competence
    C. Recognition of mutuality
    D. Congeniality
V. Deliberation
    A. Speaking rights and responsibilities
        1. agenda setting
        2. reformulation
        3. informing
        4. articulation
        5. persuasion
        6. voting
        7. dissent
    B. Listening rights and responsibilities
        1. comprehension
        2. consideration

Group Power

In his most recent work, *Democracy and Its Critics*, Robert Dahl insists that in a democracy, "the people must have the final say." Democratic groups must have jurisdiction over the items that appear on their agendas. After all, the fundamental meaning of democracy is self-government, and meaningful governance requires power.[4]

If a group has no power, its meetings can never be democratic. If a factory work team can make suggestions but not policy, it would be misleading to say that the team's deliberations are democratic. If the team had control over work schedules but not product design, it could deliberate democratically about times but not products. Merely discussing products is insufficient: "Democracy involves debate and discussion, but these are not enough if they remain inconclusive and ineffective in determining actual policies."[5]

Given the primary importance of power in defining small group democracy, it is necessary to specify the meaning of this elusive word. I broadly construe power as the capacity to influence the future behavior of objects or the behavior, beliefs, and emotions of living beings, including oneself. One can use power to do something, or to prevent or delay something from being done. When one's power is directed inward, it is the power to do something by and for oneself (e.g., the willpower to quit smoking). When one's power is directed outward, power is exerted against, over, or with someone or something else.[6]

Power resides both in individuals and in groups. Individuals have the power to accomplish things by themselves, but sometimes an individual's power is inconsequential unless combined with the power of others. Imagine yourself trying to carry a grand piano up a staircase single-handedly. The feat is impossible for one person, but a dozen people—none of whom has the individual power to move a piano—can do it by combining their strength.[7]

It is important to emphasize that power includes influence over one's own behavior. The ultimate aim of consciousness-raising groups is often social change, but the immediate goal is making individuals aware of the behavioral choices before them—the previously unacknowledged power they have in their own lives. Catharine A. MacKinnon explains that women's participation in consciousness-raising groups reveals to them that patriarchy depends upon traditional daily social behaviors. Women have the power to change the structure of male supremacy, because it has always depended upon their compliance. "Although it is one thing to act to preserve power relations and quite another to act to challenge them," MacKinnon explains, "once it is seen that these relations require daily acquiescence, acting on different principles, even in small ways, seems not quite so impossible."[8]

When power is thought of in this way, it loses many of its usual connotations. Power does not have to imply domination and subordination, nor does the use of power necessarily entail coercion, violence, or corruption. Power can signify an individual or collective capacity that does not rob others of their abilities. Any egalitarian, peaceful social movement will have a great deal of power, derived neither from a superior status in an institutionalized hierarchy nor threat and intimidation. Power lies in the collective will of the movement, and the decisions and actions made with this force can be nonviolent and noncoercive.[9]

In any case, it is not enough for a democratic group to have power. A demos distributes its power among the group members. Everyone in a small democratic group must have some form of influence or control, and all members must *ultimately* have equal power with regard to group policies. Some members may be more influential than others, and they may make more decisions by themselves or in committees. But final group authority must be divided evenly among group members, through a procedure like consensus or majority rule.[10]

Following this principle, a teachers' union could give day-to-day authority over dues collection to a treasurer or finance committee, while still retaining final authority over the budget and every other union policy. The union always has the power to overrule any decision made by the single member or committee.

Inclusiveness

The teachers' union example leads to another issue. Assume, for the moment, that the union members have equal final authority. If untenured teachers are excluded, is the group democratic? If the union makes decisions that do not affect the untenured faculty, it might be democratic. On the other hand, if untenured teachers must pay whatever dues the union decrees, were the union's dues set democratically?

Dahl calls this a question of *inclusiveness*. People who are significantly affected by the decisions of a demos ought to have full and equal decision-making power within it. Unfortunately this seemingly straightforward requirement presents a paradox: which comes first, the scope of the demos's power or its membership? If a group agrees to make decisions that affect only its members, it avoids this problem; however most groups, like the teachers' union, make decisions that directly and indirectly affect many nonmembers.[11]

For the vast majority of groups, there is no easy solution to this problem. Groups can meet the criterion only by degree. In light of this difficulty, I suggest a clarification of the principle of inclusiveness: a democratic group strives to include those people who are *profoundly* affected by its decisions, invite those *significantly* affected, and at least consider the views of those *marginally* affected.[12]

A cooperative running a bookstore, for example, might decide that all of its managerial decisions have a profound effect upon the members of the collective (a.k.a. the employees), so every staff member has equal decision-making power at the store's biweekly planning meetings. The staff discovers that its decisions also significantly affect both volunteers and customers, so the staff informs volunteers and customers of upcoming meetings and welcomes their attendance. Since the store's policies marginally affect the larger community and local authors, the staff decides to hold an annual community meeting (disguised as a festival to encourage attendance) and posts a sign inviting authors to speak at any time with the staff.

This example shows an attempt to bring people into direct, face-to-face contact with the group, but inclusion can also mean considering the views and concerns of people not physically present. With this in mind, the cooperative could establish a general rule of never making crucial decisions when a staff member was unable either to attend a meeting or to vote by proxy. The staff could also keep in touch with volunteer and customer feelings and opinions on a day-to-day basis, then raise these concerns during biweekly planning meetings. The staff could also keep the larger community in mind when making its decisions.[13]

This broad definition of inclusiveness must be qualified in two respects. As John Burnheim argues, "Nobody should have any input into decision-making where they have no legitimate material interest." By "material," Burnheim aims to exclude "intrusive desires about how others should fare." Thus the book co-op pays no heed to the religious zealots who are offended by the store's books on bisexuality. By "legitimate," Burnheim rejects interests that are not "based on entitlements that are morally sound." Thus the co-op's donations committee refuses to consider requests for financial assistance from an organization that engages in unethical activities. In both cases, the zealots and the organization are "affected" by the group's decisions, yet the groups are excluded on the grounds that their affected interests are either intrusive or illegitimate.[14]

In addition Dahl argues that a demos "must include all adult members of the association except transients and persons proved to be mentally defective." Under exceptional circumstances a demos can exclude people even if their legitimate material interests are profoundly and directly affected by group decisions. These exceptions include infants and (in some cases) young children, persons who are just passing through the group's jurisdiction, and people, such as those with severe mental disabilities, who are utterly incapable of making sound decisions on their own behalf or as members of a group.[15]

Commitment

Small democratic groups have goals other than democracy, but all of these are secondary to the goal to reach decisions through a democratic process.[16] As Joshua Cohen argues, the members of a demos must share "a commitment to coordinating their activities within institutions that make deliberation possible and according to norms that they arrive at through their deliberation."[17] Group members must internalize democratic values and respect group decisions that are both reached democratically and consistent with democratic principles.

A democratic group develops a set of bylaws or unwritten group norms that protect it against undemocratic maneuvers, and both new and old members need to learn and appreciate the letter and spirit of these procedures. When new members are included in the group, it is important that they develop a strong commitment to the democratic features of the group's decision-making process.[18]

If a group member does not like a democratic decision and refuses to follow it, the member can voluntarily withdraw from the group or accept some penalty for refusing to follow the decision. This requirement guards against those group members who adhere to democratic principles only when they like the group's decisions.[19]

It is important to stress that fully democratic decisions must be arrived at democratically and have no effects inconsistent with democracy. The decision-making process cannot involve undemocratic actions—such as letting a group facilitator or chair make autocratic decisions, or scheduling a meeting at a time meant to exclude a member who holds a dissenting opinion. Also, the group decision must not contradict the principles of small group democracy. For instance, a group decision is undemocratic if it institutes an exclusionary membership policy or places all ultimate authority in the hands of one group member. More generally, political philosopher James Fishkin requires democratic groups to adhere to the principle of nontyranny: they must not allow the majority to rob the minority of its democratic rights. The moment a group makes such a decision, it becomes less democratic.[20]

This highlights the need for a firm commitment to the democratic process. Groups can establish their own set of democratic principles in an oral tradition or in written bylaws, but no matter how precise, these principles always have to be interpreted. If members do not make the effort to reflect upon, practice, and internalize their democratic group norms, their interpretations may be well intended but undemocratic.

For example, a parliamentary group might not challenge or override an autocratic decision of the chair. A community development organization might interpret inclusiveness in increasingly narrow terms, excluding all but an inner circle of members. In both cases, the groups might think their processes and decisions are consistent with democratic principles, but they are not. A firm commitment to the democratic process might prevent such misinterpretations.

Relationships

Besides sharing a commitment to democracy, the members of a small democratic group enjoy a special kind of relationship with one another—a way of relating that is consistent with and conducive to the democratic process.[21] Relationships form through shared experiences and the exchange of words carrying relational meanings for group members.

Formalized salutations and polite forms of address are some of the most obvious ways our words convey relational messages. Even when a group reviews a treasurer's report, members are often subtly discussing how they think and feel about the treasurer, other group members, and the group as a whole. The utterance "That was an excellent report" does more than reassure the treasurer of her fiscal acumen.[22]

According to John Dewey, a fully democratic group respects both the individuality and competence of every member of the demos. The words and deeds of group members create a friendly atmosphere that recognizes the bonds that hold the group together.[23] Jane Mansbridge adds that when there is a relative conflict of interest among the members of the demos, mutuality and congeniality ought to play a lesser role. Groups with contradictory interests might deemphasize these forms of relationship, because in such groups there is a greater potential for using appeals to cohesiveness and friendliness as means for manipulating the membership.[24]

A neighborhood improvement group consisting of like-minded neighbors might place greater emphasis on member relationships, because all members of this voluntary association share the common goal of improving neighborhood parks and assisting members of the community. In this group, cementing friendships and emphasizing common identities only strengthens the group. In a city council, though, there might be sharp conflicts of interest, say, between developers and those favoring an end to urban development, and between suburbanites and inner-city residents. Although the council needs a minimum of shared identity and fellowship to proceed democratically, appeals to commonality can disguise real conflicts of interest. It is possible for such a group to move toward common interests over time, but an honest adversarial relationship is better than a false unity.

Having established these general criteria, we can consider the four forms of relationship in more detail. For the most part each manifests itself in the form of verbal and nonverbal communication, so I discuss each as a form of talk.[25]

Acknowledging Individuality

Recognizing a person's individuality begins with differentiating a member from the group as a whole. When one acknowledges the individuality of a group member, one addresses the person as an individual and explicitly affirms the person's individual identity and interests in relation to those of the group. Similarly, one can acknowledge one's own individuality: "That's all I can give right now while I'm a student, and that's the choice I've made."

The opposite is the denial of a member's individuality—the assertion that a member's identity and interests are or should be subordinate to those of the group as a whole. For instance, at one group meeting I observed, a member insisted that her personal needs were paramount at the moment—that she had chosen to act according to her own interests. To this another member responded, "A collective is not where everybody can do what they want and get their needs met, and struggle for their needs, but rather what a collective needs to be is a unit that works for the collective."[26]

In *Rethinking Democracy*, Carol Gould explains why it is important that democratic group members acknowledge one another's individuality. Democracy, she writes, can be "fully effective only if … people generally relate to each other as equals and with respect for each other's individual differences and interests. For the very process of participatory democratic decision making entails such reciprocal recognition."[27]

Affirming Competence

As a member of a demos, one assumes that no one else is a more competent judge of what is in one's own interests. More important, one generalizes this assumption to others, so that individual group members are seen as their own best judges. "You know yourself better than I do" is a clear affirmation, whereas "Maybe I should decide for you" questions this form of competence.[28]

This idea derives from Dahl's "strong principle of equality." In accordance with this principle, the members of a demos assume that all other members are qualified to participate in making the group's collective decisions. At the very least, members assume that no members "are so definitely better qualified than the others that they should be entrusted with making the … decisions."[29]

It seems reasonable to go a step further. Democratic groups assume that all members are capable of judging what is best *for the group*. Members will sometimes misjudge what is in the group's best interest, but no member is thought so superior at such judgment that other members are deemed incompetent. As Chai Ling, a student leader of the Chinese prodemocracy movement, explains, "Each must have simple faith in other people's intelligence and ability to choose."[30] A group member could affirm the competence of others by simply saying, "I think we should hear from everyone on this, because we all have different visions of the future of this organization."

Recognizing Mutuality

Mutuality is "the willingness to be connected, to take on another's well being, to recognize oneself in the other," so affirming mutuality consists of highlighting the interconnection and common identity of group members.[31] Referring to others as "the group" and "the team"—or even simply "us" or "we"—can constitute a recognition of mutuality. More explicitly, the speaker can ask members to think and act as a group: "We need as a group, as a collective, to figure out a way to get beyond the resentment that taints future negotiations about those same things."[32]

Just as Carol Gould identifies the importance of individuality, she also stresses the need for recognizing how our individual identity is connected to our social relations. In her view, a member of a demos is an individual, yet the individual's identity *as a group member* comes from social relations—from membership in a social group. Thus people require "reciprocal recognition" to establish their individuality. The members of the demos all reciprocally recognize one another's membership so that they may identify *themselves* as a part of the demos. Any one member's identity as a part of the whole is contingent upon the identities of the others.[33]

Congeniality

As defined herein, congeniality is the development and preservation of positive emotional relationships and a neighborly or friendly group atmosphere. It includes expressions of kindness, empathy, sympathy, and praise. *Congeniality* may be the best word, because it covers a wide range of positive communication—from formal cordiality and acquaintance to more intimate and informal friendliness and companionship.

Congeniality can be expressed with humor, such as when a member of a group I observed once joked about the cleanliness of the cellar: "I still think we should just give everybody a shovel and start digging out the basement." It can also take a more direct form, such as when another group member remarked, "I'm just ever so grateful that Steve and Amy and Ray put in the time that they did to get us to this point."[34]

The opposite of congenial talk is rude, hostile, or belittling communication. It can appear in subtle forms, such as a condescending or threatening tone of voice, or in a more blatant manner: "I have to ask you all and beg and plead if I want to even take off a fucking weekend." Sometimes this negative speech is a combination of word choice and tone, as in the following quip, which the speaker delivered rapidly and loudly: "Sometimes I get kinda frustrated with us, because we just want to do everything for the political pureness of it."

Congeniality aids small group democracy the way a lubricant greases gears, soothing irreconcilable conflicts of interest or moving individual group members toward a common vision. Mansbridge points out that Aristotle and other theorists have conceived of democracy as nothing less than the political extension of friendship.[35] In less unified groups, Barber suggests that congeniality can serve as a substitute for friendship: "A neighbor is a stranger transformed by empathy and shared interests into a friend—an *artificial* friend, however, whose kinship is a contrivance of politics rather than natural or personal and private."[36]

If a discussion of congeniality seems too far afield from more traditional conceptions of the democratic process, one need only turn to the stodgy classic *Robert's Rules of Order*, whose innumerable conventions are partly aimed at maintaining decorum. This emphasis on civility, if not friendship, parallels the commonplace expectation that citizens should show tolerance toward one another in a large-scale political system.[37]

Deliberation

Healthy relationships provide an appropriate setting for open and constructive deliberation: discussion that involves judicious argument, critical listening, and earnest decision making. A deliberative process includes a careful examination of a problem or issue, the identification of possible solutions, the establishment or reaffirmation of evaluative criteria, and the use of these criteria in identifying an optimal solution.[38]

Some modern democratic theorists have tried to revitalize conventional understandings of democracy by emphasizing the role of deliberation in the democratic process. In *Deliberation and Democracy*, Fishkin argues that democracy means more than political equality. Advocates of democracy, he writes, have focused their energy on building "a system which grants equal consideration to everyone's preferences and which grants everyone appropriately equal opportunities to formulate preferences on the issues under consideration."[39] Such equality is essential, but it does not encompass the full meaning of democracy. In Fishkin's view, equating democracy with political equality "neglects the deliberation needed to make democratic choices meaningful." Our preferences are not always well developed: if they are "unreflective or ignorant," they "lose their claim to political authority over us." Since it is through collective discussion and judgment that our preferences become reflective and informed, deliberation is necessary "if the claims of democracy are not to be de-legitimated."[40]

Joshua Cohen is another modern theorist who emphasizes the importance of deliberation. Cohen argues that a fully democratic group uses an "ideal deliberative procedure" that has four main features. First, participants view themselves as bound only by decisions arrived at through legitimate deliberation. Second, the members of the demos put forward their reasons for advancing, supporting, or criticizing proposals. Third, the process is designed to treat participants equally, and there are no power or resource differences that "shape their chances to contribute to deliberation" or "play an authoritative role in ... deliberation." Finally, "ideal deliberation aims to arrive at a rationally motivated *consensus*." There is no promise that reasoned argument will lead to a consensus, and a democratic process may end in a majority vote. But regardless of the demos's method of decision making, a full consensus can be viewed as the *ideal* outcome.[41]

When one imagines democratic groups, one might think that the members of such groups speak for roughly equal periods of time. But is it important that all ten members of a collective speak the same amount? Or is it essential that all members have equal opportunities to speak? If one person speaks far more than any other, there may be a problem. The problem, though, is that this speaker is taking away others' opportunities—not that the speaker is simply talking the most. Similarly, if a group member hardly ever speaks, this member may lack adequate speaking opportunities. Again, it is the presence or absence of opportunities—not the silence—that is at issue. Inevitably some members will speak more than others, and the members of small democratic groups have a right to remain silent.[42]

Thus, equality of opportunity is important in democratic groups. As Dahl argues, members of the demos "ought to have an adequate opportunity, and an equal opportunity, for expressing their preferences as to the final outcome," as well as "for placing questions on the agenda and for expressing reasons for endorsing one outcome rather than another."[43]

These opportunities need to be readily apparent to each member of the demos. They should be "manifest" or "displayed," such that all members of the demos recognize the existence of their opportunities.[44] For instance, a group might formally give opportunities to all, yet never remind shy members that they are welcome to speak. A group might have a system for taking speaking turns, yet never fully explain the system to new members.

For opportunities to be meaningful, members must also have at least minimal communication skills.[45] If some members cannot speak the group's language, dialect, or jargon, their opportunities to speak are meaningless. If the group encourages conversational spontaneity (e.g., interruptions and digressions), members who cannot hold the floor under such conditions may be unable to use their opportunities to speak. If a group member can speak the language and take the floor but is inarticulate, the chance to speak may amount to nothing more than the chance to become frustrated with one's own inability to speak clearly and forcefully.[46]

Like anything else, this notion of equal opportunities can be taken too far. It is not necessary for every group member to be able to speak at every moment. Timely interjections are sometimes productive, and groups sometimes need to interrupt long-winded speakers. Similarly, time pressure often makes it necessary for democratic groups to limit each member's speaking turns. The point is that over time and across different topics, speaking opportunities should be equal.

But what if no member has the opportunity to say even a few sentences? In this scenario, opportunities are equal but inadequate. If there are insufficient opportunities to communicate with one another, deliberation—careful and thorough discussion—is impossible. Under such conditions a small group might choose to vote in a democratic manner, but the constraints on deliberation move it far from the democratic ideal.[47]

With the rights to equal and adequate opportunities come certain responsibilities. Members of the demos always have the chance to speak, but there are times when they also have a responsibility to speak. A fully democratic decision is impossible if a member of the demos has withheld information that would cause the group to take a different course of action. A group is equally impaired if a member irresponsibly manipulates other group members into accepting a decision they would otherwise oppose.

Having outlined these general principles, we may distinguish the different forms of speaking that characterize democratic deliberation: agenda setting, reformulating, informing, articulating, persuading, voting, and dissenting. In turn, each of these forms of talk is defined and related to other aspects of the democratic process.[48]

Agenda Setting

Broadly defined, the agenda consists of the issues a group discusses during a meeting. Members can set the agenda by placing, removing, or altering the priority of items on the agenda. For instance, a member might ask that the group postpone an issue until a future meeting. More subtly, one can influence the pace at which the group moves through one or more agenda items. Suggesting that the group devote an hour to a given item might lead the group to consider that issue carefully and, as a consequence, give little or no attention to items at the end of the agenda. In a democracy, Dahl explains, "The demos must have the exclusive opportunity to decide how matters are to be placed on the agenda."[49] Agenda setting is a vital form of talk, for there can be no debate until an issue is placed on the agenda.[50] Agenda setting is the means by which the demos decides what issues are of immediate concern. If the full membership of the group is not involved in setting the agenda, the concerns of some members will be ignored in any subsequent (undemocratic) discussion.

Consequently, Barber explains, the agenda of a demos is never permanently set:

Strong democratic talk places its agenda at the center rather than at the beginning of its politics. It subjects every pressing issue to continuous examination and possible reformulation. Its agenda *is*, before anything else, its agenda. It thus scrutinizes what remains unspoken, looking into the crevices of silence for signs of an unarticulated problem, a speechless victim, or a mute protester.[51]

Reformulation

Reformulation is the redefinition or reframing of an issue that is already on the agenda and under discussion. Reformulation includes both semantic alterations (e.g., rephrasing a problem) and changes in the content of a proposal (e.g., integrating two solutions into one). As an example, two workers at a paper mill might have two different ideas for spending a windfall profit. One might want to invest in technology that reduces the mill's waste, and the other might prefer an investment that reduces production costs. A third worker might then reformulate the issue by joining the two seemingly competing ideas into a single money-saving pulp recycling plan.[52]

Reformulation, as Barber defines the term, amounts to "language"—the metaphors and terms that define the experiences of the past, the realities of the present, and the possibilities of the future. Barber goes so far as to insist, "We may redistribute goods and make power accountable, but if we reserve talk and its evolution to specialists [or any elite few] ... then no amount of equality will yield democracy."[53]

Informing

One of the most common forms of speech during deliberation is the exchange of information among group members. Here *informing* means providing information relevant to an agenda item under discussion without attempting to express one's views or persuade the group to reach a particular decision.[54]

If group members fail to present the pertinent information they possess, they may jeopardize democratic deliberation. Their silence could distort other members' perspectives and result in uninformed deliberation and judgment. Withholding information could also cause the group to make decisions with unforeseen results that are either undemocratic or unproductive.[55]

These dangers make it apparent that informing is sometimes more of a responsibility than a right. In a fully democratic group, members always volunteer whatever information they believe the group needs to make an informed decision. Small democratic groups have tacit Freedom of Information Acts that grant members access to pertinent information, but they also expect members to share such knowledge long before anyone would have to search for it.[56]

This requirement must not be exaggerated and misunderstood. There always exists useful information that is unknown to all of the group's members, and it is not incumbent upon the group to seek out every last bit of information. Group members are responsible only for providing relevant information that they know or have at hand.

Articulation

Articulation involves expressing one's perspective with regard to an issue on the agenda, without clear persuasive purpose and before a decision has been reached on the issue. When articulating, speakers are presenting their opinions, interests, and ideas. For example, in a community group's strategy session, a speaker might tell the other group members that she dislikes censorship. The speaker's aim, in this case, might be for other group members to understand her point of view—not to embrace it.[57]

The ability to articulate cannot be taken for granted, because people do not always have a clear perspective and the ability to express their point of view. Learning how to recognize and distinguish between self-interest and the interests of the group is an important skill, as is learning how to transform unreflective and disparate opinions into sound group judgments. In general, articulation serves democracy by bringing forward the minority and majority views of the group and filling the well of ideas from which the demos draws.

This form of speech is particularly important when "the perspectives of some citizens are systematically suppressed" during deliberation. Whether such suppression is due to social or psychological pressures, the demos should aim to "insure the expression of ... excluded perspectives." Although groups might ideally seek a consensus based upon common ground, the more fundamental goal might be "to try to insure that those who are usually left out of ... discussions learn to speak whether their perspectives are common or not."[58]

However, articulation can amount to more than the expression of one's opinion. Mansbridge explains that democratic deliberation includes a form of articulation analogous to "thinking out loud":

> Preferences themselves, let alone interests, are not given. They must be tentatively voiced, tested, examined against the causes that produced them, explored, and finally made one's own. Good deliberation must rest on institutions that foster dissent and on images of appropriate behavior that allow for fumbling and changing one's mind, that respect the tentativeness of this process. Only such safeguards can help participants find where they want themselves to go.[59]

Thus articulation presents a speaker's point of view, but it can also play a vital role in the formation of a viewpoint.

Persuasion

Agenda setting, reformulation, and the other forms of speech set the stage for debate, and the centerpiece of this debate is persuasion. As defined herein, persuasive speech is intended to influence the views of other members of the demos with regard to an agenda item. Persuasion aims to create, reinforce, or change other members' feelings, attitudes, and beliefs about an issue.[60]

Michael Walzer, a lifelong advocate of democracy, explains why persuasion plays such an important role in democratic deliberation:

> Democracy puts a premium on speech, persuasion, rhetorical skill. Ideally, the citizen who makes the most persuasive argument—that is, the argument that actually persuades the largest number of citizens—gets his [sic] way. But he can't use force, or pull rank, or distribute money.... And all the other citizens must talk, too, or at least have a chance to talk.... Citizens come into the forum with nothing but their arguments. All non-political goods have to be deposited outside: weapons and wallets, titles and degrees.[61]

But democracy needs more than mere persuasion. If no restraint is put upon attempts to persuade, there is no guard against deceptive or manipulative discourse. With this purpose in mind, Cohen insists that in a deliberative democracy, members of the demos "are required to state their reasons" when presenting their views on proposals.[62] Bruce Ackerman adds a "consistency requirement": the reasons a person gives at one time must remain consistent with the reasons given to justify other claims.[63] More fundamentally, Dahl insists that arguments should be backed by systematic research and self-reflection.[64] This requirement of reflection is particularly relevant to arguments that include emotional appeals. Groups reach decisions through both thought and feeling, and just as reasoning can be superficial and uninformed, so can emotions arise from mood and circumstance more than heartfelt convictions.

There are many linguistic devices and strategies that members of a democratic group are wary of using. Euphemisms, loaded words, and jargon often conflict with the need for clarity and precision. Using clever grammar to disguise arguments or dodge questions also undermines the need for explicit debate. In addition simplistic, ritualistic, metaphoric, and mythic discourse can forge genuine consensus and unity, but these rhetorical strategies are often used to intoxicate or mystify. They can oversimplify situations and obscure real and important differences in members' perspectives and interests. Concealed and distorted messages make it more difficult for participants to deliberate in an informed, reflective manner. When oratory slips into sophistry, the respectful exchange of perspectives and ideas becomes nothing more than a winner-take-all competition among manipulators.[65]

One might object to these restrictions, arguing that they need to be balanced with a recognition of the speaker's present situation and goals. In this view, democratic ends can justify undemocratic methods of persuasion. However, as rhetoric scholar Robert A. Kraig argues, it is dangerous to permit speakers to weigh seemingly just ends against unjust means unless the ends-means distinction is brought under scrutiny:

> If we take a longer-term perspective, one that looks beyond particular rhetorical situations, then the ends and means of rhetoric are not as distinct.... The character of a community, a movement, an institution, or a nation, is in many respects the product of the rhetorical transactions by which it is constituted and maintained. In this sense, dehumanizing rhetoric leads to dehumanized institutions....*Rhetorical means are not merely the neutral instruments of the rhetor's immediate political ends but are the building blocks of the future.*[66]

Since every attempt at persuasion affects both listener and speaker, members of the demos restrain themselves from using manipulative discourse, both because of its unethical character and its long-term damage to the character of the demos.

Voting

Although rarely described as a form of communication, voting is simply the formal means of expressing preferences with regard to a set of alternative positions on an issue. This includes preliminary tallies, such as straw polls, and decisive balloting or voice votes, anonymous (secret ballot) and public (raised hand or voice vote) forms of expression, and consensual and majoritarian methods of decision making. Voting is required only at the decisive stage of deliberation, and a demos can choose among a wide variety of democratic voting methods (see chapter 3).[67]

Voting is the only form of democratic talk that democratic theorists universally recognize as essential, because without the vote, all other forms of deliberation become virtually meaningless. As Dahl writes,

> At the decisive stage of collective decisions, each citizen must be ensured an equal opportunity to express a choice that will be counted as equal in weight to the choice expressed by any other citizen. In determining outcomes at the decisive stage, these choices, and only these choices, must be taken into account.[68]

Dissent

Even after a proposal has passed, some members might choose to present a dissenting opinion, reminding the others of the minority viewpoint. This amounts to articulating a preference for a position that lost in a decisive vote. Like voting, dissent is an essential feature of any theory of democracy. After a group reaches a decision, there must be an opportunity for disagreement, whether it consists of lingering doubts or steadfast opposition.

This form of democratic speech allows those who opposed a group decision to put their formal dissent on record for future reference. It has been underappreciated by those who hold that articulation is significant only prior to the decisive stage of voting. This is unfortunate because, as Barber explains, "it is in the aftermath of a vote that dissenters may feel the greatest need to speak their pain." The dissenter says, " 'I am part of the community, I participated in the talk and deliberation leading to the decision, and so I regard myself as bound; but let it be known that I do not think we have made the right decision.' " This does not change the decision, but it does "bear witness to another point of view" and thereby keeps the issue, at least informally, on the agenda.[69]

Listening

Speaking is only one half of the deliberative process. As Frances Moore Lappé and Paul Martin DuBois insist, "The first art of democracy is active listening."[70] Unless group members are listening, there is little point in talking, because deliberation is not taking place. Imagine a planning group in which the treasurer talks over everyone's head. The other members are missing out on information that they may need to make a fully informed decision. Alternately, if one group member refused to listen to the treasurer's arguments, the group may have difficulty arriving at anything close to a consensus. Therefore it is important to understand the role of both comprehension and consideration in small group democracy.

Comprehension

Comprehension is the successful understanding of another person's speech. In a demos the listener must be able to understand the speaker's words, the ideas the speaker is presenting, and the gist of the speaker's message. Comprehension is essential for the democratic process, because it is the means whereby one comes to understand others' (and one's own) views.

This form of listening is essentially a right. The members of a demos have equal and adequate opportunities to comprehend what others say. If unable to comprehend the words or ideas of other speakers, group members are doubly deprived. It becomes more difficult for them to see an issue from the perspective of the group as a whole. They are also denied access to information and insight that could help them develop their own individual perspectives. Therefore the group needs to exercise a right to understand the language of the demos—a right to be spoken to in intelligible terms.[71]

Fishkin gives a glimpse of what full comprehension might look like, drawing upon David Braybrooke's conception of "logically complete debate." In such a debate, "the participants, turn by turn, raise proposals and invoke arguments for them," and they take the time necessary to address these proposals and arguments. "As the issue moves toward resolution," writes Braybrooke,

> every participant is aware at every stage of every ingredient still current in the debate—every proposal outstanding; the arguments still pressed on its behalf; the distribution among the participants of favor for the various proposals and of opposition to them, and as well the distribution of conviction respecting the various arguments and of doubt.[72]

Consideration

It is more common, and equally important, to think of listening as a responsibility. If group members did not listen, they would undermine the very idea of discussion and dialogue. Consideration can amount to passive listening, such as sitting and attending to what another member says. When members carefully weigh one another's statements, brief silences often fall after a person speaks "to give time for what has been said to make its own appeal."[73] Consideration can also take a more active form, such as a verbal request for more information or a series of probing questions to clarify a speaker's statements. These active forms of consideration are particularly valuable when the listener is unsure of what the speaker is trying to say.

Robert Bellah and the coauthors of *The Good Society* focus their conclusion on the importance of paying attention to one another and our surroundings: "When we are giving our full attention to something, when we are really attending, we are calling on all our resources of intelligence, feeling, and moral sensitivity."[74] Barber also places great value on this form of listening. "Without it," he writes, "there is only the babble of raucous interests and insistent rights vying for the deaf ears of impatient adversaries."[75]

It is important to distinguish active consideration from passive capitulation. Consideration must be reciprocal, and it need not result in agreement with the speaker. Group members need to be willing to consider arguments, listening with an openness to consider the reasons given, but whether or not they reach full agreement is uncertain.[76]

In fact, sometimes respectful consideration can change the mind of the speaker rather than that of the listener. This has been one of the results of the Learning Project, a national program for community organizing and outreach. Organizers working in the program have found that careful listening and probing questions can cause speakers to reconsider their views on issues as polarized as the sources of poverty and crime.[77]

Conclusion

To summarize, small group democracy involves a somewhat powerful and inclusive group, with a membership committed to the democratic process. A demos maintains healthy, democratic relationships and practices a democratic form of deliberation. Once again, this definition amounts to an unattainable ideal, and one might question the usefulness of such a utopian vision. Dahl answers this question after presenting his own criteria for an ideal democratic procedure:

> One might ... wonder whether any system can hope to meet the criteria fully. And, if not, of what relevance are the criteria?... In the real world, no system will fully meet the criteria for a democratic process.... However, the criteria serve as standards against which one may compare alternative processes and institutions in order to judge their relative merits. The criteria do not completely define what we mean by a good polity or good society. But to the extent that the democratic process is worthwhile, then the criteria will help us to arrive at judgments that bear directly on the relative worth or goodness of political arrangements.[78]

Notes

Portions of this chapter are reprinted with the permission of Sage Publications from John Gastil, "A Definition of Small Group Democracy," *Small Group Research* 23 (1992): 278–301.

1. Mary Parker Follett, *Creative Experience* (New York: Longmans, Green, and Co., 1924), 225–6.

2. I have discussed the writings underlying this definition in greater detail in "A Definition of Small Group Democracy"; "Democratic Deliberation: A Redefinition of the Democratic Process and a Study of Staff Meetings at a Co-Operative Workplace," *Masters Abstracts* 30–04M (1992), 1114 (University Microfilms No. 1348177); "Undemocratic Discourse: A Review of Theory and Research on Political Discourse," *Discourse & Society* 3 (1992): 469–500. These previous definitions differ from the present one: I have clarified the nature of power, inclusiveness, commitment, and deliberation and highlighted the importance of obtaining adequate information during group discussions.

In previous writings ("Democratic Deliberation" and "Undemocratic Discourse") I discussed democratic deliberation with reference to all social scales. My primary purpose in presenting this model is to fill the void of theories of small group democracy. To the best of my knowledge, no published work has attempted to provide a detailed definition of democracy in small-scale systems. Many democratic theorists ignore small group democracy altogether by defining democracy in a way that limits it to large-scale representative political systems; for example, see Larry Diamond, ed., *The Democratic Revolution: Struggles for Freedom and Pluralism in the Developing World* (New York: Freedom House, 1992): 26; Milton Fisk, *The State and Justice: An Essay in Political Theory* (Cambridge: Cambridge University Press, 1989), 166; John A. Wiseman, *Democracy in Black Africa: Survival and Renewal* (New York: Paragon House, 1990), chap. 1.

Sidney Verba's *Small Groups and Political Behavior* (Princeton, N.J.: Princeton University Press, 1961) is one of the only modern works focusing on democracy and the small group, but his purpose was to understand the small group's role in large-scale democracy—not the small group as a democracy in and of itself. The most theoretical work to date on the subject may be Jane Mansbridge's *Beyond Adversary Democracy* (Chicago: University of Chicago Press, 1983), which elaborates and illustrates the unitary model of democracy through case studies of small democratic groups. One might argue that Jean Jacques Rousseau, in *The Social Contract and Discourses* (New York: E.P. Dutton & Co., 1950), presents a theory of small-scale democracy, but he discusses medium social scales (i.e., a thousand to ten thousand people) and fails to address in detail the features of face-to-face deliberation. Moreover, Rousseau's theory of deliberation is seriously flawed: see Bernard Manin, "On Legitimacy and Political Deliberation," trans. Elly Stein and Jane Mansbridge, *Political Theory* 15 (1987): 338–68.

3. For example, see Joshua Cohen, "Deliberation and Democratic Legitimacy," in Alan Hamlin and Philip Pettit, eds., *The Good Polity* (New York: Basil Blackwell, 1989), 22. Quentin Skinner identified one of the most important reasons for defining democracy as an ideal. Calling a political system a democracy "serves to commend the recently prevailing values and practices of a political system like that of the United States, and it constitutes a form of argument against those who have sought to question the democratic character of those values and practices": "The Empirical Theorists of Democracy and Their Critics: A Plague on Both Their Houses," *Political Theory* 1 (1973): 303–4.

Alternatively, the use of the term *democracy* to describe existing institutions can cause the term to lose legitimacy in step with the institutions. Thus critic Manning Marable can proclaim that "American democracy has failed," simultaneously rejecting the system and the term. Fortunately Marable and other critics often reject one form of democracy and suggest another as an alternative; see Marable's *The Crisis of Color and Democracy: Essays on Race, Class, and Power* (Monroe, Maine: Common Courage Press, 1992). This form of criticism preserves the value of the word but complicates its meaning. Once again, the problem stems from using the term to refer to an existing institution rather than an ideal. For criticism of the idealist approach I embrace, see Samuel Huntington's contribution to the movement "to make democracy less of a 'hurrah' word and more of a commonsense word"; *The Third Wave: Democratization in the Late Twentieth Century* (Norman, Okla.: University of Oklahoma Press, 1991): 7.

4. Robert Dahl, *Democracy and Its Critics* (New Haven, Conn.: Yale University Press, 1989), 113. For an excellent summary of this work, see David Held, "The Possibilities of Democracy," *Theory & Society* 20 (1991): 875–89.

5. Anthony Arblaster, *Democracy* (Open University Press: Milton Keynes, 1987), 98. Arblaster adds, "Accessibility and a readiness to listen are not ... incompatible with a fundamentally authoritarian structure of power and government. Nor is making a show of consultation and participation, when what is being looked for is essentially a ratification of decisions already taken" (ibid.). For an example of groups with the trappings of democracy but no real power, see William Graebner, "The Small Group in Democratic Social Engineering, 1900–1950," *Journal of Social Issues* 42 (1986): 137–54.

6. This definition borrows from an insightful discussion of power by Douglas W. Rae. In further agreement with Rae, I would add that power is the knowing capacity to influence; one must be aware of one's causal role to say that one's influence constitutes power. "Knowing Power: A Working Paper," in Ian Shapiro and Grant Reeher, eds., *Power, Inequality, and Democratic Politics* (Boulder, Colo.: Westview Press, 1988), 17–49.

Note that if *power* includes forms of influence over emotions and beliefs, the term has wide applicability. Therapy and consciousness-raising groups, for instance, are powerful even if they focus on changing how people think and feel more than how they behave. This distinction may be largely academic, however, since people who change their emotional and cognitive perception of the world are likely to behave differently as a consequence.

7. I thank Gail Pietrzyk for permitting me to use an adaptation of her piano metaphor. A more mathematical definition of group power is provided by Andrew King in *Power and Communication* (Prospect Heights, Ill.: Waveland Press, 1987); he argues that group power can be defined as the product of a group's mass (number of people and amount of resources) and its unity or cohesion.

8. Catharine A. MacKinnon, *Toward a Feminist Theory of the State* (Cambridge, Mass.: Harvard University Press, 1989), 102; see also chap. 5. For more on women's consciousness-raising groups, see Sara M. Evans and Harry C. Boyte, *Free Spaces* (New York: Harper & Row, 1992), chap. 3; Virginia Sapiro, "The Women's Movement and the Creation of Gender Consciousness: Social Movements as Socialization Agents," in Orit Ichilov, ed., *Political Socialization, Citizenship Education, and Democracy* (New York: Teachers College, 1990), 266–80. For a case study of a consciousness-raising group in the gay community, see James W. Chesebro, John F. Cragan, and Patricia McCullough, "The Small Group Techniques of the Radical Revolutionary: A Synthetic Study of Consciousness Raising," *Speech Monographs* 40 (1973): 136–46. Paulo Freire's writings on liberatory education in Latin America provide a more general conception of consciousness raising in small groups; see *Pedagogy of the Oppressed* (New York: Seabury Press, 1970).

9. Numerous writings in the past ten years have distinguished among different forms of power: threat, exchange, and integrative power (Kenneth Boulding, *Three Faces of Power* [Newbury Park, Calif.: Sage, 1990]); actualization and domination power (Riane Eisler, *The Chalice and the Blade: Our History, Our Future* [San

Francisco: Harper & Row, 1987]); power as more than a means of coercion or domination (Nancy C. Hartsock, *Money, Sex, and Power* [Boston: Northeastern University Press, 1983], chap. 9); sustainable and nonsustainable power (Frances Moore Lappé and Paul Martin DuBois, "Power in a Living Democracy," *Creation Spirituality* [September/October 1992]: 23–5, 42); power over, power to, and power with (Starhawk, *Truth or Dare* [New York: Harper & Row, 1986]).

10. On the importance of equal power, see Peter Bachrach, *The Theory of Democratic Elitism: A Critique* (Boston: Little, Brown, 1967), chaps. 6 and 7. Any provisional inequalities in power that the group creates must be subject to justification. If a group member questions an inequality, the group or the individual with greater power must be able to justify its existence; see Bruce Ackerman, *Social Justice and the Liberal State* (New Haven, Conn.: Yale University Press, 1980), 4–8. On the difficulties surrounding the establishment of fully equal power, see Andrea Baker, "The Problem of Authority in Radical Movement Groups: A Case Study of a Lesbian-Feminist Organization," *The Journal of Applied Behavioral Science* 18 (1982): 323–41; Mansbridge, *Beyond Adversary Democracy,* chap. 17.

11. Dahl, *Democracy and Its Critics,* 126–30. The problem of inclusiveness is faced not only by small groups and communities but also by nations. For this reason, it becomes necessary to explore models of international democratic decision making; see David Held, "Democracy: From City-states to a Cosmopolitan Order," *Political Studies* 40, Special Issue (1992), 10-39.

12. C. George Benello (*From the Ground Up* [Boston: South End Press, 1992], 51) recognizes the necessary interplay between inclusiveness and the distribution of power. All those affected by group decisions "must have a say in the decision-making process.... The trick is to create a system with sufficient delegation of authority and internal differentiation so that not everyone is involved in all decisions all the time."

13. Michael Walzer, in *Radical Principles: Reflections of an Unreconstructed Democrat* (New York: Basic Books, 1980), chap. 7, insists that there will always be people falling within the boundaries of inclusiveness who will not attend meetings. In particular, he asks militant activists to respect those who choose to attend few (if any) meetings. Their absence does not justify their exclusion, it only complicates the representation of their interests.

14. John Burnheim, *Is Democracy Possible? The Alternative to Electoral Politics* (Berkeley: University of California Press, 1985), 5.

15. Dahl, *Democracy and Its Critics,* 129. When people are deemed incompetent to participate in group deliberation, the group must—to the best of its ability—still take their interests into account. In this vein, some environmental activists have argued that fully democratic groups should take the interests of other species and all forms of life into account. See Van Andruss, et al., eds., *Home! A Bioregional Reader* (Philadelphia: New Society Publishers, 1990), 70, 95–99.

16. Teresa Labov provides an example of a co-op that sacrificed its principle of openness to the community (inclusiveness) in order to satisfy its other three principles—cooperativeness, commitment to the group, and harmony.

"Ideological Themes in Reports of Interracial Conflict," in Allen D. Grimshaw, ed., *Conflict Talk* (Cambridge: Cambridge University Press, 1990), 139–59.

17. Cohen, "Deliberation and Democratic Legitimacy," 21. Carol Gould (*Rethinking Democracy* [Cambridge: Cambridge University Press, 1988]) also stresses commitment to the democratic process and responsibility for carrying out group decisions. A more extreme statement is provided by Mahatma Gandhi: "A democrat must be utterly selfless. He [sic] must think and dream not in terms of self or party but only of democracy" (quoted by S. M. Tewari in Krishna Kumar, ed., *Democracy and Nonviolence* [New Delhi: Gandhi Peace Foundation, 1968], 30). By contrast, I argue only that one ought to make a commitment to the democratic process *prior to* (not to the exclusion of) other commitments to people and principles.

18. There are at least two different rationales for using formal group bylaws and similar regulations. First, they may be designed to make a subversion of the democratic process too costly. If such rules have force, they function in the same way that laws against criminal violence restrain malevolent people; see Kenneth Boulding, "Perspectives on Violence," *Zygon* 18 (1983): 425–37. Second, one can view rules as self-restraints that a group of well-meaning but imperfect people voluntarily impose upon themselves as protections against making hasty, undemocratic decisions during moments of weakness. In *Democracy and the Ethical Life: A Philosophy of Politics and Community*, 2d ed. (Washington, D.C.: Catholic University of America Press, 1990), chap. 10, Claes G. Ryn presents this view with regard to the role of constitutions. Jo Freeman applies this principle to small groups, insisting that groups must formalize their procedures to safeguard democracy. "The Tyranny of Structurelessness," in Fellowship for Intentional Community and Communities Publications Cooperative (eds.), *Intentional Communities: A Guide to Cooperative Living* (Evansville, Ind.: Fellowship for Intentional Community; Stelle, Ill.: Communities Publications Cooperative, 1990), 76–77.

Critics of bylaws often contend that formal rules are unrealistic. In this view, a group should not try to codify norms that, in reality, must constantly be redeveloped and "owned" by the group members. Ultimately bylaws can undermine commitment by replacing personal conscience and organic group norms with impersonal, stale doctrine. Thus a 1656 Quaker document on business meeting policy reads, "These things we do not lay upon you as a rule or form to walk by ... for the letter killeth but the Spirit giveth light" (quoted in Francis E. Pollard, Beatrice E. Pollard, and Robert S. W. Pollard, *Democracy and the Quaker Method* [London: Ballinsdale, 1949], 47).

19. Since no group fully realizes the democratic ideal, an individual is never strictly obligated to follow group decisions. Philosophical anarchists make this argument with regard to governments; however, the potential for small groups to approximate the democratic ideal is much greater than it is for large political systems. If one thinks of obligation in incremental (as opposed to dichotomous) terms, one can recognize that a group's greater embodiment of democratic principles should inspire a proportionately stronger sense of obligation. For a strong defense of philosophical anarchism, see A. John Simmons, *Moral Principles and Political Obligations* (Princeton, N.J.: Princeton University Press, 1979).

20. James Fishkin, *Democracy and Deliberation* (New Haven, Conn.: Yale University Press, 1991), 34–35.

21. Those who wish a simpler definition of democracy might argue that these relational features should be viewed as conducive to (rather than part of) small group democracy. On the contrary, many democratic theorists have stressed the relational component of a fully democratic process (e.g., Benjamin Barber, *Strong Democracy* [Berkeley: University of California Press, 1984]; Carol Gould, *Rethinking Democracy* [Cambridge: Cambridge University Press, 1988]). The different forms of relationship presented herein draw heavily upon Barber's discussion of "strong democratic talk" in *Strong Democracy*, 173–198. For a clarification with regard to mutuality see Benjamin Barber, "Reply," *Dissent* 32 (1985): 385. For a brief synopsis see Benjamin Barber, "Political Talk—and *Strong Democracy*," *Dissent* 31 (1984): 215–22.

John Dewey has gone even further by arguing that democratic governance is a means toward a democratic form of relationship among people; see David Fott, "John Dewey and the Philosophical Foundations of Democracy," *Social Science Journal* 28 (1991): 29–44; John D. Peters, "Democracy and American Mass Communication Theory: Dewey, Lippman, Lazarsfeld," *Communication* 11 (1989): 199–220.

22. One of the early and most provocative works on relational communication is Paul Watzlawick, Janet Beavin, and Don Jackson, *Pragmatics of Human Communication: A Study of Interactional Patterns, Pathologies, and Paradoxes* (New York: Norton, 1967). Therein the authors coined the now infamous phrase, "One cannot *not* communicate" (p. 51). The argument was that interaction always has a meaning and an impact on the relationship. Moreover, Samuel Bowles and Herbert Gintis, in *Democracy and Capitalism: Property, Community, and the Contradictions of Modern Social Thought* (New York: Basic Books, 1986), especially chapters 5 and 6, argue that people's actions and interactions constitute them as persons. Thus one's sense of individuality, competence, or group identity can come into existence through proclaiming and interactively affirming its existence.

As I briefly discuss in "Undemocratic Discourse" (p. 473), the relational aspects of democratic discourse resemble existing politeness theories. See Penelope Brown and Stephen Levinson, "Universals in Language Usage: Politeness Phenomena," in Esther N. Goody, ed., *Questions and Politeness: Strategies in Social Interaction* (Cambridge: Cambridge University Press, 1978), 56–289; Robin T. Lakoff, "The Logic of Politeness; Or Minding Your p's and q's," in C. Colum et al., eds., *Papers from the Ninth Regional Meeting of the Chicago Linguistic Society* (Chicago: Chicago Linguistic Society, 1973), 292–305; Tae-Seop Lim and John W. Bowers, "Face-work: Solidarity, Approbation, and Tact," *Human Communication Research* 17 (1991): 415–50.

23. John Dewey, *The Public and Its Problems* (Athens, Ohio: Swallow Press, 1927), 154. See also Peters, "Democracy and American Mass Communication Theory," 218. The implicit metaphor in the term *atmosphere* is only a surface feature of the deep literature on the ecology of human interaction. In this view the maintenance of a hospitable group environment is essential to sustaining certain forms of human interaction—one of which, I argue, is democratic interaction. On the

ecology of human communication, see C. David Mortensen, "Communication, Conflict, and Culture," *Communication Theory* 1 (1991): 273–93.

24. Jane J. Mansbridge, *Beyond Adversary Democracy* (Chicago: University of Chicago Press, 1983), 4–5. See also Jane J. Mansbridge, *Beyond Self-Interest* (Chicago: University of Chicago Press, 1990) and "Feminism and Democracy," *The American Prospect* 1, no. 2 (1990): 126–39.

25. Some of the examples of relational talk are excerpts from staff meetings at Mifflin Street Community Co-op, which I discuss in chapters 4 and 5.

26. Kenwyn K. Smith and David N. Berg discuss the tensions between the individual and the group in terms of seven paradoxes that small groups face. "A Paradoxical Conception of Group Dynamics," *Human Relations* 40 (1987): 633–58. Although groups are more commonly associated with the development of a social or group identity, P. G. Friedman suggests that groups can play a vital role in developing a person's sense of individual identity. "The Limits of Consensus: Group Processes for Individual Development," in Gerald M. Phillips and Julia T. Wood, eds., *Emergent Issues in Human Decision Making* (Carbondale, Ill.: Southern Illinois University Press, 1984), 142–60.

27. Gould, *Rethinking Democracy*, 257. For an application of the reciprocity principle to large-scale democracy and mass communication systems, see Dianne E. Rucinski, "The Centrality of Reciprocity to Communication and Democracy," *Critical Studies in Mass Communication* 8 (1991): 184–94.

In the above quote, Gould uses the term *participatory democracy*. This term corresponds to a broad branch of democratic theory that emphasizes the role of public participation in the decision-making process. Prominent writings in this tradition include: Barber, *Strong Democracy*; C. B. Macpherson, *The Life and Times of Liberal Democracy* (Oxford: Oxford University Press, 1977); Mansbridge, *Beyond Adversary Democracy*; Carole Pateman, *Participation and Democratic Theory* (Cambridge: Cambridge University Press, 1970), and *The Disorder of Women* (Cambridge: Polity Press, 1989); Mark Warren, "Democratic Theory and Self-Transformation," *American Political Science Review* 86 (1992): 8–23.

Critics have viewed the participatory theory of democracy as dangerous (e.g., Samuel Huntington, "The Democratic Distemper," *Public Interest* 41 [1975]: 9–38), unrealistic (e.g., Daniel C. Kramer, *Participatory Democracy: Developing Ideals of the Political Left* [Cambridge, Mass.: Schenkman Publishing, 1972]), and antagonistic to a more deliberative conception of political decision making (Claus Offe and Ulrich K. Preuss, "Democratic Institutions and Moral Resources," in David Held, ed., *Political Theory Today* [Stanford, Calif.: Stanford University Press, 1991]: 143–71).

28. Like the other forms of democratic relationship, the affirmation of competence manifests itself in the form of communication among group members. Thus the character of a group's talk can indicate the degree to which members' competence is collectively affirmed. This view parallels Ackerman's neutrality principle, which forbids speakers from asserting that they are morally superior to other members of the collective. *Social Justice and the Liberal State*, 10–12, 15–17.

29. Dahl, *Democracy and Its Critics*, 98. The assumption of competence relates to the question in Figure 1.1 about the capability of group members to represent their own interests and participate in democratic deliberation.

30. Quoted in Robin Morgan, "Chai Ling Talks with Robin Morgan," *Ms.* (September/October 1990): 14. In addition to believing others are competent, one must also presume that oneself is competent at representing one's self-interest and the interests of the group. This belief in oneself is closely related to self-esteem, which plays a vital role in democracy. As Gloria Steinem explains, self-esteem allows a person to trust her own beliefs and conscience. In this way, "Self-esteem plays as much a part in the destiny of nations as it does in the lives of individuals.... Self-esteem is the basis of any real democracy" (*Revolution from Within* [Boston: Little, Brown, 1992], 9–10). For a mixture of views on the recent emphasis on self-esteem, see the series of articles in the *Utne Reader* (January/February 1992), 89–99. Political philosophers have also paid a great deal of attention to self-esteem in recent decades. See John Rawls, *A Theory of Justice* (Cambridge, Mass.: Harvard University Press, 1971): 440–46; Michael Walzer, *Spheres of Justice* (New York: Basic Books, 1983), 272–80.

31. Quote from David Spangler, cited in Corinne McLaughlin and Gordon Davidson, *Builders of the Dawn: Community Lifestyles in a Changing World* (Shutesbury, Mass.: Sirius Publishing, 1986), 298.

32. If one is skeptical that such things as word choice can affect a person's group identity, see Samuel L. Gaertner et al., "Reducing Intergroup Bias: The Benefits of Recategorization," *Journal of Personality and Social Psychology* 57 (1989): 239–49. In addition, Ernest Bormann shows how the sharing of group stories can develop mutuality when narratives are jointly developed and understood by group members: "Symbolic Convergence Theory and Communication in Group Decision-Making," in Randy Y. Hirokawa and Marshall Scott Poole, eds., *Communication and Group Decision-Making* (Beverly Hills, Calif.: Sage, 1986): 219–36.

33. Gould, *Rethinking Democracy*, 106. The tension between individuality and community has received a great deal of attention in recent sociological and philosophical writings, spawning a group of scholars who see themselves as communitarians. See Robert N. Bellah, Richard Madsen, William M. Sullivan, Ann Swidler, Steven M. Tipton, *Habits of the Heart: Individualism and Commitment in American Life* (New York: Harper & Row, 1985); these same authors move from a descriptive to a more prescriptive tone in *The Good Society* (New York: Alfred A. Knopf, 1991). For philosophical essays, see Michael J. Sandel, ed., *Liberalism and Its Critics* (New York: New York University Press, 1984), part 2. For recent communitarian writings one can refer to the new journal *The Responsive Community*.

Mutuality encompasses an identification with others, which some intriguing social scientific experiments suggest constitutes much of the basis of altruistic behavior. See C. Daniel Batson, et al., "Negative-State Relief and the Empathy-Altruism Hypothesis," *Journal of Personality and Social Psychology* 56 (1989): 922–33; C. Daniel Batson et al., "Five Studies Testing Two New Egoistic Alternatives to the Empathy-Altruism Hypothesis," *Journal of Personality and Social Psychology* 55 (1988): 52–77.

Some may argue that whatever its virtues, mutuality has its drawbacks. For instance, Irving Janis has suggested that group cohesion can contribute to the practice of groupthink or faulty collective decision making and judgment (Irving L. Janis, *Groupthink* [Boston: Houghton Mifflin, 1982]). However, the most comprehensive review of the research on groupthink has found no association between group cohesion and the existence of groupthink; Won Woo Park, "A Review of Research on Groupthink," *Journal of Behavioral Decision Making* 3 (1990): 229–45. In fact a recent meta-analysis has found that, on average, social scientific experiments show a positive relationship between cohesiveness and group productivity: Charles R. Evans and Kenneth L. Dion, "Group Cohesion and Performance: A Meta-analysis," *Small Group Research* 22 (1991): 175–186.

34. Just as some have argued that cohesive groups are unproductive groups, some have argued that happy people tend to be lousy decision makers because they fail to reason systematically. Fortunately this dim view of the human condition has not received strong empirical support; see Diane M. Mackie and Leila T. Worth, "Processing Deficits and the Mediation of Positive Affect in Persuasion," *Journal of Personality and Social Psychology* 57 (1989): 27–40.

35. Mansbridge, *Beyond Adversary Democracy*, 9.

36. Barber, *Strong Democracy*, 189; see also Barber, *The Conquest of Politics* (Princeton, N.J.: Princeton University Press, 1988), 147–150. See also Rawls's discussion of the principle of fraternity: *A Theory of Justice*, 105.

37. Michael Walzer argues that democratic citizens are expected to "be tolerant of one another. This is probably as close as we can come to that 'friendship' which Aristotle thought should characterize relations among members of the same political community"; *Radical Principles*, 62. At the very least, democratic citizens avoid bursts of rudeness toward their fellow citizens. As an example of the rending effects of such incivility, note the insightful comments of a parking lot attendant, lamenting the behavior of some drivers: "The rudeness, especially as it is so often directed at me, rankles. There is … an evolutionary process at work in this distinctly urban rudeness: a perhaps natural shyness or insecurity aggravated by big-city emotional distance; this becomes reserve, becomes suspicion, becomes indifference, becomes finally incivility, and, at its extremes, inhumanity"; Mark Heisenberg, "A View from the Booth," *Utne Reader* (January/February 1993): 134.

38. This definition draws on the work of small group researcher Randy Y. Hirokawa; "Group Communication and Decision-Making Performance: A Continued Test of the Functional Perspective," *Human Communication Research* 14 (1988): 487–515. Similar views of deliberation are provided by John Dewey, *How We Think* (New York: Heath & Co., 1910); Charles R. Beitz, *Political Equality: An Essay in Democratic Theory* (Princeton, N.J.: Princeton University Press, 1989), 114; Charles W. Anderson, *Pragmatic Liberalism* (Chicago: University of Chicago Press, 1991), esp. 164–5, chap. 10.

Not surprisingly, the satisfaction of Hirokawa's functions generally correlates with sound decision making; see Hirokawa, "Group Communication and Decision-Making Performance." More generally, interactive methods of group decision making (as opposed to the noninteractive techniques some practitioners have employed) tend to result in higher-quality group decisions, better average individual decisions, and an "assembly effect" (a group decision better than any one individual's decision or combination thereof): Brant R. Burleson, Barbara J. Levine, and Wendy Samter, "Decision-Making Procedure and Decision Quality," *Human Communication Research* 10 (1984): 557–74.

39. Fishkin, *Democracy and Deliberation*, 30–31.

40. Ibid., 25, 29. Other recent writings on the importance of deliberation in the democratic process include Anderson, *Pragmatic Liberalism*; Barber, *Strong Democracy*; Michael Briand, "Value, Policy, and the Indispensability of Politics" (Kettering Foundation, Dayton, Ohio, 1991, manuscript); Cohen, "Deliberation and Democratic Legitimacy," and his review of *Democracy and Its Critics* in the *Journal of Politics* 53 (1991): 221–5; Bernard Manin, "On Legitimacy and Political Deliberation"; Mansbridge, "Feminism and Democracy"; David Mathews, *What Is Politics and Who Owns It?* (Dayton, Ohio: Kettering Foundation, 1992); David Miller, "Deliberative Democracy and Social Choice," *Political Studies* 40, Special Issue (1992): 54–67; Beitz, *Political Equality*, 114–16; John S. Dryzek, *Discursive Democracy: Politics, Policy, and Political Science* (Cambridge: Cambridge University Press, 1990). For criticisms of deliberative democracy, see Sanders, "Against Deliberation"; Thomas Christiano, "Freedom, Consensus, and Equality in Collective Decision Making," *Ethics* 101 (1990): esp. 166–8.

The body of literature on the public sphere parallels the deliberative view in many respects. The work that has received the most attention in this literature is Jurgen Habermas, *The Structural Transformation of the Public Sphere: An Inquiry into a Category of Bourgeois Society*, trans. Thomas Burger with Frederick Lawrence (Cambridge, Mass.: MIT Press, 1989). For a review of this work, as well as criticisms and extensions, see Craig Calhoun, ed., *Habermas and the Public Sphere* (Cambridge, Mass.: MIT Press, 1992). For an attempt to build a theory of democracy centered on discourse and the public sphere, see Dryzek, *Discursive Democracy*.

41. Cohen, "Deliberation and Democratic Legitimacy," 22–23. In an earlier essay Cohen presents an essentially similar model of deliberative democracy and examines the economic system that would accompany it; "The Economic Basis of Deliberative Democracy," *Social Philosophy & Policy* 6 (1988): 25–50.

42. One reason people value their silence is that it allows contemplation. As Robert Scott writes, "Orwell's *1984* depicts a society in which the freedom of thought is even controlled, because one cannot contemplate, one is constantly inundated with party slogans and government Newspeak words.... *Winston Smith, although he was nearly continually quiet, had no right to silence*" ("Rhetoric and Silence," *Western Speech* 36 [1972]: 154).

On the other hand, "Silence is oppressive when it is characteristic of a dominated group [or subgroup], and when the group is not allowed to break its silence by its own choosing"; Adam Jaworski, "How to Silence a Minority: The Case of Women," *International Journal of Soc. Lang.* 94 (1992): 27. In Quaker meetings it is customary to call for a few minutes of silence and reflection both before meetings and in the case of strong controversy. To have the intended effect, such silence "must be willingly agreed, and not felt as a kind of hostile constraint"; Pollard et al., *Democracy and the Quaker Method*, 44.

43. Dahl, *Democracy and Its Critics*, 109. Alice Sturgis, in her elaboration of the principles underlying parliamentary procedure, calls this the "right of discussion." She writes, "Each member of the assembly has the right to speak freely without interruption or interference provided the rules are observed. The right of members to 'have their say,' or to 'have their day in court,' is as important as their right to vote"; *Standard Code of Parliamentary Procedure*, 3d ed. (New York: McGraw-Hill, 1988), 9.

44. Cohen, "Deliberation and Democratic Legitimacy," 21.

45. This notion of meaningful opportunities is analogous to Rawls's discussion of the worth of liberty, which depends upon one's ability to take advantage of one's rights and liberties; *A Theory of Justice*, 204–5.

46. This discussion is based, in part, on Habermas's notion of communicative competence. See Jurgen Habermas, *Legitimation Crisis*, trans. T. A. McCarthy (Boston: Beacon Press, 1975), and *Communication and the Evolution of Society* (Boston: Beacon Press, 1979). For critical discussions of Habermas's concept, see Anthony Giddens, "Jurgen Habermas," in Quentin Skinner, ed., *The Return of Grand Theory in the Human Sciences* (Cambridge: Cambridge University Press, 1985), 121–39; T. A. McCarthy, "A Theory of Communicative Competence," *Philosophy of the Social Sciences* 3 (1973): 135–56. Anderson, in *Pragmatic Liberalism* (199–202), provides a more concrete definition of deliberative competence. For an extension of this idea to media use and large-scale democracy, see Oscar H. Gandy, "The Political Economy of Communication Competence," in Vincent Mosco and Janet Wasko, eds., *The Political Economy of Information* (Madison, Wis.: University of Wisconsin Press, 1988), 108–24. For social scientific theory and research on interpersonal and small group communicative competence, see James C. McCroskey and Virginia P. Richmond, "Communication Apprehension and Small Group Communication," in Robert S. Cathcart and Larry A. Samovar, *Small Group Communication*, 5th ed. (Dubuque, Iowa: William C. Brown Publishers, 1988), 405–20; Malcolm R. Parks, "Interpersonal Communication and the Quest for Personal Competence," in Mark L. Knapp and Gerald R. Miller, eds., *Handbook of Interpersonal Communication* (Beverly Hills, Calif.: Sage, 1985), 171–201; Dean E. Hewes et al., "Interpersonal Communication Research: What Should We Know?" in Gerald M. Phillips and Julia T. Wood, eds., *Speech Communication: Essays to Commemorate the 75th Anniversary of the Speech Communication Association* (Carbondale, Ill.: Southern Illinois University Press, 1990), 130–80.

47. Dahl, *Democracy and Its Critics*, 109, stresses the combination of equal with adequate opportunities.

48. The distinctions among the different forms of speech draw heavily upon Barber, *Strong Democracy*, 178–97.

49. Dahl, *Democracy and Its Critics*, 113. The large-scale analogy is the relatively amorphous national "agenda." The media plays a crucial role in setting the nation's agenda; for a discussion see David Protess and Maxwell McCombs, eds., *Agenda Setting: Readings on Media, Public Opinion, and Policymaking* (Hillsdale, N.J.: Lawrence Erlbaum Associates, 1992); Marc Raboy and Peter A. Bruck, eds., *Communication for and against Democracy* (New York: Black Rose Books, 1989);

Robert Entman, *Democracy without Citizens* (Oxford: Oxford University Press, 1989).

50. I use the term *debate* almost interchangeably with *discussion* and *deliberation*. Some writers choose to draw a stark contrast between debate and other words, such as *dialogue*. Shelley Berman does this, painting a rather dim portrait of debate; see "Comparison of Dialogue and Debate," *Focus on Study Circles: The Newsletter of the Study Circles Resource Center* (Winter 1993): 9; for similar contrasts, see Bruno Lasker's *Democracy through Discussion* (New York: H. W. Wilson Co., 1949): 16–18, passim; Pollard et al., *Democracy and the Quaker Method*, 26–27. I recognize that group debates can become disruptive, divisive, or downright dangerous, but they can also be respectful and productive. By using debate as a synonym for deliberation, discussion, and dialogue, I wish to emphasize that fully democratic group meetings may commonly involve the constructive disagreements and arguments that can make debate a worthwhile activity.

51. Barber, *Strong Democracy*, 182.

52. Lappé and DuBois ("Power in a Living Democracy") use the term *political imagination* in a sense that is similar to reformulation, as I have defined it. It also corresponds to what media scholars call "issue framing." As an example of the importance of issue frames, Shanto Iyengar has studied the effects of different thematic frames on one's view of poverty. Iyengar explains that "how people think about poverty" depends on

> how the issue is framed. When news media presentations frame poverty as a general outcome, responsibility for poverty is assigned to society-at-large; when news presentations frame poverty as a particular instance of a poor person, responsibility is assigned to the individual. Similar framing effects are documented in the 1986 General Social Survey where the amount of public assistance deemed appropriate for a poor family varies with the description of the family.

"Framing Responsibility for Political Issues: The Case of Poverty," *Political Behavior* 12 (1990): 19.

53. Barber, *Strong Democracy*, 193.

54. This parallels the "right of information" that underlies democratic parliamentary procedures: "Every member has the right to know the meaning of the question before the assembly and what its effect will be"; Sturgis, *Standard Code*, 9; see also Manin, "On Legitimacy and Political Deliberation," 351–3. A similar principle underlies some laws in large-scale political systems, such as the Freedom of Information Act in the United States. Along these lines James P. Love recently discussed the progress of a plan to create a computer service providing citizens with access to government information; see "Democratizing the Data Banks: Getting Government Online," *The American Prospect*, no. 9 (1992): 48–50. For an even more ambitious proposal to "provide equal opportunity for every citizen to gather information" on questions of interest, see Michael Margolis, *Viable Democracy* (London: MacMillan Press, 1979), 161–9.

55. The failure to establish and draw upon an adequate information base can prove quite costly. Moreover, if a group member possesses faulty information,

communicating it to the rest of the group can be counterproductive. See Randy Y. Hirokawa and Dirk R. Scheerhorn, "Communication in Faulty Group Decision-Making," in Randy Y. Hirokawa and Marshall Scott Poole, eds., *Communication and Group Decision-Making* (Beverly Hills, Calif.: Sage, 1986), 63–80; Dennis S. Gouran and Randy Y. Hirokawa, "Counteractive Functions of Communication in Group Decision-Making," in *Communication and Group Decision-Making*, 81–90.

56. The responsibility to make important information public is a clearly recognized principle among advocates of large-scale democratic government. As communication scholar Jay Blumer writes, democratic theory holds that "ordinary citizens should be sufficiently equipped, informationally, to hold decision-makers effectively to account"; "Communication and Democracy: The Crisis Beyond the Ferment Within," *Journal of Communication* 33 (1983): 169. See also Gandy, "The Political Economy of Communication Competence"; Edward Herman and Noam Chomsky, *Manufacturing Consent* (New York: Pantheon, 1988); Raboy and Bruck, *Communication for and against Democracy.*

57. Even if a speaker adds no new information or argument to the discussion, there is intrinsic value in the simple act of articulating one's own perspective on an issue. This process can connect the individual with both the group and the content of the group discussion; it can help people understand one another as well as the subject at hand. For this reason, Follett suggested holding public "experience meetings" that would connect detailed policy information with people's daily lives; *Creative Experience*, chap. 12.

58. Sanders, "Against Deliberation", 23–24. The meaning of *articulation* used herein parallels Sanders's notion of testimony, which she views as a corrective for the excessive emphasis on deliberation.

59. Mansbridge, "Feminism and Democracy," 136. Similarly Pollard et al. (*Democracy and Quaker Method*, 23) insist that "the very attempt to state an idea clearly may clarify it in the mind of the person who holds it."

60. This definition of persuasion comes from Gerald R. Miller, "On Being Persuaded: Some Basic Distinctions," in Michael Roloff and Gerald R. Miller, eds., *Persuasion* (Beverly Hills, Calif.: Sage, 1980), 1–28. For a review of research on persuasion, see Miller's "Persuasion," in Charles R. Berger and Steven H. Chaffee, eds., *Handbook of Communication Science* (Newbury Park, Calif.: Sage, 1987), 446–83.

61. Walzer, *Spheres of Justice*, 304. See also Ackerman, *Social Justice and the Liberal State*; Manin, "On Legitimacy and Deliberation."

62. Cohen, "Deliberation and Democratic Legitimacy," 22.

63. See Ackerman, *Social Justice and the Liberal State*, 4, 7, 11.

64. Dahl has tried to show a connection between the deliberative view and his "criterion of enlightened understanding." This criterion asks that one be able to provide reasons for one's view, but it also requires that to the extent possible, citizens in a demos must undertake (1) systematic research and (2) self-reflection. "My 'reasons,'" Dahl writes, "might meet all the public tests of acceptability and yet not be good reasons—not in my interests—because they are based on an

impoverished understanding of my own needs and wants"; "A Rejoinder," *Journal of Politics* 53 (1991): 230.

65. These examples are taken from John Gastil, "Undemocratic Discourse: A Review of Theory and Research on Political Discourse," *Discourse & Society* 3 (1992): 469–500. The emphasis on a rational basis for persuasion parallels a distinction made in the literature on persuasion between systematic, reasoned attitude change and changes due to heuristic or unconscious processing of peripheral cues, such as the features of the speaker. For an inventory of heuristic processes relied upon by professional persuaders, see Robert B. Cialdini, "Compliance Principles of Compliance Professionals: Psychologists of Necessity," in Mark P. Zanna, James M. Olson, and C. Peter Herman, eds., *Social Influence: The Ontario Symposium*, vol. 5 (Hillsdale, N.J.: Lawrence Erlbaum, 1987), 165–84; on the effects of emotional appeals, see Ira Roseman, Robert P. Abelson, and Michael F. Ewing, "Emotion and Political Cognition: Emotional Appeals in Political Communication," in Richard R. Lau and David O. Sears, eds., *Political Cognition* (Hillsdale, N.J.: Lawrence Erlbaum, 1986), 279–94; on the effects of fear appeals in particular, see Franklin J. Boster and Paul Mongeau, "Fear-Arousing Persuasive Messages," in R. N. Bostrom, ed., *Communication Yearbook 8* (Beverly Hills, Calif.: Sage, 1984), 330–37.

For some, the potential for manipulation makes democracy altogether undesirable. Thus Thomas Hobbes described democracy as "no more than an aristocracy of orators, interrupted sometimes with the temporary monarchy of one orator." Reflecting on this quote, Walzer agrees that "democratic politics is a monopoly of politicians." By contrast I take the view that appropriate norms and group procedures might preclude outright dominance by the most verbally gifted members of the demos. At the very least, such dominance is far from inevitable even in less than fully democratic groups. Quotes from Walzer, *Spheres of Justice*, 304.

66. Robert A. Kraig, "The Hitler Problem in Rhetorical Theory: A Speculative Inquiry" (University of Wisconsin-Madison, 1992, manuscript), 42–43. Kraig argues for striking a balance between ends and means, stressing the long-term effects of one's present means. In this view, "The practical application of rhetorical ethics ... can be understood as a perpetually unresolved dialectic. A rhetor would be ethical when he/she struggled to discover good and effective means of persuasion in any given case" (p. 42). For a similar view of ends and means, see Peter Bachrach and Aryeh Botwinick, *Power and Empowerment: A Radical Theory of Participatory Democracy* (Philadelphia: Temple University Press, 1992), 118–119.

67. This conception of voting must be distinguished from definitions that limit it to majority rule. Julia T. Wood, for example, distinguishes between consensus and voting as methods of making decisions. "Alternative Methods of Group Decision Making," in Robert S. Cathcart and Larry A. Samovar, *Small Group Communication*, 5th ed. (Dubuque, Iowa: William C. Brown Publishers, 1988), 185–91.

68. Dahl, *Democracy and Its Critics*, 111.

69. Barber, *Strong Democracy*, 192f. The importance of dissent is shown by the ingenuity and determination of subordinate political discourse. Members of

subordinate groups frequently attempt to express their opposition even at the risk of severe punishment by authorities. See James C. Scott, *Domination and the Arts of Resistance: Hidden Transcripts* (New Haven, Conn.: Yale University Press, 1990), especially chapter 6. In cases of inescapable oppression, people have no threat of "exit"—only the power of "voice" (what I call dissent). In democratic groups the commitment to the democratic process implies a willingness to rely upon voice rather than exit so long as the group remains democratic. See Albert O. Hirschman, *Exit, Voice, and Loyalty* (Cambridge, Mass.: Harvard University Press, 1970).

70. Lappé and DuBois, "Power in a Living Democracy," 42. Other authors have also noted the transformative effects of listening and being heard. See Trena M. Cleland, "Living Democracy," *In Context*, no. 33 (1992): 35–36; Harry C. Boyte, *Commonwealth* (New York: Free Press, 1989), 148. For an extended discussion of different kinds of listening and their role in democracy, see Michael Osborn and Suzanne Osborn, *Alliance for a Better Public Voice* (Dayton, Ohio: NIF Institute, 1991).

71. Once again this relates to Dahl's aforementioned criterion of enlightened understanding (*Democracy and Its Critics*, 111–12). On the importance of Dahl's criterion and the dynamic character of preferences (or interests), see James G. March, "Preferences, Power, and Democracy," in Ian Shapiro and Grant Reeher, eds., *Power, Inequality, and Democratic Politics* (Boulder, Colo.: Westview Press, 1988), 50–66.

72. Braybrooke quoted in Fishkin, *Democracy and Deliberation*, 36–37.

73. Pollard et al., *Democracy and the Quaker Method*, 45.

74. Bellah et al., *The Good Society*, 254.

75. Barber, *Strong Democracy*, 175.

76. See Mansbridge, "Feminism and Democracy."

77. Lappé and DuBois, "Power in a Living Democracy," 42. On listening affecting the listener, see also Brenda Ueland, "Tell Me More: On the Fine Art of Listening," *Utne Reader*, no. 54 (November/December 1992): 104–9.

78. Dahl, *Democracy and Its Critics*, 131.

3

MORE THAN ONE
WAY TO DECIDE

The Committee for Peace in Guatemala takes pride in its method of decision making. Weekly meetings of volunteers are run by consensus, and the group has never needed to use a formal voting procedure. Each Tuesday night a different facilitator is named, and this member plays a very active role, guiding discussion and discerning when a consensus is emerging. Every meeting also has a watchdog, a member who makes certain that the facilitator does not rush the meeting or intimidate individuals. All group members are also responsible for noting any early signs of discord, but meetings are usually harmonious.

Across town, the Guatemalan Relief Society holds a different kind of meeting. They pride themselves on their highly skilled, almost ritualistic use of Robert's Rules of Order. *A chair is elected each year, and this individual oversees each monthly meeting-of-the-whole, as well as the two biweekly committee meetings. Meetings are fast paced, even though all critical votes are taken by secret ballot. The authority of the chair is rarely questioned, but members say this is because of the group's clear understanding of* Robert's Rules *rather than any sheepishness on the part of the membership.*

THESE TWO HYPOTHETICAL groups are similar to different groups I have joined or observed. If they existed in the same town and had overlapping goals, it is quite possible that each group would dislike the other's method of decision making and claim that only its own group procedures are fully democratic. Such a claim is unwarranted, because equally democratic groups can and do use different procedures. There is room for variation within the boundaries of small group democracy.

Three methods of decision making used in small democratic groups are consensus, majority rule, and "proportional outcomes."[1] Consensus tries to reach an agreement acceptable to all group members, whereas majority rule allows the passage of proposals supported by only a majority of the membership. In the proportional outcomes method, decisions are segmented and distributed in proportion to the prominence of different views. This is analogous to proportionally representative electoral systems, whereby parties receive a share of parliamentary seats in proportion to their percentage of the vote. Each of these methods fits within a democratic framework, and what follows is a discussion of their general features, their advantages, and their liabilities.

Consensus

> Consensus ... stresses the cooperative development of a decision with group members working together rather than competing against each other. The goal of consensus is a decision that is consented to by all group members.... Full consent does not mean that everyone must be completely satisfied with the final outcome—in fact, total satisfaction is rare. The decision must be acceptable enough, however, that all will agree to support the group in choosing it.[2]

> — Center for Conflict Resolution

The business meetings of the Religious Society of Friends (Quakers) are commonly cited as an example of small group consensus. Consensus logically follows from the Quaker view of spiritual knowledge. Believing that all persons have "that of God" within them, Quakers use consensus to draw out and integrate the insights of each individual, arriving at the best possible approximation of the truth. Quakers have found this method effective for addressing issues such as the opposition to war, the abolition of slavery, and the marrying of same-sex couples. For centuries, Quakers have used consensus in face-to-face groups ranging in size from five to two hundred members.[3]

The biweekly meetings of Friends Co-op, a housing cooperative I lived in for two years, provide an example of a semiformal style of consensus. The meeting facilitator began by reading a proposal from the agenda and opening the floor for discussion. After members had spoken their minds, the facilitator or another member tried to find a consensus. Members registered their agreement by nodding, verbally assenting, or silently wiggling their fingers (sometimes referred to as "Quaker applause"). In the event of continuing disagreement, the group tried to find alternative solutions or a temporary resolution.[4]

Consensus relies upon information, articulation, and persuasion to clarify and change the minds of group members, and it often utilizes compromise to reach an agreement.[5] Each group member provides different perspectives, puts forward information, ideas, feelings, and

---

Friendly Advices on the Conduct of Quaker Meetings for Business

These guidelines, purportedly written by William Bacon Evans, are adapted from the Powell House Newsletter *1 (August 1964). I thank Christopher Densmore for bringing them to my attention.*

1. Suitably prepare thyself for business session by previous group or individual waiting upon the Lord [prayer or meditation].

2. Seek not for information in open business session which thou shouldst have discovered by reading reports and minutes.

3. Let not certain Friends be known for their much speaking. Brevity is desirable in meetings for business as in meetings for worship.

4. If thou art tempted to speak much and often, exercise restraint lest thy speaking be not "in the Spirit."

5. Having spoken on a matter of business, it is well for thee to refrain from speaking again till after others have had full opportunity to voice their concerns.

6. Thou shouldst exercise care lest thy presumed convictions be only "points" or even prejudices.

7. Beware lest thou confuse thy own desire with the leading of the Spirit.

8. Should thy concern not meet with the general approval of the meeting, in common courtesy and in true humility withdraw thy concern that the meeting may act in some measure of unity.

9. Temper thy speech with tenderness and forbearance, that Friends may "feel" the promptings of the heart.

---

arguments, and listens carefully to what the others have to say. When there are conflicts of interest or desire, members try to reconcile divergent views, often agreeing on a reformulated version of a popular proposal that failed to reach consensus.

In the event of protracted disagreement, consensus groups continue to look for unanimity, but group members also accept the possibility of a deadlock. If agreement cannot be found or time pressure forces an immediate decision, dissenters can register their views without blocking consensus. There is a wide spectrum of dissent, ranging from disagreement without "standing in the way" to blocking consensus by vetoing a proposal.[6]

However, consensus must be distinguished from a simple "veto power" decision rule. Consensus is based on the desire to find common ground, whereas the veto power model works with a mutual distrust and an unwillingness to compromise. The United Nations Security Council exemplifies the veto system, since its members are unwilling to accept any decision that goes against their national interests. The impetus for negotiation is to prevent intolerable gridlock, rather than to create a sense of shared goals and mutual respect.[7]

There are many advantages to using consensus as a means of reaching decisions in small democratic groups.[8] Consensus is the surest safeguard against an unequal distribution of power. In theory, all group members have full power. In practice, members who abuse the blocking privilege often find themselves constrained by informal social pressures, so a balance is kept between a member's autonomy and the need for compromise.

Consensus can also bolster members' commitment to democracy. It radically empowers group members, often making them aware of both their autonomy and their responsibility to the group. Through consensus, group members can come to cherish their democratic rights and duties. At the very least the feeling of satisfaction that comes from consensus decision making can enhance members' appreciation of the democratic aspects of the process.[9]

Member relationships in consensus groups may be nurtured, because the relational aspects of small group democracy are the foundation of consensus. Individuality, competence, mutuality, and congeniality are historically associated with the use of consensus decision making, so it is more likely that consensus groups will direct energy toward maintaining a healthy relational atmosphere.[10]

Consensus also safeguards equal and adequate opportunities to speak. Consensus assumes that the minority viewpoint is crucial, so members may go out of their way to draw out quieter group members. Listening may also be enhanced, since consensus relies upon members understanding and considering what each other says. Without such listening it becomes far more difficult to arrive at a decision acceptable to all group members.[11]

In addition, consensus is designed to increase members' commitment to the group's decisions. A group member may enthusiastically implement a decision, because the group made a favorable compromise to ensure consensus. Or the member may willingly implement a decision after recognizing that it was the best decision upon which the group could agree. Since no decision is reached until all members can accept it, everyone is directly responsible for the group's decision.[12]

Despite these potential advantages, consensus has its pitfalls. Like any method of decision making, consensus works better in theory than in practice. Its drawbacks are its vulnerabilities—ways the process can fail if members do not have adequate experience, knowledge, or discipline. Over a period of months, groups using consensus can mature substantially, reaching increasingly sound decisions by incorporating member information and perspectives.[13] Initially, however, problems are more likely.

The most adept members of a group can manipulate the shades of disagreement used in consensus to alter a group decision. People may tend to approach consensus with a bias against disagreement and conflict, so members can induce agreement with their view by threatening a conflict if challenged.[14]

Consensus can also take a long time.[15] A group might have a two-thirds majority from the outset, yet many meetings could pass before the majority or minority change their views and reach an agreement. Possible side effects of such a time-consuming process include frustration, missed opportunities, and a weakened commitment to group procedures. The extra time taken to reach one decision also takes time away from deliberations on other issues.[16] Even if most group members are ready for change, existing policies remain intact if no decision is reached. As Jane Mansbridge points out, "*Not* making a decision ... *is* making a decision to leave the status quo (which may be oppressive, or just inefficient) unchanged."[17]

Majority Rule

Whereas consensus is often identified with groups such as the Quakers, people typically associate majority rule with representative bodies such as the U.S. Senate, which has some general features. Discussion is framed by a set of written procedures—often based upon *Robert's Rules of Order*—and monitored by a chair and/or parliamentarian. Members have the power to extend or set limits on discussion by requiring simple or two-thirds majorities to call for votes, table proposals, etc.; decisions are reached through formal voice votes or written ballots.

This parliamentary stereotype overlooks the variety of ways democratic groups can use majority rule. Even *Robert's Rules of Order* emphasizes the need for the group to tailor procedures to the skills and styles of its membership. Groups governed by majority rule can choose to proceed more informally by speaking without specified turns and changing proposals without a lengthy amendment process. Also, there are different kinds of majorities. A simple majority (i.e., more than 50 percent of the votes) is most commonly thought of as majority rule, but majoritarian decisions can be based on three-fifths, two-thirds, three-fourths, and any other fraction greater than one half and less than unanimity. Groups can use these different majority rules to give minority opinion more power on certain issues and procedures.[18]

Just as consensus has its strengths, so does majority rule. This form of decision making is a means of ensuring equal power without giving group members absolute vetos. When group members disagree even after deliberation, majority rule provides a way to resolve the dispute fairly without favoring the status quo.[19]

Speaking opportunities are also likely to be equal when governed by majority rule (e.g., requiring a two-thirds majority vote to close debate); discussion continues until most group members have had their say. Differing views are also likely to be aired if speaking turns are alternated between those favoring and opposing the proposal under discussion. Even if one's chances to speak are not adequate or equal in a given instance, they may become so over time.

The same procedures that ensure speaking opportunities also allow quick decisions when a clear majority is known to exist. In addition, the ability to close debate and take a decisive vote when there is not full agreement eliminates the bias toward the status quo. Majoritarian groups sometimes use a two-thirds vote to revoke an existing policy, but often a simple majority can revise policy. In either case the group's policies are likely to reflect the views of current majorities. As with consensus, these strengths are most prominent when members are experienced with the group's method of decision making.

Just as the limitations of consensus are exacerbated by inexperience, the hazards of majority rule are most prominent when members are unfamiliar with group procedures. Members of a group using majority rule sometimes find themselves in a permanent minority, and this situation can become intolerable if exploited or ignored. The group membership may be divided into two or more blocs, with one being a dominant majority and voting as a majority on a wide range of group proposals. Although the majority may be only seven of the ten group members, it will prevail ten out of ten times because of the nature of the system. If members find themselves stuck in a permanent minority, their commitment to making decisions democratically may wane. Their participation may begin to feel like voluntary servitude more than an opportunity to work with a group of equals.[20]

Even with a changing majority, this method of decision making can lead to tense relationships among group members. Majority rule often works as a zero-sum game: one subgroup's victory is another's defeat. If the process becomes highly competitive, adversaries may begin to question one another's mutuality and competence, and group discussions can turn into hostile debates.[21]

Just as it can splinter a group, majority rule—when combined with elaborate parliamentary procedures—has a tendency to fragment issues by requiring "a series of often confusing motions, seconds, points of order, and reconsiderations." Such a procedure "has severe limitations in helping a group get a sense of the whole of an issue and in setting some common direction for dealing with it."[22]

Finally, the ability of majorities to close debate by vote can be abused to silence a minority viewpoint. Once a clear majority is identified, those holding the prevailing view may not listen patiently to the minority. Considering others' arguments presumes the need to work together, but majorities have no short-term need to hear minority opinions.[23]

Proportional Outcomes

In the proportional outcomes method decisions are designed to reflect the proportions of the group membership that hold different views. Whereas compromise commonly occurs within both consensus and majority rule methods, the proportional outcome method institutionalizes the spirit of compromise.

This method has intuitive appeal, because it embodies basic principles many people learn at an early age. Studies of children in Western countries have found that as they grow older, children gradually develop the ability to distinguish between permanent and shifting group majorities. When a few group members are always in the minority, older children more routinely give the minority a proportional share of influence.[24]

This is easiest to do when decisions lend themselves to simple division. Imagine a group of five children at a summer camp deciding what to do for ten hours. If each of the proposed activities, such as board games, can be accomplished in two hours, each child may decide how the group will spend two of its ten hours.

In other cases groups can make compromises and concessions so that those in the minority are given compensation in proportion to their share of the membership. In the previous example, two children in the minority may agree to do an activity that takes the full ten hours, but only if they get double desserts at lunch or the chance to make the next decision for the group.

When a minority faction of a group is extremely small relative to the majority, a proportional outcomes approach can go even further. The group might give the minority limited veto power, a disproportionate amount of representation, or even equal representation (just as each state, regardless of its population, receives two seats in the Senate).[25]

In a way, proportional outcome schemes are a cross between majority rule and consensus. As in majority rule, unanimity is not required. Just as majorities get their power by virtue of their size, the relative size of voting blocs determines their influence. Like consensus, the proportional outcomes method is based on the premise that all members, including those in the minority, ought to play a role in shaping the final group policy.[26]

These similarities correspond to some of the strengths of proportional outcomes. The method can have many of the advantages associated with consensus—encouraging positive relationships and careful deliberation. It can also reap the benefits of majority rule, since it is egalitarian, allows quick decisions, and reduces the bias toward the status quo.

The unique advantage of this method is that decisions can often be divided proportionally, or compromises can be made across issues rather than within a single issue. While this is possible with other methods, it is built into the basic principles of the proportional system.[27]

Just as the proportional outcome scheme combines the potential strengths of consensus and majority rule, so does it share their weaknesses. To the extent that the system emphasizes unanimity, it can invite manipulation and excessive delays. If it leans toward quick decisions, it can result in fewer speaking opportunities and inattentiveness.[28]

Using proportional outcomes also has a tendency to factionalize groups, even more so than majority rule. In majority rule, minority blocs have a clear incentive to build coalitions; otherwise, they can become isolated and powerless. In the proportional outcome system, subgroups are never powerless, since they receive a degree of influence commensurate with their size. This makes it easier for a group to split into separate and permanent group factions, a condition that limits the group's mutuality, deliberative capacity, and ability to implement truly collective decisions.

Beyond Head Counting

Whether groups rely upon consensus, majority rule, or proportional outcomes, they will all have to devise ways of polling or registering the views of the membership. Head counting is perhaps the simplest means of polling. Other forms include secret or open ballots and preliminary techniques, such as the straw poll. When a chair in a parliamentary group asks for yeas and nays, she is collecting verbal ballots for and against a proposition. When a facilitator in a consensus group says he senses that the group favors a proposal, he is implicitly asking for group members to cast their ballots, either expressing their assent with silent nods or presenting their veto with a verbal objection. All democratic groups use polling techniques, and it is useful to explore the methods groups use to get beyond mere head counting.[29]

Polls or ballots on two or more alternatives can be structured in many ways. Consider a school board deciding between two proposed budgets (A and B). In its final vote the board might allow votes for A, B, or abstention. Alternatively, it might require that a member propose one of the two budgets and vote with a yes/no/abstention format. These systems may seem identical, but in some situations they can have different results. If on the first ballot, budget A is rejected, the bylaws of the group may make it impossible (or difficult) to reconsider A. This puts pressure on the board to pass B to avoid the possibility of having no budget for the coming year. If the budgets were considered simultaneously, the vote might have shown a majority favoring A.

Notice that in the above structure, abstentions are counted as absent votes. In a forced-choice structure, by contrast, anything but a yes is counted as a de facto no vote. This may seem a minor difference, but it is not. While serving on the Wisconsin Student Association Senate I witnessed occasions on which the vast majority of the senators cast abstentions (or failed to vote at all) because they were uninformed, undecided, and/or uninterested. Under such conditions a proposal would occasionally pass on something like a three-to-one vote in a senate with twenty-five members present. Had the forced-choice structure been in effect, all votes with fewer than thirteen yeas would fail with twenty-five senators present. To its credit, the same senate used the forced-choice structure only for critical issues, such as constitutional amendments and calls for impeachment.

A democratic group can also make polls more sensitive to the full diversity of views. Preferences and judgments, like attitudes in general, are quite complex, and subtle polls can allow members to express shades of agreement and disagreement. When confronted with two choices, a person might be 40 percent in favor of one, 20 percent in favor of the other, and 40 percent undecided.[30] If given ten votes to distribute, a member could vote in accordance with these conflicting feelings. Alternatively, a ballot might have five or seven choices, ranging from "strong yes" to "strong no," analogous to the seven-point scales used in survey research.

Polls can even distinguish among identical preferences that are based on different reasons. A majority may favor budget A but not for the same reason. When polls allow members to choose among different rationales as well as different items (e.g., "Yes because of x" versus "Yes because of y," or simply "Yes because of—"), groups can receive valuable information. After such a poll a group might decide to reverse or postpone a decision because there are contradictory reasons behind supporting it. If half of a political action group wants to hold a demonstration involving civil disobedience to recruit new members and half wants to hold it to test the mettle of the membership, going ahead with the demonstration might prove disastrous, as members would be working at cross-purposes.

Groups can also restructure their polls to take multiple alternatives into account. Some decisions require choosing among multiple proposals, and group members might favor two or three out of ten possible decisions. Groups choose among multiple alternatives when they need more than one of something (e.g., electing four representatives), but this can also be done when only one proposal or candidate will be selected.[31]

To choose among multiple alternatives, members might rank all available choices or give them each ratings ranging from one to three.

Earlham '85 Polling Method

Instructions

1) Mark the ballot to indicate which, if any, of the candidates is your first choice.

2) For each of the other candidates, mark the ballot to indicate whether you find the candidates acceptable or unacceptable (or, if you prefer, mark neither).

Ballot

	1st Choice	Acceptable	Unacceptable
Candidate A	_____	_____	_____
Candidate B	_____	_____	_____
Candidate C	_____	_____	_____
Candidate D	_____	_____	_____

Tallying Method

To win, a candidate must obtain both (1) a majority of the first choice votes and (2) first choice or acceptable votes on a majority of ballots. (If no candidate meets these two conditions, the two candidates with the most first choice votes participate in a runoff election. If a runoff produces no winner, new candidates might be nominated.)

Rationale

The first of these requirements ensures that the winning candidate is the first choice of a majority of voters who have strong preferences. The second requirement ensures that the candidate is also acceptable to a majority of those voting. In a divisive and competitive race, it is entirely possible that a candidate could win a majority of first choice votes yet prove unacceptable to a majority of voters.

Members could also have the chance to vote yes or no for each choice, with the final tally adding yes votes and subtracting no votes. In 1985 the Earlham College student government elections used yet another alternative, asking voters to identify the candidates they preferred as well as those they found "acceptable."[32]

Polling procedures can also require that the group take more than one vote. This allows members to respond to the information they receive on the first poll. If members are stating both positions and rationales on the first poll, the group might discover that it needs to address some factual or moral question before taking the final poll. In the earlier school board example, a preliminary vote can be taken on the two budgets to make certain that one will pass in the final poll, avoiding the possibility of a deadlock. Preliminary polling techniques such as these assume that a relatively formal method of articulation can help move deliberation forward. An early poll forces members to probe their own views or opinions, and it makes them aware of the views of others.

With any of these polling strategies, it is possible to vote by speaking, raising hands, or writing on ballots. The latter two techniques allow simultaneous voting, and (unless group members close their eyes) only written ballots allow secrecy. Research on sequential straw polls, in which, one by one, members state their positions, shows how the order in which members vote can affect the outcome. If the fifth person in a nine-person group happens to vote after four "yea" votes, she becomes a little bit more likely to go along with the yeas than she would be otherwise. To avoid this problem, members can vote secretly or simultaneously, possibly in a round-robin to elaborate their views after stating their general positions.[33]

Unfortunately, all of these polling techniques are subject to error and abuse. The more complex the poll, the more chance there is for confusion, which results in inadequate opportunities to express final preferences. More elaborate polls are also easier to distort, since group members can exaggerate the extremity of their views. Members can vote for their preferred candidate or proposal and vote against all the others—even if they know the others are also fine choices. In multiple polling schemes, members can manipulate the final poll through deceptive votes in preliminary tallies. For instance, a member may want to block a proposal with a veto without having to listen to the counterarguments of other group members. This member can support the proposal during the straw poll, then veto it during the final vote taken at the end of the group's scheduled meeting time.[34]

The extra time and thought that the more complex polls require make them appropriate for groups able to present their views honestly and situations where time permits reflection. Perhaps experimenting with the full variety of polling techniques is the best way to determine which ones best suit a group under different circumstances.

Mixing Methods

A spirit of experimentation is also a good approach to integrating various polling techniques with the different methods of decision making. Ideally, groups can find ways to draw upon the strengths of each polling strategy and decision-making method, adapting their procedures to changing memberships, issues, and situations.

For example, the board of directors for Madison Community Co-ops allows board members to vote as favoring, opposing, objecting, or abstaining. An objection blocks consensus, and the proposal is either tabled or discussed further. Eventually the objection can be overridden through majority rule. If there is no objection, yeas and nays are counted and the majority decides the verdict. One exception to this process is that any procedural motion, such as a call for recess, is voted on through simple majority rule.

A precursor to the board's procedure is Martha's Rules of Order, developed at a residential housing cooperative. A group using Martha's Rules tries to work toward a full consensus among group members, but if necessary the group can override one or two objections to a proposal with a simple majority vote. If three or more group members object, the override requires a two-thirds majority, and the issue is tabled until the next meeting to allow time for reformulation and compromise on the proposal.

Martha's Rules also formalize the group's ability to measure the degree to which an individual supports a proposal. One can say, "I am comfortable with the proposal," or merely, "I can live with the proposal." If there are competing proposals, the distinction between these two degrees of support can be decisive, but usually the distinction merely gauges how enthusiastically the group supports a proposal. This particular method is just one more example of how groups can adjust and combine different methods of decision making and polling to meet their current needs.[35]

Notes

1. It is important to stress that small group democracy encompasses different decision rules, including consensus and proportional outcomes, because "tyranny of the majority" is so closely associated with the democratic process. On the historical association of democracy with simple majority rule see Robert A. Dahl, *Democracy and Its Critics* (New Haven, Conn.: Yale University Press, 1989), 171–73.

2. Quote from Center for Conflict Resolution, *Building United Judgment* (Madison, Wis.: Center for Conflict Resolution, 1981), 1. For an academic history of consensus, see W. K. Rawlins, "Consensus in Decision-Making Groups: A Conceptual History," in Gerald M. Phillips and Julia T. Wood, eds., *Emergent Issues in Human Decision Making* (Carbondale, Ill.: Southern Illinois University Press, 1984), 19–39. For the history of consensus in political theory and a critical evaluation of it, see Douglas W. Rae, "The Limits of Consensual Decision," *American Political Science Review* 69 (1975): 1270–94. For a more positive view see Kirkpatrick Sale, *Human Scale* (New York: G. P. Putnam's Sons, 1980), 501–4.

3. On Quaker decision making see Michael J. Sheeran, *Beyond Majority Rule* (Philadelphia: Philadelphia Yearly Meeting, 1983); Francis E. Pollard, Beatrice E. Pollard, and Robert S. W. Pollard, *Democracy and the Quaker Method* (London: Ballinsdale, 1949). On the usefulness of the Quaker method for other groups, see Pollard et al., ibid., chap. 5. On other quasidemocratic decision-making procedures with a heavy spiritual influence, see Corinne McLaughlin and Gordon Davidson's *Builders of the Dawn: Community Lifestyles in a Changing World* (Shutesbury, Mass.: Sirius Publishing, 1986). It should be noted that many Quakers do not view their decision-making process as an example of consensus or democracy. For these Friends the religious element makes the Quaker process distinct; for example, see the letters under "Not Just Consensus" in *Friends Journal* (February 1993), 5.

One unique feature of the Quaker method, different from other versions of consensus in use, is the powerful role of the clerk of the Meeting. Sheeran (*Beyond Majority Rule*) writes at length about the clerk's responsibility for "discerning" the "sense of the meeting"—and the potential for abusing this responsibility. Some Quaker meetings have procedural safeguards against a clerk's ability to distort decisions, such as a one-fifth vote to overrule the clerk's decision; see, for example, Pollard et al., *Democracy and the Quaker Method*, 144.

4. Consensus can be used with a set of highly structured procedures or a more anarchistic approach. For examples of each, see McLaughlin and Davidson's descriptions of Philadelphia's Movement for a New Society and the Auroville Community in South India; *Builders of the Dawn*, 162–68, 173–78. Bruno Lasker (*Democracy through Discussion* [New York: H. W. Wilson Co., 1949], p. III) describes at length a methodical discussion procedure that draws upon consensus principles. As a cautionary note, at least one investigation has found that inexperienced consensus groups using unstructured discussion methods have more difficulty integrating the information held by different group members; Garold Stasser and William Titus, "Pooling of Unshared Information in Group Decision Making: Biased Information Sampling During Discussion," *Journal of Personality and Social Psychology* 48 (1985): 1467–78.

5. Advocates of consensus sometimes give compromise a pejorative meaning, contrasting it with the pursuit of a genuine common ground. It is in this sense that Pollard et al. insist that Quaker business meetings do not have "any special tendency to result in mere compromise between different points of view"; *Democracy and the Quaker Method*, 61.

6. Sheeran, *Beyond Majority Rule*, 65–71. On blocking consensus and the alternatives to blocking, see Center for Conflict Resolution, *Building United Judgment*, chap. 5.

7. On full veto power and the U.N. Security Council, see Jane J. Mansbridge, *Beyond Adversary Democracy* (Chicago: University of Chicago Press, 1983), chap. 18. In Julia T. Wood's terminology, the U.N. format is closer to negotiation than consensus, because it involves no attempt to find common ground or create a collective identity; see "Alternative Methods of Group Decision Making," in Robert S. Cathcart and Larry A. Samovar, *Small Group Communication*, 5th ed. (Dubuque, Iowa: William C. Brown Publishers, 1988), 187–88.

8. RoLayne S. DeStephen and Randy Y. Hirokawa point out that most of the research on consensus and small groups treats consensus as an outcome—a product of group discussion rather than a group process. Thus the majority of studies on small group consensus are not relevant to the question of how the consensus *process* affects groups and their members. See "Small Group Consensus: Stability of Group Support of the Decision, Task Process, and Group Relationships," *Small Group Behavior* 19 (1988): 227–39.

One variable I do not discuss is the "productivity" of groups using a consensus, majority rule, or proportional outcomes decision method. Productivity is a rather broad variable, and the few studies that have compared majority rule and consensus are far from conclusive on the question. See Randy Y. Hirokawa, "Does Consensus Really Result in Higher Quality Group Decisions?" in Gerald M. Phillips and Julia T. Wood, eds., *Emergent Issues in Human Decision Making* (Carbondale, Ill.: Southern Illinois University Press, 1984), 40–49. Consensus may be more advantageous in a group negotiation context, since it tends to result in more mutually beneficial decisions. Two recent studies have produced evidence supporting this view: Leigh L. Thompson, Elizabeth Mannix, and Max H. Bazerman, "Group Negotiation: Effects of Decision Rule, Agenda, and Aspiration," *Journal of Personality and Social Psychology* 54 (1988): 86–95; Elizabeth Mannix, Leigh L. Thompson, and Max H. Bazerman, "Negotiation in Small Groups," *Journal of Applied Psychology* 74 (1989): 508–17.

Like these two articles, the vast majority of social scientific studies cited herein have been conducted with groups of college students. In the typical design the group members have little or no experience working with one another. These factors make many studies somewhat artificial, a problem that has plagued research on small groups for decades, as small group communication scholar Ernest G. Bormann has observed on more than one occasion: "The Paradox and Promise of Small Group Research," *Speech Monographs* 37 (1970): 211–16; "The Paradox and Promise of Small Group Research Revisited," *Central States Speech Journal* 31 (1980): 214–20. This conventional methodology also makes it more difficult to generalize the findings to the full variety of group settings—most of which do not consist of three or four unacquainted college students discussing a hypothetical problem for one or more hours.

Nonetheless the careful research design in many of these studies makes their findings suggestive or, at the very least, thought-provoking. I encourage readers to conduct their own inclusive and contextually sensitive research on small group democracy. There is little research on the subject, and careful study of existing groups would greatly improve our understanding of the democratic process in small groups.

9. A wealth of evidence supports the notion that, on average, group members are more satisfied with the consensus method than majority rule. See Charlan Nemeth, "Interactions Between Jurors as a Function of Majority vs. Unanimity Decision Rules," *Journal of Applied Social Psychology* 7 (1977): 38–56; Martin F. Kaplan and Charles E. Miller, "Group Decision Making and Normative Versus Informational Influence: Effects of Type of Issue and Assigned Decision Rule," *Journal of Personality and Social Psychology* 53 (1987): 306–13. A similar study reports the same findings and also notes that even group members holding the minority viewpoint were more satisfied with the decisions reached in consensus groups than in those using majority rule: Norbert L. Kerr et al., "Guilt Beyond a Reasonable Doubt: Effects of Concept Definition and Assigned Decision Rule on the Judgments of Mock Jurors," *Journal of Personality and Social Psychology* 34 (1976): 282–94.

10. See L. Kelly and C. Begnal, "Group Members' Orientations toward Decision Processes," in Gerald M. Phillips and Julia T. Wood, eds., *Emergent Issues in Human Decision Making* (Carbondale, Ill.: Southern Illinois University Press, 1984), 63–79.

11. However, critics of consensus maintain that the process suppresses conflict, preventing the airing of minority viewpoints. In this view, majority rule is a better method for ensuring that the minority has its say. Gideon Falk finds evidence supporting this view in "An Empirical Study Measuring Conflict in Problem-Solving Groups Which Are Assigned Different Decision Rules," *Human Relations* 35 (1982): 1123–38. In a similar study Gideon Falk and Shoshana Falk also argue that majority rule is better than a unanimity rule at minimizing the influence of the most powerful group member: "The Impact of Decision Rules on the Distribution of Power in Problem-Solving Teams with Unequal Power," *Group and Organization Studies* 6 (1981): 211–23.

12. Studies finding greater commitment to consensus group decisions include Nemeth, "Interactions Between Jurors"; Dean Tjosvold and Richard H. G. Field, "Effects of Social Context on Consensus and Majority Vote Decision Making," *Academy of Management Journal* 26 (1983): 500–506.

13. Warren Watson, Larry K. Michaelsen, and Walt Sharp, "Member Competence, Group Interaction, and Group Decision Making: A Longitudinal Study," *Journal of Applied Psychology* 76 (1991): 803–9. Some critics hold that consensus is inherently flawed. For a brief, impassioned argument against consensus, see D. G. Clark, "Consensus or Stalemate?" *National Parliamentarian* 53, no. 1 (1992): 7.

14. Anne Gero identifies the existence of an "antidisagreement norm" in her study of business and social work students. "Conflict Avoidance in Consensual Decision Processes," *Small Group Behavior* 16 (1985): 487–99.

15. Quantitative studies of inexperienced groups support this view. For instance, comparisons of majority rule and consensus mock juries have found that consensus groups take more time to reach decisions: Nemeth, "Interactions Between Jurors"; Kerr et al., "Guilt Beyond a Reasonable Doubt"; Charles E. Miller, "Group Decision Making under Majority and Unanimity Decision Rules," *Social Psychology Quarterly* 48 (1985): 51–61. In addition, qualitative studies of experienced consensus groups such as the Clamshell Alliance have found that the

process tends to take more time; see Gary L. Downey, "Ideology and the Clamshell Identity: Organizational Dilemmas in the Anti-Nuclear Power Movement," *Social Problems* 33 (1986): 357–73.

The simplest theoretical explanation for why consensus takes longer than majority rule is that it is usually easier to get a smaller number of people to agree; thus, in groups of equal size, consensus requires more people to agree (or, at least, accept a decision). Benjamin Radcliff, "Majority Rule and Impossibility Theorems," *Social Science Quarterly* 73 (1992): 515.

16. The argument that time spent on one issue takes it away from deliberation on another comes from Thomas Christiano, "Freedom, Consensus, and Equality in Collective Decision Making," *Ethics* 101 (1990): 167.

17. Jane J. Mansbridge, "A Paradox of Size," in C. George Benello, *From the Ground Up* (Boston: South End Press, 1992), 166. To counterbalance the tendency to favor the status quo, a group can put expiration dates on its decisions. Caroline Estes explains that Alpha Farm makes "temporary decisions on a number of occasions, usually trying the decision for a year and then either making a final decision or dropping it entirely": "Consensus Ingredients," in Fellowship for Intentional Community and Communities Publications Cooperative, eds., *Intentional Communities: A Guide to Cooperative Living* (Evansville, Ind.: Fellowship for Intentional Community; Stelle, Ill.: Communities Publications Cooperative, 1990), 81. This "favoritism toward the status quo" can also be viewed as caution, which is entirely appropriate in many contexts. For instance, a study using actual jurors found that after watching a videotaped trial, groups using consensus were more likely than groups using majority rule to reach not-guilty or hung verdicts (relatively cautious, compared to guilty verdicts): Robert Buckhout, Steve Weg, and Vincent Reilly, "Jury Verdicts: Comparison of 6- vs. 12-Person Juries and Unanimous vs. Majority Decision Rule in a Murder Trial," *Bulletin of the Psychonomic Society* 10 (1977): 175–78.

18. For this insight I owe thanks to Mary Giovagnoli. The classic on parliamentary procedure is Henry M. Robert, *Robert's Rules of Order Newly Revised* (Glenview, Ill.: Scott, Foresman, 1990). A popular, more streamlined alternative is Alice Sturgis, *Standard Code of Parliamentary Procedure*, 3d ed. (New York: McGraw-Hill, 1988). An even more simplified and concise manual of parliamentary procedure is Hermon W. Farwell, *The Majority Rules*, 2d ed. (Pueblo, Colo.: High Publishers, 1988). For a general critique of the majority rule method of decision making in small groups, see Center for Conflict Resolution, *Building United Judgment*, 4–7.

19. This is a longstanding argument in favor of majority rule. If one presumes that people have different preferences at a given point in time, majority rule, compared to all other decision rules, is the most responsive to individual preferences (presuming the body has an odd number of members and the choice is between only two alternatives): Philip D. Straffin, Jr., "Majority Rule and General Decision Rules," *Theory and Decision* 8 (1977): 351–60. If one ignores the role of deliberation and changing preferences, this can be proven mathematically; see Straffin, "Majority Rule," and Mark Gradstein, "Conditions for the Optimality of Simple Majority Decisions in Pairwise Choice Situations," *Theory and Decision* 21

(1986): 181–87. A more readable presentation of this view is provided by Bruce Ackerman in *Social Justice and the Liberal State* (New Haven, Conn.: Yale University Press, 1980), chap. 9. Ackerman uses rather humorous dialogues to make the case for using majority rule when "good-faith" disagreements exist.

20. On the mutually reinforcing relationship between unstable majorities and pluralist politics, see Nicholas R. Miller, "Pluralism and Social Choice," *American Political Science Review* 77 (1983): 734–47. On a large social scale, Northern Ireland provides an example of the fate of a permanent minority; see Anthony Arblaster, *Democracy* (Open University Press: Milton Keynes, 1987): 70–72. When the composition of the majority does not change over time and the views of the opposition are markedly different from those of the majority, a proportional outcome scheme, discussed below, might be a more democratic method of decision making; see Arend Lijphart, *Democracies: Patterns of Majoritarian and Consensus Governments in Twenty-one Countries* (New Haven, Conn.: Yale University Press, 1984), 21–23.

21. See Alfie Kohn, *No Contest* (New York: Houghton Mifflin, 1986).

22. Robert H. McKenzie, "Learning to Deliberate and Choose," *Public Leadership Education* 4 (1991): 11.

23. In response to a majority court opinion, a dissenting Supreme Court justice expressed this view: "It is said that there is no evidence that majority jurors will refuse to listen to dissenters whose votes are unneeded for conviction. Yet human experience teaches that polite and academic conversation is no substitute for the earnest and robust argument necessary to reach unanimity." (Justice Douglass, with Justices Marshall and Brennan, quoted in Nemeth, "Interactions Between Jurors," 40.) In a study investigating this issue, Nemeth found some support for Justice Douglass's view; consensus groups engaged in more conflict, and participants were more likely to change their minds. Similarly Kerr et al., in "Guilt Beyond a Reasonable Doubt," found that in half of the mock juries using majority rule, deliberation was ended after the first decisive poll, despite the presence of a vocal minority.

More generally, the very nature of majority rule makes it more likely that minority viewpoints will emerge and be dominated by majorities. Thompson et al. ("Group Negotiation") found that majority-rule negotiation groups were more likely to form dominant coalitions and reach decisions that worked against the interests of group minorities.

24. Leon Mann et al., "Developmental Changes in Application of Majority Rule in Group Decisions," *British Journal of Developmental Psychology* 2 (1984): 275–81.

25. On the application of the proportionality principle, see Arend Lijphart, *Democracy in Plural Societies* (New Haven, Conn.: Yale University Press, 1977), 38–41. The proportional outcome approach to decision making has proven effective in the past, even for large-scale social groups, such as Switzerland and the Netherlands, both of which use "consociational" political systems that incorporate proportional outcomes. See Lijphart, *Democracies* and *Democracy in Plural Societies*; Mansbridge, *Beyond Adversary Democracy*, 265–68.

26. The proportional outcomes method is probably closer to consensus than majority rule; thus Lijphart's definition of the "consensus model of democracy,"

which includes proportional outcomes, is contrasted with majority rule. *Democracies*, pp. 23–30.

27. Mannix et al. ("Negotiation in Small Groups") conducted a direct test of the benefits of sequential agendas versus package agendas (simultaneously reaching decisions on different issues, making them part of a single agenda item). They found that package agendas resulted in more mutually beneficial decisions for the members of small negotiation groups, whether the groups used majority rule or consensus decision rules.

28. On the disadvantages of proportional outcomes and consociationalism in large-scale systems, see Lijphart, *Democracy in Plural Societies*, 47–52.

29. For a discussion on multichoice and two-step voting formats, see Benjamin Barber, *Strong Democracy* (Berkeley: University of California Press, 1984), 286–89. For a more detailed discussion of the multichoice format and its use in Switzerland, see Benjamin Barber, *The Death of Communal Liberty* (Princeton, N.J.: Princeton University Press, 1974).

30. See James Lull and Joseph Cappella, "Slicing the Attitude Pie: A New Approach to Attitude Measurement," *Communication Quarterly* 29 (1981): 67–80; Bernard Manin, "On Legitimacy and Political Deliberation," trans. Elly Stein and Jane Mansbridge, *Political Theory* 15 (1987): 350.

31. In fact the existence of multiple alternatives raises a problem for majority-rule voting. If head-to-head votes show that majorities favor A over B, favor B over C, and favor C over A, which is the preferred policy? For a clear discussion of this problem see Dahl, *Democracy and Its Critics*, 144–46. This paradox is irresolvable, but as Benjamin Radcliff argues in "Majority Rule and Impossibility Theorems," this should be seen as a limitation upon using majority rule—not as a reason to abandon such a process.

32. I thank George Gastil for providing detailed information on the "Earlham '85" ballots.

33. See James H. Davis et al., "Effects of Straw Polls on Group Decision Making: Sequential Voting Pattern, Timing and Local Majorities," *Journal of Personality and Social Psychology* 55 (1988): 918–26; James H. Davis et al., "Some Social Mechanics of Group Decision Making: The Distribution of Opinion, Polling Sequence, and Implications for Consensus," *Journal of Personality and Social Psychology* 57 (1989): 1000–1012.

34. Social choice theorists rather soberly refer to deceptive voting behavior as "strategic voting." On its unavoidability, see David Miller, "Deliberative Democracy and Social Choice," *Political Studies* 40, Special Issue (1992): 58–59.

35. Some of the details of Martha's Rules of Order have changed over the years. The namesake cooperative, Martha's Co-op, currently uses a different version. I thank Jeff Haines for clarifying the details of Martha's Rules. For brief summaries of Martha's Rules and other alternative procedures, see Center for Conflict Resolution, *Building United Judgment*, 101–6.

Some critics of procedures like Martha's Rules argue that these are an impure form of consensus, because they allow a majority to rule. In response, many ardent advocates of consensus emphasize that consensus does not require unanimity.

Defining it as such underemphasizes the importance of practices such as "standing aside" from a decision. See Virginia Coover et al., *Resource Manual for a Living Revolution* (Philadelphia: New Society Press, 1978), 52–53; Estes, "Consensus Ingredients," 80–81.

4

FOOD FOR THOUGHT: A DEMOCRATIC GROCERY CO-OP

Whatever is, is possible.[1]
—T. L. Peacock

At 6:30 on a rainy Monday evening, the small room above Mifflin Street Community Co-op fills with greetings and friendly chatter. Each of nine staff members enters carrying drinks and snacks from the grocery store below. They set their coats on bookshelves and file cabinets, then move chairs and floor cushions into a rough circle that snakes its way along desks, boxes, and the odd objects that rest against the walls. When Laura enters, she asks everyone to fill in their slots on the work schedule. She hands the schedule clipboard to Rose, who scribbles down her name a few times and passes it around the circle.

By 6:40 the appointed facilitator, Dan, has begun to go down the list of ongoing items, and one or two staff members explain what they have done since the last meeting. Yes, the bicycle rack has been purchased, but it has not yet arrived. Yes, the sign about the ongoing boycott has been posted next to the offending food item.

Next Dan reads the agenda and asks if anything needs to be changed. A forgotten announcement or two is quickly tacked on, and the staff turns to new items of business. Rose briefs the staff on a donation request, and after reaching a clear consensus, the group decides to contribute cheese and crackers to an upcoming community forum. Louis asks what should be done about a person who wants to get the volunteer discount but doesn't work his full hours. The staff agrees to make an exception, because of the person's special circumstances. And so on.

69

The day-to-day business is taken care of as time flies by—punctuated with the periodic antics of Laura and Sam, who take turns as court jester. Then, in the heart of the meeting, Dan announces that the next agenda item is work schedule policy. The jesters groan, and two more staff members look about the room nervously. Like a team of synchronized swimmers, the staff members simultaneously and uncomfortably adjust their sitting positions. There is an audible five-second pause.

The discussion begins innocently enough, with Kate reviewing last week's distribution of work shifts. Louis suggests that there was a misunderstanding about who was working on Saturday, and Sam points out that two part-time shift-workers put in a lot of time during the week. Amy expresses concern about overusing shift-workers, and other staff members agree. There's a pinch of tension as Ray explains the problem with having too many of one's shifts covered by other staff and shift-workers. Norma correctly discerns that she is the staff member on everyone's mind, and she explains why she had to swap so many shifts. Kate explains why Norma's actions upset her, and Laura, Rose, and Ray nod in agreement. Before long all have spoken their minds, a tentative resolution is reached, and the meeting continues. The tension slowly subsides, while the discussion turns to three minor business items and the remaining announcements.

By 9:00 the last agenda item is done, and the staff makes certain that all work shifts for the following week are covered. At 9:15 the meeting unofficially adjourns, and the staff members slip into their coats and walk downstairs in pairs. The last person locks the store and leaves at 10:00.[2]

THIS IS A glimpse of a typical staff meeting at Mifflin Street Community Co-op, a worker-managed grocery store in Madison, Wisconsin. During the store's more than twenty years serving the community, it has built a reputation as a politically engaged and self-conscious business. It has supported and worked with numerous political and community organizations, and it has brought its politics to its shelves, providing consumer information and alternative products. To better understand small group democracy, it is useful to take a close look at the history and current practices of this exceptional grocery co-op.

The "Owner's Manual" for members of the co-op gives insight into Mifflin's character as a "living, breathing experiment in participatory democracy, community control, and economic alternatives." Open membership and "democratic control based on one member, one vote" are its first principles. This pamphlet, available free at the checkout counter, echoes the language of the Co-op's original bylaws, adopted in 1969:

> Mifflin Street Community Co-op exists to embody a belief in community self-determination in opposition to the dominant trends in all communities in which control is increasingly concentrated outside the community and operated for profits which are not used for the

betterment of the community. Our assets ... are committed to this struggle by any means necessary.[3]

The history of Mifflin Co-op from the 1960s to the 1990s reflects a commitment to being more than just a store. The co-op, including both its storefront and second-floor rooms, has served as temporary lodging for the homeless, a community health-care center, a base of operations for organizing community celebrations and demonstrations, an information nexus for political organizers and other co-ops, a shelter from the police, an outlet for alternative products and organic produce, a brick canvas for colorful murals, and a symbol of community identity and determination.[4]

Mifflin Co-op's reputation derives more from this remarkable history than the odd brands of food stacked on its shelves and the Marxist posters adorning its interior walls. But what makes Mifflin unique is its staff meetings. According to some firsthand accounts, these meetings are a model in democratic decision making.[5]

In the fall of 1990 the Mifflin Co-op worker collective gave me permission to study its weekly staff meetings. I chose to focus on meetings because regular face-to-face gatherings are the heart of many a group's existence. The life of a small group transcends its meetings, but the times that it meets as a whole have a special importance. As anthropologist Helen Schwartzman argues, focusing on a group's meetings means looking at the center of its system—the place where shared meanings, power relations, and group norms are developed and validated or challenged. Meetings can "make, remake, and sometimes unmake" a group.[6]

I studied the co-op's staff meetings using a variety of techniques. I started with a wealth of background information, including my previous experiences at Mifflin as a shopper and volunteer. I read notes from past staff meetings and a retrospective history of the co-op, chronicled by a former staff member. At the center of the study were video and audio tapes of six consecutive staff meetings, most of which took place in the upstairs room at the co-op. I set up two video cameras and microphones in opposite corners of the room and let them run continuously during the meetings. In addition, I had numerous informal conversations with the staff, and all nine staff members completed a long questionnaire about themselves and the co-op. I followed up this questionnaire with one-on-one interviews, talking with each staff member for one to two hours. After the last interview, I met with the staff as a whole to elicit their reactions to my preliminary findings. In what follows, I draw upon each of these methods of observation, providing a multifaceted portrait of Mifflin Co-op's attempt to practice small group democracy.[7]

Group Power

The first issue that must be examined is the extent to which the staff had control over its agenda. Did the staff's decisions have concrete effects, or was the staff merely an advisory committee under the authority of some other entity?

In the co-op's bylaws, the staff—sometimes referred to as the "worker collective"—has responsibility for the "day-to-day affairs of the Co-op and the management of the store." These bylaws give the board of directors responsibility for long-range planning, budget approval, and hiring and firing of staff. The co-op's general membership—mostly customers—elects five board members, and the staff appoints two more. Committees composed of staff, board members, and community members take on other responsibilities, such as personnel review and the development of the budget.

In practice the staff's weekly meetings are the site of both day-to-day decisions and broader policy development. During the six meetings I observed, the Mifflin staff made several decisions, virtually all of which took effect immediately. The staff made half a dozen donations, changed store policies, and set work schedules.

The one exception was the staff's decision to provide "tenure incentives." Retaining long-term staff members enhances the depth of knowledge and quality of work at the co-op, so the staff proposed giving workers monetary or vacation bonuses for staying with the co-op longer. In this case the staff decision was contingent upon approval by the board of directors. Nevertheless, the board had previously informed the staff members that it would accept whatever the staff decided, so staff deliberations became decisive. The board often took this approach, and the staff regularly decided long-range co-op policies.

The staff's power is noticeably constrained, though, by external political and economic forces.[8] As for political sovereignty, the last article of the Mifflin bylaws acknowledges that the co-op's rules are subject to the laws of local, state, and federal governments. Out of necessity, co-op activities are sometimes aimed toward complying with health codes and other regulations. Although the co-op's early years involved direct challenges of the law, the store's viability requires generally obeying existing laws.

Since the co-op seeks to maintain financial stability, its stocking, pricing, and other monetary decisions are constrained by prevailing market forces. The store's comfortable profit margin, however, gives it room for flexibility. Last year's gross receipts totaled over $800,000, which allowed the co-op to maintain and upgrade the store, donate $10,000 to the community, give good wages and full health benefits to the staff, and set aside enough additional capital for investment in the co-op's future.

Aside from the amount of power, it is necessary to look at the distribution of power at Mifflin Co-op. One can crudely assess relative power by noticing the physical location of different group members when important decisions are being made. For example, at a housing board meeting I recently attended, I sat in the outer circle around the board's central table. During the meeting the board approved five new members, all of whom were present and sitting in the outer circle. After a few minutes it occurred to the new board members that they were now equal to those already on the board, so they picked up their chairs and moved to the table. The only remaining difference was that the president of the board had seated himself at the head of the rectangular table.

At Mifflin Co-op, staff members sat in a ragged circle; there was no seating distinction among them. It is no coincidence that this geometric shape is often the seating arrangement of choice among groups seeking equal power relations. In the circle there is no head of the table, and there are no rows.[9]

Another sign of even power distribution is the fact that staff members all have special assignments—areas of expertise—and they have some leeway on issues within their specialty. For instance, Sam is in charge of maintenance, and his views on maintenance issues may receive greater weight. Also he is likely to make minor maintenance decisions on his own or after consulting two or three other staff members. Nonetheless, this system of specialization does not amount to a formal division of authority. Aside from minor day-to-day decisions, all staff decisions require the approval of the staff. Even those powers delegated to committees can, if necessary, be revoked by the full staff.

Inclusiveness

While the staff had substantial power, the inclusiveness of its meetings was more ambiguous. Meetings were fully inclusive with regard to the staff: staff members had equal authority during meetings, and attendance was always high. Within the population of co-op employees, however, the meetings were somewhat exclusive.

Recalling the discussion of seating arrangements, it is always helpful to note who is not present in the meeting room when important decisions are being made. The co-op's shift-workers and general membership do not attend meetings, and their physical absence reflects their lower status and interest in the co-op. Shift-workers receive the same hourly wage as staff members and sometimes work a significant number of hours, but they rarely appear at staff meetings. These workers are hired part-time, with the understanding that their status is comparable, but not equal, to that of staff members.

This inequality, while typical of most businesses, is a controversial issue at Mifflin Co-op. A staff discussion of evaluation policy illustrates the problem that the staff/shift-worker distinction creates. Every year the staff evaluates itself and the shift-workers, and during one of its Monday night meetings, the staff discussed the possibility of changing this policy:

ROSE: Are we going to have the shift-workers evaluate each other?
KATE: Well, we want them to, but they don't want to do it.
ROSE: Really?
RAY: Scott is opposed to the concept of evaluations.
KATE: He doesn't talk to us about it. He just came up to us and said, "I refuse to fill out this evaluation."
NORMA: Well, he said that he explained it on his other form.
KATE: I just don't think that's a reasonable situation.
NORMA: Well, apparently *he* thought it was reasonable.
RAY: *Those two* have a difference of opinion.
AMY: Is Leonard going to evaluate the other shift-workers?
KATE: I don't know. He handed in a sealed envelope, and Matthew hasn't handed his back.[10]

As the excerpt shows, the staff takes the views of shift-workers into account somewhat haphazardly. The shift-workers do have the right to attend meetings, and a former shift-worker reported doing so without hesitation. Nonetheless the shift-workers do not have the same decision-making power; their judgments do not have to figure into a staff consensus.

Some staff find this system acceptable. They see the need for two levels of commitment to the co-op, one for dedicated staff and one for those seeking more temporary employment. Other staff loathe unnecessary hierarchies and view this as one of them. There is currently no proposal on the staff agenda to abolish the distinction between regular and shift-workers, but this issue is likely to resurface in coming years.

Beyond employees, the staff has tried to include customers and community members in proportion to the impact that staff decisions have upon these groups. All staff meetings are open to the general public, and people occasionally bring their concerns to these meetings. While the nonstaff have no decision-making power during staff meetings, they do have the opportunity to raise issues and offer criticisms. Also, those customers who become members of the co-op through paying an annual fee or doing volunteer work are invited to the annual membership meeting. At these meetings (one of which I attended as a voting member), the membership elects the Mifflin Co-op board of directors. In theory the membership can have a strong influence on the co-op, but membership participation is usually low. Less than 5 percent of the members attend the annual meeting, and there is not intense competition for seats on the board.

Commitment

Since the staff are most directly included in the decision-making process, it is essential that they are committed to democracy. The co-op's long-term commitment to the democratic process is apparent in the wording of its bylaws, which the staff updated in 1991. These bylaws make many of the co-op's democratic features into written, binding laws, which can be as important to a small group as a constitution is to a nation. These bylaws include a preamble that states the co-op's broader commitment to democratic participation:

> The cooperative shall function with open, democratic control of its operations exercised jointly by members and the worker collective. Maximum member participation on all levels and continual improvement in the quality of group interactions and communication are to be energetically sought. Community members shall be encouraged to become members of the cooperative, and helped to learn more about the products and operations of the co-op, with an eye toward their future, increased participation.

The staff insisted that these written words hold meaning for them. During interviews, each explained why democracy was important to them. All of the staff had previously worked in undemocratic workplaces, and they valued the power that the co-op gave them over their work environment. They also saw a connection between their appreciation of small group democracy and their commitment to making their society—and their world—more democratic. When asked what democracy meant, all members of the worker collective were able to articulate basic principles, such as the importance of placing decision-making power in the hands of the people, ensuring equality of opportunity, allowing freedom of speech, and embracing diversity.[11]

But a strong commitment runs deeper than ink on a page. A group reveals its true commitment to the democratic process in its actions. The Mifflin Co-op staff showed an active commitment in many ways. Every staff member had participated in more than one workshop on participatory decision making, and all had taken time after meetings to reflect upon the strengths and weaknesses of their decision-making processes. Part of the reason they valued their jobs at Mifflin was because of its democratic process, and they were willing to expend time and energy on its behalf. In fact they underwent obtrusive observation, completed lengthy questionnaires, and granted me interviews largely because they viewed this project as an opportunity to make their meetings and themselves more democratic.

Relationships

Beyond a shared commitment, small group democracy requires healthy relations among group members. To the extent that Mifflin Co-op staff meetings are democratic, the staff members will show a measure of congeniality toward one another and regularly affirm each other's individuality, competence, and mutuality.

A starting point for understanding relational communication at Mifflin Co-op is a glance at the general patterns of talk during Monday night meetings. One can look at what staff members say to each other and try to see the relational messages (if any) that their words convey. Such interpretation is always imperfect, since it is impossible to know precisely how a speaker's words were intended and received. Nonetheless, it is useful to begin with an overview of the staff's relational messages before turning to concrete examples.[12]

A quick accounting of the Mifflin Co-op meetings shows that staff members directed most of their positive relational talk toward the group as a whole, or to Ray, Sam, Amy, and Norma. Almost all of the hostile messages flew in the direction of Louis and Norma. Ray rarely spoke in negative terms (i.e., invalidation of a member's individuality, denial of mutuality, and hostile comments), whereas Louis, Kate, and Norma sent negative messages more often than the others. Amy, Ray, and Laura received only kind words, while Louis and Norma received far more negative than positive messages.

Every staff member except Ray and Norma directed the vast majority of their negative relational talk toward Norma. The affirming talk Norma received came largely from herself, with Ray and Dan each contributing a single affirming comment; the friendly words she received came almost exclusively from Kate. The hostile talk Louis received came from Norma and, to a lesser extent, Kate, and the affirming messages he received came from himself.

Overall patterns of nonverbal communication were similar. If a camera took photographs of the group at regular intervals, these photos would show frequent smiles, expressive speakers, and attentive listeners. Staff members usually spoke in steady speeds and at a normal pitch and volume—although lively exchanges or attempts at humor often involved rapid and fluctuating speech. The postures and movements of the staff usually appeared calm and relaxed, revealing their general comfort with the setting and each other.

Staff usually maintained their composure. Sometimes while they were delivering or receiving angry words, their emotions would surface in harsher tones and slightly higher volumes. If shouting began, other staff quickly intervened, as Rose once did when Louis began to raise his voice. More moderate emotional displays, such as soft crying or a long, frustrated pause in the midst of an impassioned speech, went uninterrupted. The bulk of the tense or hostile nonverbal behavior was directed toward or sent by Norma and Louis.[13]

A more contextualized look at Mifflin's staff meetings reveals the meaning of these general communication patterns. For the most part, relations among staff were harmonious during meetings. The most prominent recurring form of relational communication was the steady stream of friendly and humorous comments. As one example among many, the staff made light of their decision to donate cheese to an anniversary party for WORT, a community-sponsored radio station in Madison, Wisconsin:

RAY: A block of mild cheddar seems like a nice, solid donation.
ROSE: You decide, Kate.
LAURA: How exciting.
RAY: Get one of those green North Farm ones.
LOUIS: Yeah, a green and yellow cheese.

The staff also used humor to lighten up discussions of tenure incentives. The tenure incentives plan had been somewhat controversial, because it would create a difference in compensation between new and veteran staff members. Staff could not decide on a neutral term to describe the proposed policy (*tenure incentives* is my own invention), so a rather curious name emerged during one of the staff meetings:

NORMA: Okay, the last three items are evaluation schedules, Laura's long-term plans, and *turnips* for long-term commitment.
AMY: Turnips?
SAM: Mm-hmm.

Later that same meeting, Amy joined in the fun:

AMY: Okay, we had talked about some kind of plan to encourage people to stay on longer, and we didn't want to call it a reward or an incentive, so it's called "turnips for a long-term commitment." We just thought using a vegetable was safe.

By the next meeting, things had become more complicated:

LAURA: At any rate, I think we're down to turnips, folks.
RAY: And *alternative turnips*.
LAURA: Yes, like beets and rutabagas.

LOUIS: Okay, guys.
LAURA: Parsnips.
RAY: Long-term benefit alternatives!

These comments served a serious purpose by helping to maintain a friendly group atmosphere during difficult deliberations. In addition the term *turnip*, though thoroughly silly, had a rationale behind it. As Sam recently explained, the staff wanted a tenure incentive policy that defied conventional notions of threat and reward. "A turnip," he said with a smile, "is neither a carrot nor a stick, but it *is* a root vegetable."[14]

This congenial atmosphere dissipated when the staff discussed whether Norma could take another vacation. This was the only time staff members repeatedly and openly addressed the mutuality and individuality of staff members. Although this discussion was more the exception than the rule at the co-op's Monday night meetings, it deserves attention. It created tension for the entire staff, and every staff member spontaneously brought it up during their interviews.

Norma had taken off a lot of time in recent months. She frequently asked staff members and shift-workers to cover her shifts so that she could have a block of free days, and she had already taken more vacation time than the staff would have liked. The absence of a staff member puts a strain on the rest, so when the staff agreed to give Norma one more vacation during the summer, Norma promised not to do it again for several months. The understanding was that if Norma violated this agreement, she would leave the co-op.

The issue came up during the first meeting I observed. Norma asked if she could trade two of her shifts to take another vacation. After a few minutes of discussion, Ray expressed his point of view:

RAY: The great thing about the co-op is that you can take off lots of time one stretch at a time, but the people that keep working at the co-op are the ones that suffer. *They're* the ones who pick up extra shifts. *They're* the ones that take over other people's responsibilities, and they just get sick and tired of it.
SAM: And you aren't able to accomplish anything.
LOUIS: Right, in your own—
SAM: In your own specialty. I get shit done for maintenance.
AMY: If you just add that up and see how many weeks somebody has been gone, it's getting to be almost—
LAURA: A full year.
AMY: Yeah, almost a full year. And, it always creates pressure when somebody's gone. It affects everybody.

[Later in the meeting.]

AMY: I think that the rest of the staff is trying to stay within the parameters of the vacation policy, but you're looking at it a different way, saying, "There's a day here, there's a day there, and I don't fit into those parameters but everyone else does."

[long silent pause]

SAM: I guess I feel a similar way. I feel like when people are talking to you about this, I see a lot of nodding and I hear a lot of "Mm-hmm, mm-hmm," but I don't feel like a lot of it's sinking into you about why we feel the way we do. I don't feel like a lot of what we're saying registers.

During the next meeting the staff returned to the issue, and the exchanges between Norma and Kate became particularly heated:

KATE: I've just been doing training for the board of directors, and it's become very apparent to me that we have to think of *us* as being the store. This is a *collective*, and the co-op is more than a store. This isn't Food Mart, and we're not hired to just come and do our job. It's an emotional institution, and I think that that's maybe where you've gotten a little sidetracked, Norma.

I think you have done a good job. I definitely have seen improvement, and I appreciate that. And yet I think what Dan is speaking to—this resentment thing—is that you're neglecting the emotional needs of the collective, not necessarily purposely, but for lack of any knowledge of how to do it.

I know I feel tremendously alienated from you, and I don't know that it can be rectified. I don't know how we can get through all of these issues without feeling that *bond*—that "we're all in this together" sort of feeling. That's what I've felt has been lacking over the last number of months.

And it's not just coming from you. It's coming from all of us, or most of us, too. And that's why when I heard that you were considering whether or not you would resign, I was thinking that might be the easy option. Because then we don't have to try to put it all back together again. I think it's going to be difficult for me, and I know it will be difficult for you—

NORMA: I know it will be really difficult, but I've already decided that I'm not going to move on. I don't think that leaving is a solution. I mean, there might be cases where that has to be the solution. But as far as I'm concerned, if we can't get it together here—with our many shared values—then *forget* Palestine and Israel. Forget it. I just believe that it's possible, and it's worth doing it. I don't want to just bail out.

KATE: But this is not the way to start, and I can tell you that right now. This is not the way to start, and that's what I was feeling last week. If you care about this group at all, don't trade shifts like you did last week. That is not the way to mend the rift that we're feeling in this room right now.

As much as you're trying, I don't think you're seeing the heart of the issue. Or that's how it seems to me. And I know you're trying really hard, but it's just like two ships passing in the night. We're not connecting, and that makes me scared, because connecting takes a lot of time. I don't want to keep spending all this time if the ships are not going to get any closer.

NORMA: Well, I'm going to think about that some more, but I've considered it already. I feel like part of the democratic process—part of what has to happen in a collective—is that people have to learn to stand up for themselves when they feel like they're not being treated fairly.

In this excerpt, Kate initially offers encouragement by commending Norma on doing a good job at the co-op, but Kate may say this only to soften the criticism that follows. Kate explicitly questions Norma's attachment to the co-op, as well as her awareness of the norms and emotional needs of the collective. Kate portrays Norma and the co-op as "two ships passing" and fears that the ships "are not going to get any closer." Kate's feelings are so strong that she considers Norma's resignation the best possible solution, "because then we don't have to try to put it all back together again."

Norma responds to Kate's criticisms by affirming her own mutuality and individuality. Norma admits there is division in the co-op, but she insists that she is a part of the group and doesn't "want to just bail out." In her view, standing up for personal interests does not threaten the cohesion of a democratic group. Seen in this light, her actions do not reflect a separation from the co-op but only a legitimate desire to give her personal needs equal priority with those of the collective.[15]

The conflict between Kate and Norma was not resolved in this discussion, nor was it mitigated in subsequent deliberations. Ultimately Norma went against the wishes of the rest of the group by exchanging two of her shifts with Louis and one of the shift-workers so that she could take another vacation.

When I conducted interviews, I found that my own observations paralleled those of the staff. The staff believed that, on balance, relational talk during meetings was respectful and good-natured. As Ray wrote, "Most of the time, things are quite friendly with the staff. The problem comes in with the personality conflicts." Kate concurred:

> I feel very unified with most of the collective. The joking and personalness, though time-consuming and distracting, is essential to pulling the group together and making the meetings unintimidating. We learn a lot about each other and can relax into being ourselves.

The one staff member who disagreed was Norma, who felt that the relationships among staff members were not so positive. In particular she thought the staff only marginally affirmed her individuality and competence, generally denied her mutuality, and created a neutral—rather than friendly—atmosphere. She believed that the staff unfairly questioned her prioritization of personal needs, but she insisted that she should act as an individual regardless of how others talked to her. She recalled that on one of the anonymous staff evaluations she received, someone had written, "Norma should be more satisfied with where she is in life, i.e. being at work." She thought that this remark questioned her ability to know what's in her best interests. Finally, she sometimes felt individual staff members were distant and unfriendly toward her, treating her as an outsider.

Because so many of the staff enjoyed their relationships with one another, one might still consider the co-op's meetings very democratic. This assessment needs qualification, though, because of the relationship between Norma and the staff. Was Norma treated unfairly and disrespectfully? Or was the rest of the staff trying to maintain reasonable norms by constructively criticizing Norma and openly expressing their emotions? Norma believed that the staff went too far, seeking consensus and homogeneity at the cost of her individuality:

> I think their ideal Mifflin Co-op would consist of people that agree with them. They hand-pick people with shared values, and I'm just kinda outside of that. Consequently, I don't feel free to be as active. I don't feel like I'm part of a unified whole. I don't feel like I'm a part of the co-op.

According to Norma, the staff cannot accept the fact that she does not work as many hours at the co-op as most staff members. At a staff meeting before the six videotaped meetings, the staff agreed that while large differences in work hours were contrary to co-op goals, Norma and others could continue working reduced hours under a "grandfather clause." Norma argued that the co-op was violating that agreement by asking her to heighten her commitment. In her view the negative messages she received were designed, perhaps unwittingly, to drive her away or force her to bow to the will of the majority.[16]

The rest of the staff argued that Norma had given too much priority to her personal interests and too little to the interests of the co-op. Most admitted that they had lost respect for Norma as a result of this transgression, and some acknowledged having strong negative feelings toward her. Nevertheless it appeared that this hostility was directed toward Norma's behavior with regard to vacation time, not toward Norma as an individual. Remarkably, Norma received almost no negative relational talk during every other discussion. In addition, the staff tempered its negative talk with positive comments. Norma received more negative *and positive* relational messages than any other staff member.

The conflict between Norma and the staff over vacation time provided a challenging test of the relationships at Mifflin Co-op. The co-op appears to have passed this test, even in the opinion of Norma. Despite all of her concerns with the meeting process, Norma insisted that I should put her doubts in perspective:

> I really do think that staff members try to respect the idea that they shouldn't push something through against someone's will. They still really respect the fact that they don't want to be coercive, and they really do want to empathize with what somebody's saying and try to take it seriously, respect it, and integrate it into some arrangement that's agreeable to everybody. And that *does* work remarkably well.

Relations between Norma and the rest of the staff may have been tense at times, but two years have passed since I first interviewed Norma, and she remains on the co-op staff.

Opportunities to Speak

Given this relational setting, what was the character of deliberation at Mifflin Co-op? These questions will be considered in turn: Did staff members always get a chance to speak during meetings? Did speakers fulfill their responsibilities? Did staff members listen to one another?

Opportunities to set the agenda and vote are crucial, because without them one cannot directly influence what the group will discuss or what its decisions will be. Of all the forms of communication, these were the easiest to observe at Mifflin Co-op. This fact is, in and of itself, encouraging: if every group member can see how and when the agenda is set and votes are taken, any manipulation of agendas and decisions will be easier to detect.

The agenda is set during the week prior to the Monday night meeting. During each workday, staff members can write whatever items occur to them on a scrap of paper tacked or taped onto the basement door. Anything from announcements to serious issues might appear there, and no limits are placed on how much one can put on the written agenda. Then, near the beginning of each meeting, the agenda is briefly reviewed. Items can be removed or postponed, but staff members refrain from using any procedural tricks to sneak items off or onto the agenda. Similarly, the different facilitators moved through the agenda with caution, never rigidly forcing a discussion to close before the group was done deliberating.

Voting was equally straightforward. Under Mifflin's version of consensus, the facilitator's behavior varied greatly depending on the seriousness of the item. When an agenda item required a minor decision, the facilitator would usually intervene as soon as a discussion began to wander. If a staff member made a proposal the group liked, words and nods of agreement would quickly signal consensus. The facilitator would sometimes (but not always) ask if the group had agreed, and the notetaker would usually (but not always) make sure the decision was clearly stated.

When an agenda item was more significant, discussion would be relatively open-ended, and the facilitator would often keep a "speakers list." As each person indicated—with a whisper, a hand signal, or a raised eyebrow—the desire to speak, the facilitator made a mental note or wrote the person's name on a list. Names might get moved up the list if they had not spoken as much or if the present topic concerned them personally. Sometimes a speaker at the top of the list deferred to another, especially when the speaker thought it would help the flow of discussion. Depending on the issue and the number of people wishing to speak, the facilitator would stop keeping a speakers list and let the discussion proceed on its own.

As the group neared a decision, the facilitator would get a sense of the group's positions by asking every member to state their view. If a consensus appeared to exist, the facilitator might ask if any group members disagreed with the apparent consensus. If the group had not reached consensus, the group would informally decide to continue talking, postpone the issue to the next meeting, or drop the issue altogether—something that was never done during the meetings I observed.

In every case, a final decision was never made without the awareness and equal participation of all staff members present. Those unable to attend particular meetings would make certain that their views on serious issues were passed along. No important decision was made that contradicted the views of a staff member who was unable to attend that particular meeting.

Agenda setting and voting, though, are just two of the many features of democratic deliberation. It is also important to see whether staff members had equal and adequate opportunities to reformulate the agenda, provide information, articulate their views, persuade one another, and dissent after a decision was reached.

Silence is one of the clearest signs of a speaking opportunity. When a speaker finishes and no one takes the floor for a few seconds, therein lies a chance to speak. Other factors, such as the timing and context of the silence, can make it more or less of an invitation to speak, but for those who rarely interrupt, a pause provides an entry into the discussion. During Mifflin Co-op's staff meetings, such silences occurred somewhat regularly—perhaps every five minutes.

Just as silence signals the existence of an opportunity, speaking constitutes the use of one. The distribution of "speaking turns" shown in Figure 4.1 provides an indirect accounting of staff members' chances to speak during six co-op meetings. Louis, Kate, and Dan spoke most frequently, and Sam and Rose opened their mouths the least.[17]

Similarly, an examination of how long each staff member spoke reveals that only Amy, Laura, and Sam held the floor less than the average amount of time. Kate set and reformulated the agenda the most, whereas Rose, Laura, and Sam rarely did so. Louis, Kate, Norma, and Dan articulated their views most often, and Amy, Laura, and Sam did so the least. From one category of talk to the next, there is a rather consistent pattern: Kate spoke the most, while Laura and Sam spoke the least.

One can also look at the number of times during meetings that staff members verbally opened or closed opportunities for others to speak.

Figure 4.1 Number of Speaking Turns, by Speaker

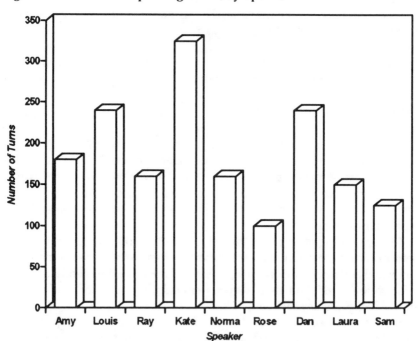

Speakers can open opportunities by explicitly requesting that another person speak ("What do you think, Dan?"). Or they can close opportunities by blatantly interrupting another speaker (excepting those instances where the interruption is a short interjection or a word of encouragement).[18]

By these calculations, the co-op staff opened over three hundred opportunities to speak during the transcribed portions of the six videotaped meetings. The people who opened the most opportunities were Kate and Dan, while Louis, Norma, and Sam opened the least. Louis cut off others most frequently, whereas Amy and Sam each made only one clear-cut interruption.

Because Kate and Dan tended to speak the most, it is significant that they were also the two people who opened the greatest number of speaking opportunities. In effect, they offered chances to speak in proportion to the larger number of opportunities that they used. Three of the staff members who spoke the least number of times—Amy, Laura, and Sam—also made the smallest number of blatant interruptions. They might have been too reserved to jump into the deliberations when others were speaking, but perhaps they simply had less desire to speak and felt no need to interrupt a speaker.

Amy, Louis, and Norma received the largest number of personal invitations to speak, while Ray received the least. Kate and Dan, the most frequent speakers, were cut off the most, and Rose was cut off least. Kate and Dan were also the only staff members cut off more times than they were invited to speak. The least vocal staff members, Laura and Sam, did not receive the most opportunities to speak, but neither were they cut off frequently.

This initial glimpse suggests the need to look closely at the speaking opportunities of Laura and Sam, two of the least vocal staff members. To judge the quality of their opportunities, I carefully examine the staff's deliberations of Norma's vacation plans and the proposed tenure incentives plan. I choose these two issues because every staff member had strong opinions about them and wished to speak. Did Laura and Sam get an equal and adequate chance to talk during these important and emotionally charged discussions?

During the first of the two deliberations on Norma's vacation, both Laura and Sam jumped into the conversation and spoke for long periods of time. Neither speaker was interrupted, and both ended with definitive statements, signaling that they had finished their speaking turns. Sam finished by saying, "I don't feel like you're seeing it from our point of view. That's where I'm at." Laura concluded, "I'd prefer to see a full-fledged commitment. And I don't know if you can do that."

During the final discussion of tenure incentives, one hour had passed and neither Laura nor Sam had explicitly endorsed one of the proposals under discussion. At this point Laura complained that the meeting was going late. "We'd better hurry it up," she insisted. "I don't know what everybody thinks, but personally, I would be in favor of Plan C." She then added, "I'd kinda like to get a sense from the people who haven't been talking so much."

Just after Laura finished speaking, Sam yawned and simply stated, "I think Plan C sounds good to me." Neither cared to elaborate, since other advocates of Plan C had already provided numerous arguments for it. It was also at this point in the discussion when Laura began a round-robin that effectively rotated speaking turns, giving members the chance to express their preferences and add any comments they wished. Overall, it appears that Laura and Sam were able to speak freely during these crucial staff deliberations. A final decision was not reached until they, and the others, had ample opportunities to participate.[19]

This positive portrayal of speaking opportunities was corroborated by the staff members, who generally believed they had sufficient opportunities to speak during meetings.[20] The only possible exceptions were Louis and Norma. Louis said he wanted more opportunities to persuade and vote on final decisions. Norma also believed she did not have a sufficient number of voting opportunities, and she claimed that relational dynamics among staff made her reluctant to reformulate, persuade, or vote.

Louis and Norma's claims are not supported by evidence from the staff meetings. Louis attempted to persuade others more often than all but one other staff member, and he was given the second highest number of personal invitations to present arguments. Louis and Norma expressed their views and interests an average amount of the time, and Norma attempted to reformulate an agenda item or persuade others no less frequently than the average staff member.

As for voting, the staff's consensus method of decision making gives equal opportunities for all staff members to express their views during the final stage of decision making. It is possible, however, that Louis and Norma are more concerned about decisions made outside of staff meetings. Other staff members might circumvent formal voting procedures and reach a "miniconsensus" without including Louis or Norma. Since this occurs outside regular meetings it presents a special problem, which I discuss at length in chapter 5.

Louis and Norma's claims may need a more subtle understanding. When I asked them why they thought they had fewer opportunities to speak, they expressed personal frustration rather than a feeling of unfair treatment. Louis explained, "We have equal access to talk....In general and in the meetings, we have equal access." In his view, no one at Mifflin "abuses" their opportunities by speaking so often and forcefully that others have little chance to talk.

Norma agreed that "every individual is responsible for using their opportunities" and that at the co-op, "opportunities are equal for everyone. On some level, it's true that I've had the perfect opportunity to speak at all times." Nevertheless, she argued, "there's another level—more of a relationship level. It has to do with how I relate to or fit in with the group the whole time I've been there. It has to do with some things that are unique to me, like my own insecurities." On this relationship level, Norma had ample opportunities to speak, but emotional conflicts made her reluctant to do so.

Did the negative relational messages directed to her during the vacation discussion leave her too upset or intimidated to speak during meetings? The evidence suggests otherwise, since she expressed herself frequently on all issues, including her vacation plans. She began the second vacation discussion with the longest speaking turn in all of the videotaped meetings. This single speaking turn was more than twice the length of the next longest one. Throughout the discussion, she responded to others' comments and forcefully presented her views.

In sum, the opportunities to speak during Mifflin Co-op's Monday night meetings appear to have been more than adequate. The equality of these opportunities is more difficult to gauge. There was undoubtedly an unequal use of opportunities, but this difference does not necessarily imply an inequality of opportunities. Perhaps the difficulty in assessing relative equality is that all staff members appear to have had several chances to speak during meetings. Since everyone had opportunities in abundance, the equality of their distribution becomes almost irrelevant.

Speaking Responsibilities

The presence of opportunities, however, is no guarantee that group members fulfilled their speaking responsibilities. Did Mifflin Co-op staff members routinely withhold pertinent information or try to manipulate one another? To answer this question, I turn to the series of decisions the co-op made regarding donations.

During the six meetings I observed, half a dozen staff decisions concerned community requests for co-op assistance. As part of its commitment to the community, the co-op donates inventory and revenue to some of the organizations that request assistance. Since the amount of food and money requested exceeds the co-op's donations budget, the staff must judge the merits of each request. To make these decisions democratically, members must provide each other with relevant information and try to persuade each other in a way that is forthright and sincere. As the following excerpts show, it appears that the staff members fulfilled these responsibilities.

During the first meeting, the staff considered a donation request from the Women's International League for Peace and Freedom (WILPF). To reach a clear decision, staff members had to weigh pertinent information and generate persuasive arguments. The following excerpt illustrates both of these:

DAN: The other donation request on the docket for tonight is the folks from Women's International League for Peace and Freedom are organizing an ad [protesting the Persian Gulf War] to go in the *Isthmus* that reads, "How many lives per gallon?" It only costs five dollars to sign on, and after paying for the ad, the five dollars goes to further efforts toward organizing for peace in the Persian Gulf.

SAM: Stephen came in from Press House with this originally and showed it to Rose and me, and Rose threw five dollars into it. I did it for myself. Rose did it as a representative of DARE, I think. Um—

DAN: Yeah, I think it would be best for Mifflin—

AMY: Yeah.

SAM: Yeah, it's not going in for a while—

DAN: Yeah, it's going in either next weekend or the following weekend, and the due date is tomorrow.

LAURA: Yeah, I'm sorry, what was it going into?

SAM: The *Isthmus*. Is it going to be a full-page ad or a half-page ad?

DAN: I think it depends on how much money they get.

KATE: Let's do it.

DAN: Okay.

KATE: So, I'll put that down as five dollars.

SAM: One of the intentions of bringing it to us as a group is they were hoping they could get more than five dollars. Do we want to just do the five as Mifflin Co-op?

LOUIS: Can't we give them ten or twenty?

RAY: Can we also give them money from our advertising account?

AMY: We could do that.

SAM: How's the advertising budget doing?

AMY: We have enough money to give it to them.

SAM: What do we *want* to give them?

AMY: I'm not sure, what do you think?

KATE: Twenty-five?

SAM: What'd you say?

KATE: Twenty.

AMY: How about twenty from advertising and five from staff donations?

KATE: Why so much, though, because if they're gonna get an ad, maybe it would be better for us to wait and give a more concrete type of aid rather than this.

DAN: I agree with that position. My feeling in general on ads is that I'd rather give twenty-five bucks to someone giving a teach-in.

AMY: But didn't they say that after the cost of the ad, the money would be used for other—

SAM: Yeah, but the ad's gonna take a lot of money.

DAN: Yeah, a full page in the *Isthmus* is like sixteen hundred dollars—

KATE: *No, really?*

DAN: Something ridiculous.

LAURA: [laughs] They may not be able to afford a *personal* ad.

KATE: You know, I think a lot of people will sign on for five bucks.

LOUIS: Let's decide something and get on with this.

SAM: Maybe ten bucks.

KATE: From marketing or advertising? Or …

DAN: Ten bucks from organizing and—

KATE: Ten from staff?

LAURA: *Five* from staff.

KATE: Five from staff.

DAN: Fifteen total. Sounds good to me.

KATE: Is someone gonna fill that out and send it in?

SAM: I'll do it.

KATE: Okay.

DAN: Okay, donations are done.

This excerpt shows the speed and impact of the exchange of information and the presentation of arguments. The discussion of the WILPF request begins with questions and informative answers, as the staff clarifies the nature of the request, the cost of advertising, and the possibility of providing money from two separate budgets. Kate and Dan then put forward an argument for limited funding, a proposal the staff ultimately accepts.

Other donation requests are handled in a similar manner. Basic information is provided spontaneously or in response to questions. Clear and concise arguments are then presented, and then the staff reaches a decision. The donation discussions average four minutes, with the longest lasting seven. The most striking feature of these discussions, and others like them, is what they *do not* include. There are no signs of concealed or delayed information, and there are no veiled or deceptive arguments. Questions are answered, and rationales are stated clearly. There are no vague, misleading, or incomplete answers, and there are none of the cues of deceptive discourse, such as incessant appeals to authority, misleading uses of pronouns and syntax, or excessive jargon.[21]

None of the staff members pointed to another as regularly withholding vital information or framing arguments in a way intended to manipulate listeners. The closest thing to an exception was Norma's concern about Kate's privileged position in the information nexus. Because of her strong commitment, high level of involvement, and varied responsibilities, Kate may have been the most informed staff member.

Norma did not indicate that Kate kept information from the staff, but she was concerned about the timing of Kate's (and others') information. Norma sometimes learned important facts during meetings, often shortly before the time when a final decision was needed. This gave her insufficient time to process and respond to the information. Norma did not feel uninformed; rather, she believed she was not informed *in time*. This issue is discussed further in chapter 5, but it should be noted at this point as a possible limitation on small group democracy at Mifflin.

Listening

Even if the staff had ample speaking opportunities that were used regularly and responsibly, fully democratic deliberation at Mifflin Co-op would be impossible if these same people were not able and willing to listen to one another. Any group that aspires to use a democratic process needs to ensure that its members have equal and adequate opportunities to comprehend one another. In turn, each member is responsible for carefully considering what others have to say.

Most of the time, Mifflin Co-op staff members understood one another during meetings. The staff had developed a language of its own, but every group member knew it. Staff members understood the technical references to features of the store or the co-op's finances, and they laughed together at both obvious and inside jokes made during meetings.

Staff members also listened to what each other had to say. Side conversations began on a few occasions, but the more serious the issue, the more likely it was that the entire staff was sitting relatively still and concentrating on the speaker's words. The give-and-take of most discussions showed that staff members were not engaging in what communication theorist Dean Hewes calls "egocentric" discussion—the artful juxtaposition of unrelated, self-absorbed comments.[22] When addressing minor agenda items, staff would quickly integrate each other's different ideas into a final proposal, and during discussions of major issues, whenever they spoke, staff members would acknowledge different points of view.

Although Norma and the staff had divergent positions on the vacation issue, they seemed to understand—if not accept—their differences of opinion. By contrast, Louis and the staff sometimes failed to understand the nature of their disagreement with regard to the proposed tenure incentives. Examining this difficulty reveals a great deal about the success and limitations of the democratic process at Mifflin Co-op.

After the initial discussions of the tenure incentives plans, it became apparent that Louis's views differed from those held by the rest of the staff. At various times Rose, Kate, Dan, and others had raised concerns about providing incentives in the form of increasing annual pay bonuses, but only Louis clearly opposed all three of the proposals for establishing monetary incentives. (The group called these proposals "Plans A, B, and C.") Louis suggested some alternative nonmonetary incentives, but the group did not clearly understand the nature of these alternatives. Nor was it clear that Louis understood the function of the monetary incentives that the other group members endorsed.

Shortly after Amy had described the monetary incentive plans, Louis let his opposition be known:

LOUIS: I think it *stinks*.

SAM: Why does it stink?

LOUIS: Just, I don't know, this is *bizarre* ... I guess that's not very descriptive.

RAY: "Stinks," "bizarre" ...

NORMA: *Why*, Louis?

LOUIS: I don't know, it just strikes me as kind of filling our pockets or something.

KATE: [sarcastically] That's what we're here on this Earth to do.

ALL: [laughter]

RAY: I don't know, I think—

DAN: At least that's what one person thinks.

LOUIS: I think the percentage—

AMY: Do you understand that—

LOUIS: I understand that, um—

AMY: It's assuming that the person becomes more valuable, well not "more valuable," but—

KATE: More *experienced*.

LOUIS: You said it! There is an assumption that you will become more *valuable* or more effective in the store. It's an assumption ...

AMY: Well, it costs a lot to keep retraining somebody to replace someone.

LOUIS: Yeah, but it doesn't cost *this* much more.

AMY: But I don't think the whole thing is just a reward for how valuable this person is, I think—

LOUIS: It sure comes off that way.

AMY: If I could finish what I'm saying, it's sort of recognizing that this is a very profitable business, and it doesn't need to be some kind of financial sacrifice for people to work here.

LAURA: I also wanted to say that just because we work in a co-op doesn't mean that our work should be devalued.

LOUIS: I never said that.

LAURA: But you said that getting money as a compensation for staying "stinks." I just think that if you're going to take this as a serious job—one you can stay at for a very long time and retire from—we need to change policy, because you can't really support yourself in your retirement on the money we make now.

NORMA: Do you have an *alternative*, Louis?

LOUIS: I think some existing models ... I don't know, I would have to look into it. I don't know, but I think there are existing models in the industry that ...

LAURA: Would you feel more comfortable if it were some kind of retirement package?

LOUIS: Yeah, that's an idea.

LAURA: You know, to me that's a great concern, not that I'm ready for *retirement*—

LOUIS: Yeah, okay, the thing that really affected me was that this was thrown at us, and this was the only thing that some of us could come up with. I feel like everybody's adopting it without looking at anything else, and it seemed like we were already passing this before we even got to discuss any other alternatives.

At the next staff meeting, the staff tried to understand and consider the alternatives Louis would prefer:

RAY: So, Louis, not to *pick on* you or anything ...

LOUIS: This is *not* a good time to pick on me anyway, so don't waste your time trying to.

ALL: [laughter]

RAY: Do you think that the staff should get any benefits aside from the ones we get now? Is *any* increase in our benefits package excessive in your mind?

LOUIS: No, not necessarily.

RAY: Okay.

LOUIS: I really have a problem with this. I think there are other alternative benefits, such as a clothing allowance or paid vacation. I really have problems with percentage numbers because they're based on ... I don't know.

KATE: Additional paid vacation is a percentage, too, it's just in a different form. I don't think that it's—

LOUIS: Right, but it's more tangible in my perspective.

KATE: But you just have different needs from other people. I need money, I *don't* need vacation. And I think that money—

DAN: That's actually a very interesting point worth pursuing. Should you have a staggered amount of time that you can take off, whether paid or unpaid? That's an idea.

LOUIS: Yeah, we'll have to remember that. I don't know, I just ... It bothers me, and right now I don't really have a clear enough head to continue my opposition to these proposals ...

As the discussion continued, confusion and exhaustion only increased. Louis tried to explain and advocate his alternatives, but the others were unable to understand his position:

AMY: I guess I'm not sure what the difference is between the existing proposals and adding another week's paid vacation after a certain amount of time, because to *me*—

LOUIS: It's not that much different, no.

AMY: It's the *same thing*. It's only that we're calling it something different.

LOUIS: Yeah.

AMY: And it's figured in the same way, too.

LOUIS: In a way, yeah. Again—

AMY: *Exactly* the same way, I don't see a difference.

LOUIS: Okay, let me clarify it. My objection is to how it's presented. It looks to me as kind of a strange animal when you compare it to everything else that we've done in the co-op with regard to benefits. It just really strikes me as a weird monkey. So, I don't know, maybe we could sit together and come up with a balance of these two ideas, instead of asking me over and over to clarify this—

RAY: It's not at all clear what—

NORMA: What your *objection* is.

RAY: I think Plan C is fine—

NORMA: Unless there's an alternative. Oops.

RAY: I've got no problems with it. I mean, I'm being a little harsh but I don't—

LOUIS: That's not harsh. You're just stating your point—

RAY: My harshness is that I'm losing patience with the discussion. It hasn't been going that long, but I can see it circling for another hour before it comes in for a landing. I don't want to discuss it indefinitely, because I just can't see where ... Okay, I don't know what I'm saying, but I don't want to continue without any forward progress.

After repeated attempts at clarification and suggestions of possible compromises, Louis and the staff seemed exhausted by the seemingly endless deliberations. The discussion ended only when Laura insisted that talking was becoming useless:

LAURA: It seems like our discussion goes in more and more and more circles, so I'm not sure if more time will yield more circles or if more time will yield an alternative—a truly *viable* alternative.

LOUIS: Why assume that it wouldn't?

LAURA: Because we've been talking and talking and talking and going in circles to circles to circles. So I can't see where our circles are going to spiral out, you know.

LOUIS: Well, *fine*. So *go*. I mean, I'm not going to block the consensus if you want it. I mean, I'm just giving you an alternative, and I still feel uncomfortable with this plan. If people are so burdened by this process or they feel so certain that this is what they want, then *go*. I'm not holding you up.

Five minutes later deliberation ended, and the group agreed to adopt Plan C. In the end, Louis and the staff did not understand each other but agreed that a decision had to be reached, even if a fully satisfactory consensus was not achieved. Louis chose to accept the decision, even though he did not approve of it. He had the opportunity to block consensus, but he elected to go along with the decision, albeit reluctantly.

These observations parallel the self-analyses provided by the co-op staff. All staff members believed that they were good listeners: they claimed to listen carefully to others and consider what was said, and they reported understanding each other most of the time. Staff said they usually had a chance to get others to clarify themselves, and they used many of these opportunities.

Aside from these general comments, some staff members noticed difficulties, such as those that emerged in the tenure incentives discussion. Dan, for instance, acknowledged that "sometimes time constraints make it hard for us to listen to explanations or, conversely, make it hard for others to have the patience to reexplain a point."

Others focused on the general difficulty of understanding Norma and Louis, particularly when discussing vacation policy and the proposed tenure incentives, respectively. Amy wrote,

> I didn't always succeed at understanding others, though I think I tried, especially with Norma and consensus and Louis and the pay raise and tenure incentives discussions. I listened, but didn't understand their points of view. I've spoken to each of them separately, during the week after the meeting, but I still don't fully understand their points.

Ray explained that he also has trouble understanding particular individuals for two reasons: "The people I have trouble understanding are the people I can't communicate well with—the people whose opinions I respect less than others. I try to understand their point, but sometimes I give up." He confided that Norma and Louis are the two people he has the most difficulty understanding.

Laura and Sam had equal difficulty understanding Louis. Laura insisted that even when she "asked him to clarify himself, it didn't really help." Sometimes she just could not understand him, no matter how hard she tried. Similarly, Sam explained that on the tenure incentives issue, Louis "will never give a concrete reason that any of us can understand. It's just the way he wants to be. He's pretty adamant about that one."

Kate also said she sometimes had difficulty understanding and seriously considering what Norma and Louis said during meetings. But she qualified this generalization:

> Some of us could do with better communication skills, but, especially for Louis, it is a deep cultural issue and not easily overcome. I find that one-on-one personal exchanges outside meetings have a lot of influence on how I perceive statements made inside meetings. Since Louis and I are good friends, I have a much better perspective on his somewhat hard to understand statements and views.

Norma and Louis also believed that the staff's inability to understand Louis may relate to his general communication skills or style. Norma noted, "I think, maybe it's ironic or something, but Louis is the person who feels most like he's not listened to. I also feel that he's the person who has the least developed skills in listening." But Louis attributed the problem to differences in *style*, not skills. He insisted that Mifflin is subject to a larger cultural bias: "If you tend not to communicate well, you will be listened to less." Louis saw himself as the victim of this bias, which I discuss in chapter 5.

In the end, it is difficult to make an unambiguous statement on the character of listening at Mifflin Co-op. Staff members acknowledged difficulty listening to Norma's views on vacation policy and Louis's opposition to the tenure incentives proposals. At the same time, the staff made a great effort to understand and consider these two members' views on these issues. The vacation and tenure incentives discussions were by far the longest of all those transcribed, and they were the only ones that lasted for more than one meeting. Norma and Louis spoke as much as (or more than) usual during these discussions, while staff members both passively listened and, in the case of Louis, repeatedly asked for clarification and elaboration.

A realistic definition of small group democracy does not ask whether a group can always reach understanding; instead, it asks whether group members are able to listen and willing to try to appreciate one another's point of view. Although Monday staff meetings did not always end in mutual understanding, staff members made an earnest effort to reach this point.

Conclusion

When this examination of listening is combined with the other components of small group democracy, the overall portrait of Mifflin Co-op is quite favorable. The staff had power over its meeting agendas, and its meetings were relatively inclusive, although some staff members questioned the distinction between staff and shift-workers. Also, staff members were strongly committed to the democratic process. Staff meetings usually maintained positive member relationships, but the vacation issue created a tense atmosphere that limited the potential for unconstrained deliberation. Staff members had adequate (and perhaps equal) opportunities to speak, and although the exchange of information among staff may have been imperfect, the staff generally deliberated in a responsible manner. Finally, staff members generally understood one another and considered what was said during meetings. Taken all around, Mifflin Street Community Co-op exemplifies many of the fundamental principles of small group democracy.[23]

Notes

1. Quoted in Seymour M. Lipset, Martin Trow, and James Coleman, *Union Democracy* (Garden City, N.Y.: Anchor, 1956), 463.

2. At the staff's request I have used pseudonyms for the names of the staff members, but not for the store. I ask that the anonymity of the staff be respected. Trying to identify the individuals herein would violate the staff's right to privacy. To maintain the anonymity of individuals, I have refrained from providing richer personal descriptions of individual staff members. These relatively impersonal presentations might leave the reader with the impression that the staff members are, in Ray's words, "worker drones." Let me assure the reader that the staff lead normal lives.

Finally, two pseudonyms have changed since I first discussed Mifflin Co-op in "Democratic Deliberation: A Redefinition of the Democratic Process and a Study of Staff Meetings at a Co-Operative Workplace," *Masters Abstracts* 30-04M (1992), 1114 (University Microfilms No. 1348177). "Laura" was previously "Lulu," and "Norma" was referred to as "Sarah."

3. Michael Bodden, "A Twenty-year History of the Mifflin Street Community Co-op" (Madison, Wis., 1990, manuscript), 3. Notice how Mifflin's decision to employ a democratic method of decision making relates to the decision tree in Figure 1.1. The staff's decisions are of concern to all group members, whose interests are considered equal. Staff are also willing to presume that each member is competent and committed to preserving the democratic process. While the staff is concerned with the store's financial prosperity, it believes that this goal is best served by using a democratic system. In addition, the staff's statement of purpose

views fully democratic decision making as an end in itself; the Mifflin staff hopes to serve as an example for other co-ops.

4. Ibid., passim. Bodden's twenty-year history of the co-op is an important document, simply because it exists. As Dennis K. Mumby explains, organizational narratives do more than "simply *inform* organization members about the values, practices, and traditions to which their organization is committed. Rather, they help to *constitute* the organizational consciousness of social actors by articulating and by embodying a particular reality, and subordinating or devaluing other modes of 'organizational rationality.'" In this sense, Mifflin Co-op's democratic features are partly a result of its historical image as a democratic organization. Dennis K. Mumby, "The Political Function of Narrative in Organizations," *Communication Monographs* 54 (1987): 125.

5. For a lengthy discussion of the process I used to select Mifflin Co-op over other groups, see John Gastil, "Democratic Deliberation: A Redefinition of the Democratic Process and a Study of Staff Meetings at a Co-Operative Workplace," *Masters Abstracts* 30-04M (1992), 1114 (University Microfilms No. 1348177), 68–72.

I have chosen to focus on a single case among many case studies of small groups, both democratic and undemocratic. For examples of communities pursuing democratic methods of decision making, see John Case and Rosemary C. R. Taylor, eds., *Co-ops, Communes, and Collectives: Experiments in Social Change in the 1960s and 1970s* (New York: Pantheon Books, 1979); Corinne McLaughlin and Gordon Davidson, *Builders of the Dawn: Community Lifestyles in a Changing World* (Shutesbury, Mass.: Sirius Publishing, 1986); Elaine Sundancer, *Celery Wine: The Story of a Country Commune* (Yellow Springs, Ohio: Community Publications Cooperative, 1973), 91–94. On Quaker business meetings, see Michael J. Sheeran, *Beyond Majority Rule* (Philadelphia: Philadelphia Yearly Meeting, 1983).

Studies of decision-making processes in community/political action groups include Case and Taylor, *Co-ops, Communes, and Collectives*; Gary L. Downey, "Ideology and the Clamshell Identity: Organizational Dilemmas in the Anti–Nuclear Power Movement," *Social Problems* 33 (1986): 357–73; Jane J. Mansbridge, *Beyond Adversary Democracy* (Chicago: University of Chicago Press, 1983); the drafting of the Port Huron Statement in James Miller, *Democracy Is in the Streets: From Port Huron to the Siege of Chicago* (New York: Simon & Schuster, 1987); Sara M. Evans and Harry C. Boyte, *Free Spaces* (New York: Harper & Row, 1992).

Among the many existing case studies of democracy in larger workplaces are those on Spain's Mondragon cooperatives: see Roy Morrison, *We Build the Road as We Travel* (Philadelphia: New Society Publishers, 1991); William F. Whyte and Kathleen K. Whyte, *Making Mondragon: The Growth and Dynamics of the Worker Cooperative Complex* (Ithaca, N.Y.: ILR Press, 1988); C. George Benello, *From the Ground Up* (Boston: South End Press, 1992), chap. 8. See also Len Krimerman and Frank Lindenfeld, *When Workers Decide: Workplace Democracy Takes Root in North America* (Philadelphia: New Society Publishers, 1991); Lipset et al., *Union Democracy*; Mansbridge, *Beyond Adversary Democracy*.

For case studies from the field of social work with relevance to small group democracy, see Judith A. B. Lee, ed., *Group Work with the Poor and Oppressed* (New York: Haworth Press, 1989). Examples of attempts to structure classrooms and schools democratically can be found in Mary A. Hepburn, ed., *Democratic Education in Schools and Classrooms* (Washington, D.C.: National Council for the Social Studies, 1983), chaps. 3, 4, and 6.

6. Helen Schwartzman, *The Meeting: Gatherings in Organizations and Communities* (New York: Plenum, 1989), 239 passim.

7. Whenever a researcher makes observations, it is important to gauge the effect of the observation process on the observed. In the case of Mifflin Co-op, the staff and I concluded that the presence of cameras did not have a large net effect on deliberation during meetings. For further discussion of this issue, see Gastil, "Democratic Deliberation," 123–26.

For additional reading on case-study methodology, see Robert K. Yin, *Case Study Research* (Beverly Hills, Calif.: Sage, 1989). On multimethod research, see John Brewer and Albert Hunter, *Multimethod Research: A Synthesis of Styles* (Newbury Park, Calif.: Sage, 1989). While my methodology involved soliciting staff feedback on several occasions, I take sole responsibility for the portrayal of Mifflin Co-op herein.

8. Like any other social entity, the staff was surely influenced by cultural forces as well. Some of these are discussed under differences in communication styles. Had I asked the staff, they probably could have identified ways in which they would like to change the store were it not for the social disapproval (and loss of customers) such changes would create.

9. I once observed a community improvement group meeting in which the group members arranged themselves in a circle, with the exception of one member who sat just outside the circle. The room permitted this woman to join the circle, but she chose to sit outside it. During the meeting group members made little eye contact with her, and the few times she tried speaking, she was usually ignored. The woman sitting outside the circle had the same formal status as the other members, yet during the meeting I observed, she was clearly an outsider, both figuratively and literally.

For information about using space democratically, see Rick Arnold, Bev Burke, Carl James, D'Arcy Martin, and Barb Thomas, *Educating for a Change* (Toronto: Doris Marshall Institute for Education and Action; Toronto: Between the Lines, 1991): 118–19. For academic discussions of the significance of seating and other features of the physical group setting, see Judee K. Burgoon, "Spatial Relationships in Small Groups," in Robert S. Cathcart and Larry A. Samovar, *Small Group Communication*, 5th ed. (Dubuque, Iowa: William C. Brown Publishers, 1988), 351–66; L. L. Cummings, George P. Huber, and Eugene Arendt, "Effects of Size and Spatial Arrangements on Group Decision Making," *Academy of Management Journal* 17 (1974): 460–75.

10. To make this chapter more concise and readable, excerpts from the transcripts have been edited. In many cases redundancies, filled pauses (e.g., "um," "uh"), and digressions have been removed, and grammatical errors have been corrected. For unedited excerpts, see Gastil, "Democratic Deliberation"; for full-length transcripts, contact the author directly.

11. A verbal commitment to democracy cannot be taken for granted. One might presume that most U.S. citizens could identify fundamental democratic principles, but in-depth interviews with citizens have revealed widely varying abilities to

articulate the meaning of democracy. See Michael Binford, "The Democratic Political Personality: Functions of Attitudes and Styles of Reasoning," *Political Psychology* 4 (1983): 663–84; Robert Lane, *Political Ideology* (New York: Free Press, 1962); Shawn W. Rosenberg, Dana Ward, and Stephen Chilton, *Political Reasoning and Cognition* (Durham, N.C.: Duke University Press, 1988), esp. chap. 4.

Some groups will openly express their disdain toward democracy, and others will hint at it. Some groups are ostensibly democratic but governed rather autocratically with the chair taking pride in dominating the group under the guise of democracy.

12. For a lengthy discussion of the coding methodology I employed, see Gastil, "Democratic Deliberation," 90–110. For suggesting additional ways of observing relational communication and deliberation, I would like to thank the Mifflin staff and some of my former students, including Kevin Fischer, Cathy Pollack, Sarah Mohs, and Brian Costigan.

13. This brief description of nonverbal behavior at Mifflin Co-op does not do justice to the rich information that is available in a group's nonverbal behavior. See Peter A. Anderson, "Nonverbal Communication in the Small Group," in Robert S. Cathcart and Larry A. Samovar, *Small Group Communication*, 5th ed. (Dubuque, Iowa: William C. Brown Publishers, 1988), 333–50.

14. On the importance of the term *turnip*, see n. 19, below.

15. The tension between individuality and mutuality is commonplace in many small egalitarian groups. The section on unequal involvement and commitment in chapter 5 provides further discussion of this problem at Mifflin Co-op. For examples of this tension in other groups, see McLaughlin and Davidson, *Builders of the Dawn*, 62–65. For a theoretical discussion of this tension, see Kenwyn K. Smith and David N. Berg, "A Paradoxical Conception of Group Dynamics," *Human Relations* 40 (1987): 633–58.

16. Amy, Kate, and others questioned Norma's interpretation of the grandfather clause. I investigated the matter by reading records from past co-op meetings, but these proved inadequate. The notes from the crucial meeting are not sufficiently precise to resolve the issue. This underscores the importance of thorough note taking during meetings.

17. The numbers in Figure 4.1 compensate for imbalances in absences and the performance of facilitation and note-taking duties. See Gastil, "Democratic Deliberation," 108–10.

18. On the importance of interruptions and their varied forms in group discussions, see Lynn Smith-Lovin and Charles Brody, "Interruptions in Group Discussions: The Effects of Gender and Group Composition," *American Sociological Review* 54 (1989): 424–35.

19. Sam and Laura may have spoken less than others, but they were capable of influencing the group. These two were candidates for group clown, since they had developed a knack for playing with language and drawing laughter. As just one example, Sam and Laura played a role in popularizing the term *turnip*, a name that has become the sole label for the co-op policy I have called "tenure incentives." As Robert D. Rossel argues,

> Laughter is an acknowledgment by others that an individual has momentarily gained the upper hand against the conventions of language, and thus of reality by means of linguistic artistry—for the moment persuading the rest that things are not as they seem....One indicator of the pecking order in a group may be a simple assessment of whose statements are laughed at by whom....In addition, some individuals are more capable than others of coining words that capture the moment and go on to become widely distributed tokens in the group....This ability to coin new words and cultivate special meanings that become part of the group vocabulary is often associated with the ability to get people to laugh.

"Word Play: Metaphor and Humor in the Small Group," *Small Group Behavior* 12 (1981): 130–33.

20. During the six meetings I observed, staff members never dissented, but since the co-op made most decisions through consensus, this is not surprising. Nevertheless, dissent does occur on occasion. Under its system of consensus, the co-op allows a staff member to accept a decision without endorsing it. This happened in the case of tenure incentives, with Louis accepting but disagreeing with the final decision. After the last meeting I observed, Louis *did* choose to express his disagreement with the decision after it had been finalized. As a result, the staff reopened the issue for further discussion and revised its policy.

21. On the use of these and other linguistic devices in political discourse, see John Gastil, "Undemocratic Discourse: A Review of Theory and Research on Political Discourse," *Discourse & Society* 3 (1992): 469–500.

22. Dean E. Hewes, "A Socio-Egocentric Model of Group Decision-Making," in Randy Y. Hirokawa and Marshall Scott Poole, eds., *Communication and Group Decision-Making* (Beverly Hills, Calif.: Sage, 1986), 265–91.

23. Despite its success with democratic procedures, I refrain from calling Mifflin Co-op, or any other existing group, a democratic group since the democratic ideal is unattainable.

PART II

PRACTICING SMALL GROUP DEMOCRACY

5

IMPERFECT INVENTORY: OBSTACLES TO DEMOCRACY AT MIFFLIN CO-OP

IF THE FIRST half of this book paved a yellow brick road to small group democracy, the second considers the host of hazards in the path—the proverbial wicked forests, clumsy companions, and fields of poppies. In this chapter, I continue with Mifflin Street Community Co-op, looking beyond its successes to examine the obstacles to small group democracy at the co-op. One can learn a great deal by scrutinizing these problems because the co-op has come impressively close to the democratic ideal. The co-op has already met and surmounted many obstacles in its pursuit of democracy, so the barriers it continues to face are likely to be pervasive and formidable.[1]

In my observations and conversations with staff members, certain difficulties kept reappearing: long meetings, unequal involvement in the group and unequal commitment to its goals, cliques and miniconsensus, unequal communication skills, different communication styles, and personal conflicts. This chapter discusses all of these problems, identifying their characteristics, the ways they undermine the democratic process, and the means by which Mifflin Co-op, and other groups, can address them.

Long Meetings

Oscar Wilde once grumbled that the only problem with socialism was that it "would take too many evenings." For many groups, the problem isn't the frequency of meetings so much as their duration.[2] The staff members of Mifflin Co-op openly admit that their co-op proves no exception to this rule. As Ray said, "The democratic process breaks down after two hours, and often ... our meetings go more than two hours." The meetings begin at 6:30 P.M. on Mondays, and by 8:30, many staff members are tired. In Ray's view, the exhaustion makes meetings increasingly disjointed and unproductive. Since members do not grow weary at the same rate, their participation levels also begin to diverge.[3]

Excessive meeting length places two obstacles in the way of a group that seeks to be democratic. Relationships can become strained: members who grow tired more easily may become angry and bored, as Ray did during the videotaped meetings, and those who are still full of energy may resent the more tired staff members. In addition, fatigue makes the distribution of opportunities increasingly unequal, and it may even make opportunities entirely inadequate for the group's most weary members.[4]

Although not all staff members recognized the effects of long meetings on the democratic process, they generally acknowledged that meeting length had become excessive. They pointed out that sometimes people speak too long, and even before 8:30, people are too easily distracted. Louis said

> some people will sometimes speak more than they really need to. Instead of aiding the discussion, their comments become more disruptive. I try to be very brief and concise in what I have to say. That's partially because I grew up in New York City, and you don't just jabber away—you say what you need to say and get it over with.

Staff members considered distraction an even more serious problem. Amy, who could remember well-facilitated meetings from years past, said that rambling discussions were increasingly bothering her. Now, she complained, meetings are "less democratic, because different people have different levels of distraction. Some people might want to get everything off the track more than other people."

The staff offered a variety of suggestions when asked how they might solve these problems. To prevent excessive talking, Dan suggested that the staff should place limits on the discussion time allotted to each issue. In addition, Ray suggested that before speaking,

> We have to self-facilitate to determine whether our comments will be relevant or lead the discussion astray. Self-facilitation aids the democratic process by keeping things focused, streamlined, efficient, but not impersonal. It's important to be efficient so that people don't get burned out.

When self-facilitating fails, Kate said that staff members need to be able to say, "Okay, we've heard your view." Louis agreed, saying that individual members need to gain the confidence "to come forward and say, 'Okay, you're just talking too much.'" This is the facilitator's job, but if "the facilitator's not on top of things," someone else will have to do it.

To reduce the amount of distraction during meetings, Dan suggested that the co-op continue to look for a better meeting time. If meetings were held at a time when people were more alert, members would not be distracted as easily. Regardless of when they meet, Norma added that staff members should come to staff meetings more prepared. For instance, when the co-op is answering donation requests,

> If people would prepare more, everything could be cut down by at least a third. If someone would be responsible for summarizing donation requests and making a recommendation, then it could take us three minutes to deal with requests instead of twenty.

During meetings, Laura suggested, staff members ought to write down things that come to mind; otherwise, ideas get forgotten or muddled. Quickly writing down thoughts has the added advantage of making it easier to pay attention. Once the words are written, one's mind is no longer preoccupied with remembering what to say.

Finally, Amy stressed the role of the facilitator. Self-facilitation is important, but the facilitator designated for a given meeting should actively guide the discussion. She believed that the meetings were "straying" more than they used to because they were not as "tightly facilitated." The facilitator must be willing to interrupt speakers who stray from the issue and suggest the direction in which aimless discussions need to go. Otherwise, meetings can drift into the late hours of the night.

Unequal Involvement and Commitment

The Mifflin Co-op staff believes that democracy thrives in an egalitarian setting, and staff currently enjoy many forms of equality. Every member of the worker collective has the same hourly wage, job benefits, and decision-making power at the co-op. Staff members are also somewhat equal in their commitment to the co-op's goals.

Nevertheless there are some inequalities in staff involvement and commitment to the co-op. With regard to equal involvement, Louis explained, "We are all equal, and we emphasize the idea that no one has power over other people." However, "By my observation, some people are developing greater power over others at Mifflin, and I feel that it's due to their amount of time in the co-op."

Louis later explained that "some people" referred to Kate. Kate has worked the longest at the co-op, so she is most knowledgeable on almost every subject discussed during meetings. Currently she also has the broadest range of special responsibilities at the co-op, and she works more hours in the store than anyone else.

Like Louis, Norma expressed concern about Kate's high level of involvement in the co-op. She told a story about how one of her friends visited Mifflin and told Norma, "Kate's the boss." Norma has come to agree with her friend and sees Kate as the top of an unofficial hierarchy of involvement:

> There is ostensibly no power structure and everything's egalitarian, and that's part of what I was proud to tell my friends and my parents and my family. But it's really not that way, and I'm not sure it ever *can* be that way. My experience at the co-op has shown me that. I think that in organizations, people get power even though they don't set out to get power deliberately. There's no malevolence or anything like that.

Regardless of their intentions, if one or two members of a democratic group become relatively powerful, more than the equality of final decision-making authority is at stake. Imbalances in influence and expertise can limit less powerful members' ability to obtain and understand information relevant to group decisions. In addition, the more powerful individuals are more likely to take away others' opportunities to talk by dominating both the establishment and discussion of the agenda.

It is unclear exactly when and to what degree unequal involvement undermines the democratic process at Mifflin Co-op. Norma identified Kate as the staff member with disproportionate power, yet Kate does not appear to have dominated the agenda-setting process or staff deliberations. It is difficult to characterize Kate's use of power outside of meetings, per se, as undemocratic. When Kate began working at the co-op it was in financial and physical disrepair. Kate played a central role in revitalizing the store and developing co-op policies that are still in effect. Upon her arrival Kate was given wide latitude by a grateful staff, but in recent years Kate and other staff intentionally expanded the size of the worker collective from five to nine. Each time a new member has joined, Kate has willingly yielded more of her authority. Even Norma acknowledges that over the years, Kate may have yielded a greater amount of power than she possesses today.

Strict equality of group involvement is nonexistent. What matters is the degree to which some are more involved than others.[5] If the danger posed by unequal involvement increases with the level of disparity, Mifflin Co-op's relatively minute power differences do not appear to jeopardize its democratic process at present.[6]

Unequal *commitment*, however, may pose a more serious problem. Ray pointed out the relationship between commitment and involvement:

The more that people are involved in the process, the more concerned they are. That, in and of itself, makes for more equality, more of a shared burden, and more shared assumptions of how much work something is. If people are equally committed to the co-op, then they're equally involved and concerned about the co-op decisions and their ramifications for themselves and for the store as a whole.

The difference is that a staff member can be only marginally involved in the store's day-to-day activities yet remain totally committed to the co-op's goals. This is the case with Dan, who works only a few hours at the co-op every week. Ray explained,

Dan is as committed to the ideals of the co-op as much as anyone else, easily. But he's not as involved with the store as anyone else—he's the *least* involved. He's probably spent more time thinking about philosophical co-op issues than anyone else. *That's* where his level of commitment comes in.

Most of the staff contrasted Dan with Norma. Norma works the second fewest hours per week and probably has the least commitment to the co-op. She has openly acknowledged that Mifflin Co-op is a lower priority in her life than it is for other staff members.[7] This lower level of commitment has led to personal conflicts with staff. During one Monday night meeting, Rose expressed this concern to Norma:

I think what people talk about is feeling like you don't have the store prioritized in the same way that other people do. It's just a matter of where the priority is, and it feels like your relationship with your boyfriend is prioritized over the store. It *does* conflict with how we see each other's commitment to the store, because I feel like the store is my *first* commitment. And so it's hard to work with people that have a different commitment than me.

Laura expressed the same feelings to Norma: "A limited commitment makes for odd power plays and strange things. I'd prefer to see a full-fledged commitment, and I don't know if you can do that."

This inequality of commitment obstructs the democratic process by fostering an unfriendly group atmosphere, as illustrated by the hostile exchanges between Norma and the rest of the Mifflin staff. Staff members find it difficult to affirm the legitimacy of Norma's personal interests; instead, they view her as somewhat selfish and openly question her individual needs and desires. Since Norma does not share the staff's level of emotional and philosophical commitment to the co-op, many staff find it difficult to view her as a full member of the group. At best staff address her as though she is, as Louis put it, "on probation." In addition, friendly relations between the staff and Norma are diminishing, since many staff have become frustrated with her "lack of commitment."[8]

When asked how they might address these inequalities in involvement and commitment, most of the staff believed that the inequalities had to be removed, not accommodated. In the case of Kate and Norma, staff suggested that Kate work less and that Norma either take on a greater commitment or quit. What can be done if these individuals do not voluntarily take these actions? Again, the staff identified only one solution: firing. In the case of Norma, a number of staff members have not only asked Norma to consider resigning, they explored the possibility of firing her. This was something so extraordinary for the co-op that, at the time, its bylaws contained no dismissal procedure.

Other groups may not wish to take such drastic measures. After all, it is only extreme differences in commitment and involvement that undermine small group democracy. If the inequalities are moderate a group might find them tolerable, and a group with more extreme imbalances might find ways to lessen them. If this fails, desperate action may be necessary; however, the inclusiveness criterion cautions against firing or excluding members of a democratic group.

Cliques and Miniconsensus

Since speaking and listening are central features of democracy, communication problems often interfere with the democratic process. Communication is limited by the fact that we can be in only one place at one time; by choice and circumstance, we inevitably speak with some people more than others. Also, speaking and listening are acquired skills, and communication is nothing more than guesswork among people following similar linguistic rules. We can be certain neither of being understood nor of fully understanding anyone else. In small groups, these inherent limitations of human communication can obstruct small group democracy in the form of cliques, miniconsensus, unequal levels of communication skills, and different communication styles.

Mifflin Co-op staff members recognized the value of talking outside of meetings, but they also stressed the hazards it presents for the democratic process. Communicating outside of meetings allows individuals to work through issues before meetings by exchanging information, developing opinions, and coming to understand other viewpoints. This can contribute to shorter and more friendly meetings. At the same time, these seemingly innocuous gatherings can result in serious schisms, as the group divides into separate factions resembling the cliques that exist outside the meetings. People may come to meetings with set opinions they developed beforehand, and they may become reluctant to reiterate viewpoints they already explained to many—but not all—group members.

Talk outside meetings can create factions because it almost never involves the entire group. At the co-op, it consists of informal exchanges involving two or three staff members working in the store or spontaneous conversations between friends at social encounters outside the store.[9] Those not present in these casual encounters come to meetings lacking information that was distributed informally outside of the meeting.

Norma and Dan typically lack the information that others have, because they work at and visit the store least often. Their lack of information sometimes makes it difficult for them to comprehend meeting deliberations. Dan can usually compensate for day-to-day information with his years of experience at the co-op, but Norma, who is relatively new, has more difficulty following the discussion when she is uninformed.

This leads to another problem: when staff members repeatedly request information during a meeting, staff can become angry or frustrated. The person requesting information might feel angry because the group did not provide necessary information beforehand. Norma expressed this feeling, complaining that she resents having to wait until meetings to receive information relevant to the meeting agenda. Other staff sometimes get frustrated when they have to listen to information they have already received. For instance, Amy once criticized Rose for failing to obtain relevant information before a meeting. In addition, Sam pointed out that even when staff members recognize the importance of providing someone with information during a meeting, tension still builds over the lengthening of the discussions.

In any case, conversations outside meetings provide more than information to those who take part in them. Sam said that they also keep staff members up to date with each other's feelings, concerns, and ambitions. From passing comments to significant shared experiences, these interactions create "a good bond between us and allow us to understand each other more fully.... We see each other every day, or at least five of us do," he explained, "and with that comes a certain closeness."

A problem arises because these informal interactions involve a subgroup of the staff. The rest of the staff can become "outsiders," lacking the sense of mutuality shared by the cohesive subgroup. At Mifflin Co-op it appears that Norma often falls outside of the informal communication network that exists outside meetings. Norma works as much as Rose and more than Dan, but Rose and Dan frequently interact with the other staff members as friends. As Amy describes it, there is a certain "resistance" to Norma from the rest of the staff. Even when Norma is in the store, Laura explained, some staff try to avoid her.

The formation of cliques or the social exclusion of an individual group member can lead to misunderstandings and hostility. A spirit of comradeship and a common identity may grow stronger for everyone except the excluded individual. In addition, if the members of a subgroup have already defined an issue beforehand, they may try to prevent another member from reformulating this agenda item during the meeting. Louis expressed a concern about this in the case of Kate and Ray. He feared that their premeeting discussion of the tenure incentives proposals may have narrowed the scope of the deliberation during meetings.

By the time a meeting begins, a subgroup may have gone even further, reaching an agreement among themselves. A "miniconsensus" is not always detrimental to the group. Sometimes staff have to make quick decisions outside of meetings, such as when an unexpected delivery arrives. Also, the staff regularly designates committees of two or three members to make decisions during the coming week.

A miniconsensus is counterproductive when it is informal and unspoken. In these cases, a subgroup might mistakenly believe that an issue has already been resolved and try to end debate prematurely, closing other group members' opportunities for reformulation, articulation, and persuasion. As Dan said, "If small groups of people achieve consensus on an issue outside of a meeting, [they may] assume it is dealt with, while others have not had a say in the decision."

To address these problems, staff members proposed lessening information inequalities. Norma suggested that instead of "taking it out" on her and Dan for lacking information, the co-op "could accommodate disparate hours." Clipboards, logbooks, and other forms of written communication would allow her and Dan to keep up-to-date. Others viewed such a system as time-consuming and cumbersome; they placed responsibility for the problem on the staff members who work the fewest hours. Kate, for instance, argued that either Mifflin should hire only full-time staff, or part-time staff should be responsible for gathering pertinent information themselves. "We've discussed this a lot over the years," she added, "and it's my main argument for having folks work at least twenty-five hours a week, ideally full time, just so this 'information hierarchy' doesn't exist."

Neither of these solutions addresses the problem of subgroup cohesion and miniconsensus. Making every staff member equally involved in the store might mitigate these difficulties, but they would remain. Pairs and subgroups inevitably form bonds distinct from those of the full group, and this becomes a serious problem when personal conflicts result in the conscious exclusion of one or more individuals from the informal interaction network. At the very least, group members can remain aware of this potential problem, but groups can also organize fully inclusive social activities to maintain positive relationships among all group members.

Differences in Skills and Styles

One might expect that members of an egalitarian cooperative would all possess highly developed communication skills. The reality is that there are openly acknowledged skill differences among the workers at Mifflin Co-op. Some staff are comfortable and skilled in group settings, but others are relatively reserved and inarticulate. Some are able and willing to jump into a heated debate, whereas others hesitate to enter such a discussion. When skilled and extroverted staff talk among themselves during a meeting, quieter members can feel intimidated. If not invited into the discussion, they might withdraw briefly.

Sam explained that some members, usually newer ones, have not yet overcome patriarchal and hierarchical norms that stunt the development of the skills necessary for democratic decision making: "A lot of people are very used to being led.... *It's easier to be led than ... to be in the forefront." Amy concurred:*

> We come from cultures that are not democratic—we've been raised in families with strict hierarchies, not only between parents and children, but sometimes between siblings too. Our educations have often been regimented, and we have not been taught that our individual opinions are important to the larger group. Decisions about how our society functions were made long before we were born, and we're made to fit in—not to value the different visions we create.

> Participating in a democratic experience is rare, but powerful. We all bring the dynamics of our past into the process at Mifflin. We come with unacknowledged personal agendas and different levels of need for hierarchy. We have different levels of personal or political commitment to the worker-managed workplace, and we have different levels of desire to take responsibility for it.

"Individual personalities have a great impact," Amy explained. "Some of us have little experience expressing our opinions or expecting to have them listened to. Some of us have difficulty expressing our feelings." Kate, one of the more articulate staff members, agreed: "Some people aren't as good at communicating their needs and ideas as others."

Inequalities in speaking skills can result in an inequality of opportunities, with the more skilled perceiving and receiving the greater number of opportunities to talk. More agile speakers may have more success interrupting, holding the floor, and redefining the discussion. Over time, these individuals could become even more skilled through practice, while less skilled group members could become increasingly reticent. Some group members can become accustomed to talking, while others become resigned or accustomed to remaining silent.

To prevent this, the co-op tries to develop the abilities of those with weaker communication skills by drawing them out and encouraging them to speak their minds during meetings. Louis explained that new members need to become used to being a part of a participatory democracy. The staff tries to empower new members by "actually asking people [to speak] and making it a very friendly environment, so that people feel free to discuss things."

This method for empowering new members is similar to the strategy used to develop the skills of long-term members. Kate said that the staff tries to draw out quieter members. She will sometimes ask others for their opinions, or she will nonverbally encourage them through a visual cue, such as well-timed eye contact. As an example, she said that with a glance, she might reassure Sam that he is safe to express emotional displeasure with something Louis has said.

Staff stressed the means by which more reserved members can enter a heated, fast-paced debate. The meetings are typically informal, with people speaking whenever they wish, but if a member clearly signals a desire to speak by raising a hand, the facilitator will call on that person when the current speaker is finished. Also, Laura pointed to round-robins, in which group members give their opinions in turn. These can be used at any juncture, but they are often used toward the end of an intense discussion. These remove the heat of debate and give members a clear, uninterrupted opportunity to express themselves.

Some of the quieter group members attested to the effectiveness of these empowerment strategies. Louis, for example, believed that his experiences at Mifflin staff meetings have made him "much better at communicating." He now feels more skilled in group settings as well as in one-on-one conversations.

The staff also relies upon a self-sufficiency ethic: skilled members are expected to make allowances for the others, but to some extent, other members have to fend for themselves. Sam used Kate as an example: "There are things Kate does which cause people to feel intimidated. And so far as I'm concerned, that's something that other people need to work out for themselves." He admitted being intimidated by her when he first arrived at the co-op, but he believed he could overcome it only through personal growth. Norma, who has been most intimidated by Kate, agreed, insisting that she was responsible for getting over her intimidation. At some point, staff argue, the less skilled have to take it upon themselves to develop their skills and transcend the feelings of inferiority or intimidation they may feel in the presence of more skilled peers.[10]

Differences in communication styles present another set of problems for small group democracy. An important difference between skills and styles is that one style is not necessarily "better" or "more developed" than another. For the most part, Norma explained, people are just the way they are, and they should not have to change for democracy to exist. People should adapt to, if not appreciate, each other's differences. In Sam's words,

> You have to make allowances for the people you're with. That's part of respecting people, I think. In a totalitarian state where everyone had evolved to be the perfect model of everybody else, you wouldn't have this problem. You also wouldn't have consensus decision making.

> But everybody's different. Everyone's got their own wealth of experience to draw upon and make them who they are. I think that acknowledging and allowing for the individual is fairly critical to democratic group decisions. You need to realize that each person is who they are and that they're going to act and react in different ways.

Amy identified what she considered one of the most prominent differences in communication styles among the various members of the co-op. She called it the difference between "internal" and "external" cognitive processing:

> I definitely internalize things … I don't respond to things as immediately. I think it's more valuable to process things and internalize them—not everything, but certainly many things. But there are different personality types. Some people function better speaking out loud, and some people function better by being in touch with other levels of themselves.

Amy hastened to add that neither of these styles is "better," and both are compatible with the democratic process.

Louis described a similar style difference between himself, Amy, Norma, and Sam on the one hand, and the rest of the staff on the other. "I would just tend to believe that the one thing we do have in common is that we're perhaps more introverted than other people—more quiet, more self-analyzing." Louis argued that this difference was not an inherent problem; instead, the problem derives from a cultural bias in favor of the "extroverted" style of communicating:

> I think it's more general than Mifflin. I think it's a cultural bias in our nation that favors extroverts. Extroverts are the people we see as leaders, and we will promote them over the people that are more introverted—those who just do their work and are not outspoken in a positive way.[11]

Differences in group members' evaluations of communication styles can create problems for both democratic speaking and listening. If one of the styles becomes the group norm, those using the unconventional style may have more difficulty receiving and recognizing opportunities to speak. Regardless of whether one style dominates, group members who speak in different styles may have difficulty comprehending and considering one another's views.

To a limited extent, Mifflin Co-op has tried to address this issue. "We're somewhat conscious of it," Louis acknowledged, "but I think that the cultural bias is so strong that we simply overlook it." Sam agreed that the staff has not "made allowances" for these differences; it continues to favor the extroverted style. Failing to remedy the cultural bias is, in Louis's opinion, undemocratic:

> Democracy means that you make decisions for the whole, with the well-being of all the people involved. And if you overlook someone because he or she doesn't happen to fit in or is unable to speak out, that's not *democratic*. I think people that are extroverted need to be a little more conscious and realize that other people will not be able to communicate as well or express themselves as well and that because of this, their self-expression is hindered. Because of this unspoken bias, even their self-worth and growth will be hindered.

The solution lies in the staff members' recognizing and accepting that these differences are based on style, not skill. The group can come to understand that there is more than one way to communicate. Ultimately styles might be combined or synthesized, taking care to treat each style equally. Even if such an attempt is unsuccessful, it can build understanding and respect between those members using one style and those another.

This solution, however, may be easier to propose than implement. Louis was not optimistic: "Try as we may at Mifflin, we are part of this culture, and it's difficult to deal with sensitive issues of this nature. We're trying to work around them and with them, but it's still very cumbersome." Kate expressed a similar view regarding style differences between Louis and Amy and the rest of the staff. The staff found it important but difficult to fully appreciate members' differences in background and speaking styles. "The more we understand each other, the better our democratic process, because then we can accommodate each other's needs better." But, she added, "It's very difficult to understand someone else's experiences. Our process works on understanding, and I think you can always respect someone else, but you can't always understand them."

Personal Conflicts

The final and possibly the largest obstacle in the path of small group democracy at Mifflin Co-op is personal conflicts among the staff. The staff believes that the problem involves both the seriousness of some conflicts and the failure to confront them. Expressing a typical view, Ray thought that "animosity between some staff people and the lack of respect between them hinders our democratic process. Greater group democracy would come from the resolution of interpersonal conflicts."[12]

These conflicts can obstruct small group democracy by closing opportunities to speak, causing group members to ignore others' views, and undermining mutuality. The conflicts at Mifflin Co-op illustrate each of these problems.

Staff who have unresolved conflicts with other members sometimes have more difficulty speaking, because extreme tension can make their apparent opportunities to talk meaningless. As Norma explained, "There are times when because of whatever emotional or interpersonal dynamic was going on at the moment, it felt like a reduced opportunity to speak. I feel like there are overriding interpersonal barriers."

When these interpersonal conflicts are not addressed, members lose the respect necessary for seriously considering one another's views. Even if members consciously know that they ought to respect a person, anger or resentment may prevent them from doing so. For example, Ray said that he generally listens to other staff members,

> but if it's someone I respect less than I should, their comments tend to fly by me. I don't listen to them carefully, or I look for what's behind them. It's not an honest exchange—it's been subverted by things becoming twisted. The *truth* is key to the democratic process, and the more truthful we can be, the more honest dialogue will occur. If there's not an honest dialogue, then I don't think the democratic process is working.

Similarly, Norma said that she sometimes feels that "there's something simmering behind what [Kate] says, so I don't trust what she says. I feel like it's manipulative sometimes but not always—*definitely* not always. I just feel really defensive toward her."

If the conflict is not addressed and respect erodes, interpersonal conflicts can begin to divide the entire co-op staff. A major factor in this divisiveness is the gossip that surrounds unresolved conflicts. Norma explained, "There's some kind of taboo that interferes with the democratic process, or there's some sort of pattern of behavior where people aren't good at confronting each other, and they talk behind each other's backs." Laura admitted that she resorted to gossiping about Norma with other staff members. In the past gossip was common at the co-op, but since Norma's vacation issues came up, it has become "ten times worse." It is now more frequent and often more malicious. Laura added, "I am just so angry with her, I have lost all respect." The conflict between Laura and Norma lessened their sense of shared group identity, but the gossip replaced these weakening bonds with strong emotional barriers.

The costs of unresolved conflict are high, but staff members are often willing to pay this price rather than face their conflicts. The clearest case of this at the co-op is the clash between Norma and the rest of the staff, especially Kate. During her interview Norma began to cry as she described how the conflict worsened over time: "Things got worse and worse, in a spiral. People didn't think I was doing a good job, but they didn't confront me about it. I was scared I'd lose my job."

The two meetings in which the staff explicitly addressed this conflict were, in the opinion of every staff member, among the most stressful meetings they had ever experienced at the co-op. Unfortunately the meetings did not resolve the conflict. Norma reported that afterward, many staff members would not even talk to her and avoided her both in and outside of the store. According to Norma, Rose was unwilling to confront her in person but wrote a vicious letter to her regarding the conflict and other issues from the past. Staff members confessed that Norma's perception was accurate. As Kate put it, some staff simply lacked the emotional energy to confront Norma. The conflict was just going to "smolder."

To some extent, conflicts such as this are unavoidable and extremely difficult to "solve." As Dan cautioned, "There are times when personality issues preclude people feeling comfortable with doing or saying something.... This probably is true of any grouping of people at any given point in time." It would be hard, he added, to "legislate" this problem out of existence. "It's just something that people need to be aware of."

With this caveat in mind, the Mifflin staff offered a number of suggestions for ways the co-op and other small groups can address serious interpersonal conflicts and the strong emotions that accompany them. Staff believed that group members must try to maintain their respect for one another in the midst of emotional conflict and resist the temptation to gossip. The staff also advocated preventive medicine—the development of positive relationships among group members before disputes emerge.

Beyond these basic suggestions, staff members focused on dealing with the strong emotions that surface when a group confronts a conflict. The staff believed that anger, frustration, and resentment are a part of being human, and it is essential to express these emotions constructively, no matter how awkward and upsetting it might make group meetings. Sam thought that if these emotions were bottled in, it "would just build up stress and tension." Somehow, somewhere, staff members need to vent their emotions.

During meetings, those not involved in the conflict can facilitate the expression of emotions by the persons involved in the conflict. Rose suggested that friendly comments can reduce tension and encourage staff members to relax—to take themselves less seriously. In addition, members can directly encourage others to express their feelings. If any members appear frustrated or agitated, others can give verbal or nonverbal support and allow them to express themselves. Kate said that she, Laura, and Norma frequently performed this function. She believed that there may be a greater reluctance for male group members to take these actions.

When staff members involved in a conflict speak, they should express themselves honestly and respectfully. Kate provided an example of this "reasonable" style of emotional expression: "'That makes me really angry, and I'm going to tell you why that makes me angry.'" Sam elaborated on this idea:

> You can choose your words carefully and think before you speak. Those are things I try to work on most of the time. I'm not that good at it. You can try to phrase what you want to say so that the people you're talking to understand that you're not trying to hurt them with what you're saying—that you're just giving from yourself what you feel you need to give to the group. That's how to avoid compromising democracy because you don't want to hurt somebody.

In extreme cases, though, the feelings a staff member wishes to express may be too intense to express in a productive manner. At this point, Kate recommended, the staff member should neither speak nor sit silently but leave the room. Kate said that during her years at Mifflin, staff had done this only once or twice during a meeting. The most recent time was during the discussion of Norma's vacation plans. Kate began to confront her, and the two exchanged words for a few minutes, each taking long, uninterrupted speaking turns. Eventually Kate became so enraged that she decided it was best to leave the room. Her parting words to the group were, "I'm going to have to leave for a while. I'm afraid I'm just ... ," followed by silence.

Kate discussed the incident at length during her interview. She said it was the first time she had walked out of a meeting in her seven years at the co-op:

> I knew when I left that the things I was saying were deeper than the issue at hand. I was getting beyond the rational. I wasn't listening well, and I wasn't responding well. It was not productive for me to be involved in the conversation any longer at that point, because I was just going to make it worse.

> I think everyone knew how upset I was, and it wasn't necessary for me to go on and on, though that's a tendency that I have. So I realized it was important for me to just go and chill out a little bit. By the time I came back, I *had* chilled out a little bit. I was still just as angry, but I wasn't dealing with my anger in the same way. I felt it was more productive.

If a conflict reaches the point where it generates such powerful negative feelings, it may be necessary to deal with it outside the meeting. Staff members reported success dealing with one another in one-on-one or mediated encounters, and they planned to address all serious personal conflicts in this manner.[13]

Epilogue

During my irregular trips to grocery stores, I still frequent the Mifflin Street Community Co-op. On a recent visit I chatted with the staff about this book, and they explained how their meetings had changed since I first studied them. One staff member said I should write an epilogue on whether the co-op has become more democratic. Wouldn't it be interesting to see if any of the staff's suggestions, shown in Table 5.1, had been adopted in the past year? Obviously, I liked the idea.[14]

Since my original observations and interviews, much has changed at the co-op. Three new staff members replaced Rose, Laura, and Dan, who left the collective to pursue other occupations. In addition, the number of shift-workers was reduced to two, and they worked in the store only on Monday nights, when the rest of the staff was meeting upstairs.

The change in shift-worker policy was designed, in part, to address the inclusiveness problem. Previously, shift-workers had begun to cover so many shifts that their hours became closer to those of some staff members. A few shift-workers put in long hours but lacked the decision-making power of the regular staff. By limiting the number of shift-workers to two and restricting the number of shifts that staff can ask shift-workers to cover, the difference between the roles of staff and shift-workers has become clearer.[15]

The co-op has also made an architectural change, adding a new room above the store. The room is used as a lounge, reading room, and meeting space. Previously the staff had met in the adjoining room upstairs, which was filled with file cabinets, desks, paper, and an odd assortment of quasifurniture. The staff had also periodically met in staff members' living rooms or in a room on the nearby University of Wisconsin-Madison campus.

The staff found their new meeting room ideal. Like the old room, it provided quick access to records and to the store itself, but a member needing to open a file drawer or check the computer no longer had to disrupt the meeting and step over people sitting on the floor. The new room is far more comfortable than the old one, because it is more spacious and includes a cozy sofa and chairs.

The staff explained that such "comforts" are important for a number of reasons. The larger space makes it possible for staff to sit in a circle or ellipse and make eye contact with every person in the room. The size of the room also gives individual staff members more "personal space." Without such space, some staff members find it hard to maintain eye

Table 5.1   Some Strategies for Confronting Obstacles to Small
Group Democracy

Obstacles	Strategies/Solutions
1. Long meetings	self-facilitate facilitate others meet when everyone is wide awake come to meetings prepared be attentive during meetings, take notes
2. Unequal involvement and commitment	make levels of involvement and commitment more equal: reduce some members' levels and/or increase those of other members change the group membership
3. Communication problems a. cliques and miniconsensus	establish a means for communicating important ideas and information outside of meetings (e.g. logbook) make individuals responsible for communicating with others outside of meetings
b. unequal communication skills	encourage and assist the least skilled members in improving their skills establish procedures that make it easier for more hesitant members to speak (e.g. round-robins) create a self-sufficiency ethic that spurs members to take responsibility for augmenting their skills
c. communication style differences	try to understand and accept differences in communication styles if possible, integrate different styles into a unique group style that favors no individual style
4. Personal conflicts	try to maintain mutual respect resist the temptation to gossip about group members with others in the group build positive emotional bonds among members whenever possible be open and honest with other members help other members work through their conflicts if the conflict becomes extreme during a meeting, consider leaving the room and addressing it at a later time, perhaps with a mediator

contact or speak directly to the person sitting beside them. The personal space and good chairs also provide physical comfort. Aching backs and constant shifting can easily distract staff members during meetings, so comfortable seating makes concentration easier. If a larger space makes it easier for staff members to focus on the meeting agenda and speak their minds, the co-op has taken a step toward surmounting obstacles such as excessive meeting length and the failure to confront personal conflicts.[16]

To further address the problem of long meetings, the staff has also formalized its agenda-setting process. Under the new system, staff members still have the freedom to write down agenda items during the week, but they do so in a more organized manner. They first decide whether their item belongs under scheduling, donations, committee updates, issues, or announcements. This categorical distinction allows the facilitator to cluster similar items, and it helps focus discussion. Staff members also specify the kind of action their items require: brainstorming, a decision, a discussion, an announcement, or something else. Members then estimate the amount of meeting time their items will take and sign their names beside their items.

There is also a clearer expectation that staff members read the meeting agenda prior to the meeting itself. Required reading includes not only the agenda items but also the "cling-ons," which some staff affectionately call Klingons (one of the more excitable alien species in the "Star Trek" television series). These cling-ons include any documents that clarify an agenda item. One common cling-on is the staff's new donation request form. Now, when a group asks for a donation, the staff member receiving the request writes pertinent information on a simple form, which is then affixed to the agenda sheet.

Reading the agenda and the cling-ons prior to Monday night shortens meeting time, because it provides staff members with knowledge they would otherwise have to obtain during meetings. In the meeting I observed, however, this particular expectation was not always met. Some staff sheepishly asked for information during the meeting that had been available in the cling-ons.

Staff also reported that facilitation and self-facilitation have improved somewhat, and my observations confirmed this. Facilitators more regularly try to gauge total meeting length, then try to keep the pace of the meeting in line with this forecast. Facilitators are making a more concerted effort to avoid tangents and steer wayward speakers back on track. As for self-facilitation, staff members generally followed the advice of Sam and Kate, who recently wrote a set of meeting guidelines. Staff concentrated on what each other said and usually refrained from repeating one another's words, saying "ditto" or "what she said" instead.

One of the most dramatic changes in staff policy came in response to the problem of unequal involvement and commitment. In March 1991 the co-op staff drafted its first dismissal procedure. Under this policy the staff can "dismiss" (fire) a member of the worker collective because of a "pattern of failure to show up for work," "negligence of individual responsibilities," "consistent substandard job performance," or a "pattern of abusive behavior."

If a dismissal or probation is requested by one of the staff, the request is processed by a staff committee, which then makes a recommendation, accompanied by a clear rationale, to the board of directors. This elaborate process was designed to provide a mechanism for dismissing uncommitted and uninvolved staff. This policy has yet to be tested, but its mere existence may have a positive motivational effect on anyone whose involvement might otherwise wane.[17]

Other policy changes have been designed to prevent staff members from dramatically reducing the number of hours they work at the store. The new vacation policy specifies that staff can take up to four weeks of paid vacation, and vacations must be scheduled in advance. In addition, the staff are now restricted to trading no more than 30 percent of their shifts with other staff members. Together these policies might prevent misunderstandings and disputes like those that developed between Norma and the rest of the staff.[18]

As for communication problems, the network of communication among staff members has improved since the winter of 1990. A worker log has been placed near one of the cash registers, and staff regularly read it when they begin their work shifts in the store. Staff, as well as the two shift-workers, write in the log any ideas, experiences, or feelings they wish to share. This keeps members up-to-date on important events, and it keeps them in touch with one another's moods and concerns. An erasable marker board complements the log by providing a space for information of immediate relevance, from phone messages to notes about food deliveries. Norma and Louis, both of whom raised concerns about cliques and miniconsensus at Mifflin, agreed that the worker log and marker board improved the flow of ideas and emotions among staff members. As an added bonus, these mechanisms lessened the need to make announcements or present gripes; this may shorten the length of Monday night meetings.

Differences in communication skills and styles remain, and the addition of new staff members has tested the staff's ability to accommodate the aptitudes and eccentricities of three more people. The new staff said they felt welcome at the co-op, and during the meeting they appeared comfortable. They did not talk as often as the others, but they always joined in the group laughter and sat in relaxed postures. Most important, they spoke when issues of direct concern to them came up during the meeting. They continued to speak freely even when the meeting turned into an emotionally charged debate on whether certain staff were failing to fulfill work responsibilities and creating uncomfortable work atmospheres.[19]

As this discussion suggests, interpersonal conflicts remain at the co-op. Since my original observations, the co-op has tried to diffuse tensions and ameliorate conflicts. The staff hired a professional mediator to host a retreat at which they learned about one another's backgrounds, current lives, and future aspirations. Staff told one another the ways they preferred to communicate and how they responded to different kinds of behaviors and messages. The staff found the meeting fruitful, because it helped them understand each other's experiences and perspectives.

The staff also wrote a grievance procedure for "any complaint, problem or misunderstanding ... which has not been adequately dealt with through the normal staff interaction process." The centerpiece of the policy is finding an ombudsperson acceptable to the entire staff. Initially this third party seeks a mutually acceptable resolution to the problem. If this fails, the ombudsperson then serves as an overseer while the problem is taken to the personnel committee and then the board of directors, which makes the final decision. If used, the policy provides reluctant staff members (or shift-workers) with a clear opportunity to air their grievances.

More informally, staff still try to communicate with respect and honesty. Throughout the meeting I observed, staff showed little reluctance to ruffle feathers, but they also took time to encourage each other with comments such as, "I appreciate your concern," or, "Don't worry. I know you didn't mean for me to take it that way." Nonetheless, some staff took personal offense at each other's words; through vulgarity, strong language, and staccato hand gestures some staff expressed frustration and sadness during the discussion of the store's general work atmosphere.

A few days after the meeting, Kate mused, "What's important is not the existence of conflict, but what you do with it."[20] From this perspective, the conduct and results of the discussion were more noteworthy than the personal conflicts themselves. All staff members, including the newer ones, spoke directly and held on to their opportunities to speak—even when briefly cut off by another person. Staff spoke with confidence and conviction, and they always took time to clarify themselves and correct any misunderstandings that arose. Staff were also careful to speak only for themselves, framing criticisms with "I feel" and "I think," instead of claiming the authority of the group.

The result of the discussion was a commitment to improve the communication across different work shifts regarding shelf stocking. Staff members also reached a better understanding of what behaviors different members perceive as intimidating or hostile. They agreed to change the way they spoke to one another during work shifts, particularly during those times when the store is busiest and staff are under the greatest amount of stress.

After the staff reached these agreements the meeting continued as before, and everyone became relaxed once again. As I wrote in my notebook, it seemed that the act of meeting together had given the staff a special opportunity to question and rearrange the reality of their workplace. During these special meeting times, staff were free to speak their minds and willing to listen to what others had to say.

It might be impossible for people to relate to one another on a daily basis with such stark honesty and full attentiveness. The physical, mental, and emotional strain would be too much to bear. But if a couple of hours are set aside each week, and clear rules of conduct are established and respected, perhaps it is possible for a group of people to communicate and make collective decisions in a truly exceptional way. Perhaps the obstacles to small group democracy are never fully overcome but surmounted during brief, brilliant flashes.

Notes

Portions of this chapter are reprinted with the permission of Sage Publications from John Gastil, "Obstacles to Small Group Democracy," *Small Group Research* 24 (1993): 5–27.

1. On the logic behind this approach to case studies, see Robert K. Yin, *Case Study Research* (Beverly Hills, Calif.: Sage, 1989), 47; Michael Q. Patton, *Qualitative Evaluation Methods* (Beverly Hills, Calif.: Sage, 1980), 102–3. Since the study of Mifflin Co-op, I found additional evidence suggesting that the obstacles to small group democracy identified in this chapter are encountered by a wide variety of groups. See Gastil, "Obstacles to Small Group Democracy."

2. Oscar Wilde quoted in Michael Walzer, *Radical Principles: Reflections of an Unreconstructed Democrat* (New York: Basic Books, 1980), 129. Walzer also provides a humorous sketch of the *real* activities of Karl Marx's ideal socialist citizen, who is constantly running from one meeting to the next. Walzer's parodies have some basis in fact. Corinne McLaughlin and Gordon Davidson found that many communities have faced similar problems, which they call "workaholism" or "meeting-itis": *Builders of the Dawn: Community Lifestyles in a Changing World* (Shutesbury, Mass.: Sirius Publishing, 1986), 76–77. The problem may not be the amount of time per se but the amount of time in excess of expectations. Thus Jane J. Mansbridge argues that frequent or long meetings are not as much of a problem for groups that "expect to spend a lot of time in decision making, and can value

that time as interaction with friends." "Time, Emotion, and Inequality: Three Problems of Participatory Groups," *Journal of Applied Behavioral Science* 9 (1973): 357.

3. A cynical reader might suspect that long meetings at Mifflin Co-op reflect a desire for longer work hours and, consequently, more take-home pay. This suspicion is unwarranted, since the staff are not paid for attending mandatory Monday night meetings. As compensation for attendance, they receive the 10 percent volunteer discount at the store; however, the discount requires only four hours of work, whereas staff spend between eight and twelve hours a month in Monday meetings.

4. When taken to extremes, exceedingly long (or frequent) meetings can reduce group members' willingness to attend at all, which creates an inclusiveness problem. Some groups such as university faculty are jealous guards of their time, and if members perceive that meetings take too long, they will choose to cancel them or attend sporadically. See Daniel C. Kramer, *Participatory Democracy: Developing Ideals of the Political Left* (Cambridge, Mass.: Schenkman Publishing, 1972), 122-27.

5. On the inevitability of unequal involvement and its effects on democratic decision making, see Walzer, *Radical Principles*, chap. 9; Mansbridge, "Time, Emotion, and Inequality," 361–67; Anne Phillips, *Engendering Democracy* (University Park, Pa.: Pennsylvania State University, 1991), and "Must Feminists Give Up on Liberal Democracy?" *Political Studies* 40, Special Issue (1992): 74–75, 79.

6. When power differences are slight there may be a danger of exaggerating them and accusing marginally more powerful group members of hoarding their power. Kate said she became frustrated when she was criticized for her level of knowledge and authority in the co-op. She pointed out that she has encouraged others to take on more responsibilities, but she occasionally perceives a reluctance on the part of one or more members to become more powerful.

7. In a more recent interview, Norma speculated that her lower level of commitment to the store may have been the result of how she felt treated by the staff in the past. She said that she thought others initially viewed her as less competent and less committed, so as a result she behaved in these ways. Regardless of the veracity of the claim, it raises the issue of self-fulfilling expectations, particularly with regard to sustaining a member's commitment and competence.

8. In the view of some staff, the situation at Mifflin Co-op relates to the more general problem of apathy. Political apathy is widespread on social scales both large and small. In small groups, as in large societies, it obstructs fully participatory decision making. See Kramer, *Participatory Democracy*, chap. 6; Walzer, *Radical Principles*, chap. 9; Phillips, *Engendering Democracy*, esp. chap. 5.

9. In another group I observed, some members would conduct extended side conversations during meetings. Known as "caucusing," this practice is doubly disruptive, since it also removes the caucus members from the ongoing meeting discussion.

10. None of the Mifflin Co-op staff has a severe speech impediment, so it has not had to deal with this difficulty. I have observed a small planning board with a member who required a great deal of time and energy to speak clearly. With practice the other board members learned to understand his utterances, and they showed patience in letting him finish his sentences. Despite this difference in speaking ability, it appeared that the board member was treated as an equal member of the group. The example shows that groups are capable of accommodating wide ranges of speaking abilities.

11. The introverted style discussed by Amy and Louis has similarities with shyness or reticence. In an extreme form this amounts to a fear of speaking in groups. On the varieties and effects of such fear, as well as ways of overcoming it, see James C. McCroskey and Virginia P. Richmond, "Communication Apprehension and Small Group Communication," in Robert S. Cathcart and Larry A. Samovar, *Small Group Communication*, 5th ed. (Dubuque, Iowa: William C. Brown Publishers, 1988), 405–20.

12. Other writers have lamented the variety of personal conflicts that plague small groups and communities. See Mansbridge, "Time, Emotion, and Inequality," 358–61; McLaughlin and Davidson, *Builders of the Dawn*, chap. 3.

13. For a typology of methods for resolving conflicts, see Richard W. Fogg, "Dealing with Conflict: A Repertoire of Creative, Peaceful Approaches," *Journal of Conflict Resolution* 29 (1985): 330–58.

14. Additional suggestions for dealing with problems like those in Table 5.1 are provided in the Center for Conflict Resolution's *Building United Judgment* (Madison, Wis.: Center for Conflict Resolution, 1981), chap. 13.

15. The distinction between staff and shift-workers remains an uncomfortable one for some staff. For instance one provision of the co-op insurance policy reads, "Shift-workers at the Co-op, *though dearly appreciated*, are exempt from this policy" (italics added).

16. In seeing the connection between architecture and democracy, Mifflin Co-op joins the likes of Frank Lloyd Wright and political philosopher Benjamin Barber (*Strong Democracy*). Also see the series of articles on community planning in *Utne Reader* (May/June 1992), 93–106.

The staff's desire to sit in a circle makes sense, since people communicate more often with people facing them than with those adjacent to them. A rectangular or irregular seating arrangement reduces the number of people one can face without shifting or craning one's neck. See L. L. Cummings, George P. Huber, and Eugene Arendt, "Effects of Size and Spatial Arrangements on Group Decision Making," *Academy of Management Journal* 17 (1974): 460–75.

17. The wording of the final clause of the dismissal policy also suggests the co-op's continuing commitment to democratic deliberation: "If for some reason, the Board rejects the staff's recommendation, it must ask the Collective to reconsider the firing and *give reasons why* to the Collective. Likewise, when the Collective recommends dismissing an employee, it must *explain to the Board its reasons* for recommending the dismissal" (italics added). The stress placed on reasons parallels the emphasis on reasoned argument discussed in chapter 2.

18. In the recent past there was another staff member who had switched shifts and taken vacations in a similar manner, so some staff viewed this as a recurring problem.

19. The new staff clearly understood meeting procedures. This came partly from experience and partly from the information provided by other staff members. To aid the learning process, Sam and Kate wrote a three-page description of staff meeting procedures to complement the materials in the co-op's training manual.

20. Many authors have stressed the productive role that conflict can play in groups. Frances Moore Lappé and Paul Martin DuBois believe that "creative controversy" is critical for a democracy. "It brings to light the interests and values that must be incorporated if proposed solutions are to work"; "Power in a Living Democracy," *Creation Spirituality* (September/October 1992): 42. For a more general treatment of the social functions of conflict, see Lewis Coser, *The Functions of Social Conflict* (New York: Free Press, 1956).

6

PURSUING AN IDEAL IN LESS THAN IDEAL SETTINGS

IN MANY CASES groups cannot avoid or quickly alter their settings. Large groups, for instance, cannot simply reduce their membership in a shortsighted pursuit of small group democracy. To do so would undermine the group's inclusiveness, making it altogether undemocratic. Groups under external constraints may hope to change the larger system of power relations eventually, but they may have to work within it for a time. When groups cannot change their circumstances, there are still ways in which they can adapt to them. This chapter looks at how groups can respond to problems posed by large, geographically dispersed, and unstable memberships, as well as problems of time pressure and economic, political, and social constraints on democratic decision making.

Larger Groups and Organizations

In this book small groups are defined as ranging from three to thirty people. Thirty is an approximate upper boundary for small groups; no matter where the line is drawn, it remains arbitrary. Nonetheless it is also a useful line, because some of the problems of larger democratic groups are different in degree and kind from those faced by smaller ones.

As the number of group members increases, it becomes more difficult to maintain an even distribution of final authority in the group. Decision-making hierarchies may begin to emerge, separating lower level group members from decisions made at the top. In its most benign form this may amount to a form of representative democracy, and at the worst, the group becomes an oligarchy or dictatorship.

Even if no hierarchies form, it is likely that some members will find themselves in a permanent minority, particularly in groups run by majority rule. In a very small group, each member needs to maintain something of an alliance with every other member, because proposals will often pass or fail by a single vote. In larger groups close votes are less frequent, and after several meetings, some members may be labeled oddballs or outsiders. Even groups using consensus might face this problem if the members of the permanent minority are reluctant to block consensus.

Even without hierarchies or permanent group minorities, overall member commitment may wane. Larger groups often have more power, because they have more people and resources. However the larger the group, the lower the average member's political power.[1] As a result, members are liable to have a weaker sense of personal efficacy. Even if a group increased its power in equal proportion to its increase in size, a group member might still feel a net loss in power through having a smaller percentage of total group power. This reduced sense of efficacy could result in a lower level of commitment to the process. Just as citizens in large nations easily feel disconnected from the larger political system, so can members of larger groups feel a diminished respect for group decision-making procedures.

Relational bonds among members may also weaken. It is easier to know ten people than thirty, so it is harder in larger groups to develop a common identity and sense of belonging. As groups grow larger, friendly relations will give way to neighborly relations, as faces and the histories behind them become less familiar. Politeness among strangers may eventually replace congeniality among neighbors, but there is also the possibility that such anonymity will make relations cold or hostile.

The growing size of the group and the potential erosion of democratic relationships can contribute to a breakdown in the deliberative process. In larger groups, the equality of chances to speak may remain constant, but the adequacy of opportunities will diminish. So long as meeting length remains constant, increases in the number of speakers result in fewer speaking opportunities per person. If members find themselves identifying with different speakers, they may continue to feel that their perspectives are being expressed by de facto representatives. Even in these cases, however, the nuances of their own personal perspectives may be missed by those who speak in their place. Moreover, some members may begin to view themselves as spokespersons and inadvertently silence the members they aim (or claim) to represent. In those cases where clear subgroups do not exist, disagreements may involve such a wide range of perspectives that members find their speaking opportunities altogether inadequate.

The reduced sense of shared identity and the less friendly group atmosphere may also make members less interested in considering what others have to say. Even if members do try to understand and to appreciate one another's views, the task will become increasingly difficult as the number of viewpoints multiplies. A given member's limited attention and empathy will be divided into smaller and smaller portions per person.

Face-to-face deliberation in large groups is also complicated by the sheer number of people present during a discussion. Larger groups have greater difficulty finding spacious meeting rooms. It is even more difficult to find places where the seating arrangement is physically comfortable and allows all group members to see and hear one another easily. It is harder for speakers to convey information via handouts or simple visual aids, and speaking becomes more challenging for those group members whose apprehension grows in proportion to the size of the group.

There are a number of ways small democratic groups can adapt to increases in size. Large groups often confront potential power imbalances by using formal procedures that protect group members holding minority opinions. For instance, groups using majority rule can require significant proposals to pass with a two-thirds majority, as opposed to a simple majority. Experimentation with proportional outcomes might also prove fruitful, especially when group minorities are very small. In groups run by consensus, more emphasis must be placed upon the legitimacy of blocking a group consensus. The group does not want to encourage stalemates, but it needs to reduce the conformity pressures that can build as groups grow in size.[2]

To ensure commitment, members can remind themselves of the tradeoff between greater group power and reduced individual efficacy. If they recognize the need for a large group, they may maintain their belief that democracy is the best available means of decision making. It is also important for members to recognize that although their percentage share of group power is smaller, their absolute amount of power—as a member of a more powerful group—may be greater than it would be if the group were smaller.

Instead of relying on spontaneous social interaction, larger groups can make a concerted effort to build strong member relationships. Because of the number of members, larger groups have fewer informal "group bonding" activities involving the entire group. Instead, they might plan such events and aim for maximum attendance to avoid the development of cliques. Larger groups might also institutionalize some forms of politeness, as parliamentary groups often do, by addressing the chair when speaking and referring to one another in a respectful manner.

One way to secure adequate speaking opportunities is to organize speaking turns before meetings, such that all points of view are presented during deliberation even though people cannot speak as often or as long as they would like. For instance, if five people wish to raise a particular concern, they might discuss or draft their statement beforehand; during the meeting, one or two of them would present their view to the group as a whole.

Such caucusing, however, can exacerbate listening problems. Perhaps the best way of addressing this difficulty is to remind each other of the need to listen attentively. Some groups, such as the Quakers, maintain a slower pace by periodically pausing between speaking turns. This practice makes listening easier, but it also reduces the amount of time available for speaking.

One final means of addressing the problems faced by larger groups is to move from a direct to a representative form of decision making. A growing group might decide to restructure itself in any number of ways: it could meet once a year to elect a board, break into sections that meet bimonthly and send representatives to weekly meetings, or split into autonomous committees with distinct jurisdictions. Creative forms of representation can limit the distance between representatives and the general membership, but any such system reduces contact among members and poses the danger of misrepresentation.

One example of a group that struggled to maintain direct, face-to-face participation as it grew in size is the Clamshell Alliance, a political action group most famous for its nonviolent occupation of the Seabrook nuclear power plant. The 1979 congress of the alliance drew over one hundred people, and ongoing controversies within the organization promised to make deliberation challenging. To ensure deliberation despite the congress size, an unorthodox process was devised. The congress repeatedly split into small groups, which drafted, debated, and revised proposals. When the group met as a whole, a team of facilitators made deliberation possible. One person served as the presiding clerk, responsible for coordinating the meeting. Another was assistant clerk, keeping track of which person was next on the list of speakers. Yet another took responsibility for writing on a blackboard the names of people who signaled that they wished to speak. Any group members wishing to make procedural motions wrote a note or spoke with the two process people, who jointly decided which motions to pass on to the clerk. Finally, a timekeeper intervened if the group strayed too far from its schedule, and a "vibes watcher" monitored the group atmosphere. Numerous participants found this elaborate procedure effective, and it serves as an example of how small groups can find innovative ways of adapting their decision-making process to accommodate expanded memberships.[3]

Geographically Dispersed Groups

Some groups are not only large but also geographically dispersed, unable to meet regularly as a whole in a face-to-face setting. As telecommunications technologies continue to evolve, geographically dispersed groups may become increasingly common. Computer bulletin boards, conference telephone calls, and collective newsletters are all ways a group can meet while members reside in different locales.[4]

As people become more familiar with electronic methods of communication, it may be clearer how these technologies affect the democratic process. Current research on these media has found mixed results. The effects of interacting through computer modems or videoscreens depend upon the individuals and settings involved. Below, I simply identify some of the likely problems, because it is better to be exceedingly cautious than unduly optimistic about the potential for small group democracy in these settings.[5]

When group members are unable to meet regularly as a whole, there is a danger that group power will concentrate in the hands of one or two members. Whether intentionally or accidentally, a member may begin to make decisions for the group and wield ever-increasing influence over other members. The one or two powerful members may derive their power from their central location in a communication network. For instance, the central person may be the one who runs the computer bulletin board and plays the role of coordinator.[6]

The most powerful members can gain additional power by taking advantage of group members who consider themselves outsiders. These peripheral members, who almost never meet directly with the group, may voluntarily yield their votes or influence to centrally located group members. A powerful member could accumulate actual or de facto proxy votes and gain a disproportionate amount of influence during group meetings.

The more distant or less involved group members face another problem: powerful members might make and implement decisions long before other members hear of it. This provides them a degree of short-term autonomy that may strengthen their position against the wishes of more peripheral members. If distant members fail to curb such action, the short-term flexibility of central members may evolve into increasingly long-term leeway to take action without consulting or informing the group.

Regardless of the character of group power, members' commitment to democratic procedures may lessen if they rarely experience face-to-face meetings. Many aspects of the process, such as deliberation, will be indirect or nonexistent, so their function and importance in the decision-making process may become less apparent.

Similarly, one might expect less mutuality and congeniality in a group that never meets as a whole. Maintaining a common identity is difficult when little is done in common and few experiences are shared by the full membership. Also, friendships can be strained by the misunderstandings that arise from telephone, written, and electronic communication.

A geographically dispersed group I belong to illustrates some of these problems as well as ways they can be addressed. Every other month, five to ten of the thirty group members send a letter to a collator, who puts them into a collective letter called *Collection* and mails a copy to each member. Members have made only a few group decisions together (concerning the format of *Collection*), but we have certainly emerged as something of a group. Although we have not had formal agendas, we have had many discussions in our monthly letters, articulating our personal views and influencing one another in various ways.[7]

Collection has suffered from a lack of common experiences and an unfair share of misunderstandings. Contributors often have intentions different from those inferred by readers, and the tones of letters have been misread because of the paucity of nonverbal communication.

When communication among the members of a geographically dispersed group is too cumbersome, deliberation can become exceedingly slow. In the case of *Collection*, the space between "meetings"—sometimes nearly three months—makes the ongoing conversations somewhat unnatural. Three conversational turns (i.e., from person A to B, from B to A, and back from A to B) can take from three to seven months. This limits conversations to topics that can withstand slow-paced discussion.

One way to mitigate the unequal distribution of power is to institutionalize periodic group communication, ensuring that no members fall out of touch or take too much initiative. If possible, groups can also rotate any formal responsibilities, such as that of bulletin board host. Unfortunately such rotations may be impractical if the necessary equipment or resources are not widely available. Some members may also be unwilling to play the central role, which is the case for those members of *Collection* (myself included) who are not very interested in taking on the responsibility of collating our collective letter.

Members can try to muster commitment by encouraging one another to appreciate and respect the democratic process. A dispersed group can also try to hold regular face-to-face meetings and otherwise make itself more "real" as a group. The more it functions as a full group—however imperfectly—the more likely its members are to recognize and appreciate the democratic features it has.

To maintain a sense of mutuality and congeniality, members will have to find substitutes for face-to-face interaction. For instance, in *Collection* we have tried to lighten up our communications by submitting recipes and comics, sharing personal details, talking about our common views and experiences, writing freehand, and drawing pictures. Similarly, conversations mediated by electronic keyboards often simulate freehand script and drawings via graphics and varied fonts, as well as clever adaptations of keyboard characters—e.g., the sideways smiles used in electronic mail systems, (: .

Besides inventing substitutes, group members can take advantage of the *benefits* of impersonal means of communication. Just as "many people have the experience of expressing something in a letter that they were unable to say face-to-face," so might groups find exceptional opportunities for sharing and friendship while geographically dispersed.[8]

The pace of deliberation might be varied occasionally via alternative means of interaction. If the members of *Collection* wished to become a regular decision-making body, we might experiment with combinations of annual meetings and teleconferences. Such meetings, however, might be prohibitively expensive for some members, which would limit their inclusiveness. Alternatively, the "nominal group technique" or other low- or noninteractive meeting structures might prove useful, although they are limited in their potential for genuine deliberation.[9]

Unstable Memberships

Whether geographically dispersed or centrally located, every group has members joining and departing. This is particularly true of groups influenced by external cycles, such as the semiannual turnover at a housing co-op or the semester-by-semester changes in campus organizations. Membership changes are usually addressed without much difficulty, but some groups have membership compositions one might call unstable. These groups are always in flux, with people joining and leaving every month or every week and no member staying more than a period of months.[10]

In these groups, inclusiveness becomes a potential issue. The group has to ask itself why people are coming and going. Is the scope of the group's power changing in step with the changing membership? Is the group constantly pushing out people who really belong? Are members leaving because they find the group unproductive or unsatisfying? There is even the danger of a vicious cycle: the group's unstable membership might make it ineffective and frustrating, causing members to leave and exacerbating its instability.

Commitment can be a problem for these groups, because they have a disproportionate number of new members at any point in time. Unless new members already have a commitment to the democratic process, they may not develop one before they leave. In larger cooperative houses, for example, a few people may move in and out on a month-to-month basis, making it hard to establish democratic norms in monthly meetings. Again, a vicious cycle may emerge: the instability makes it hard to teach existing democratic norms, but the failure to teach them makes the norms less powerful.

For similar reasons, mutuality can be jeopardized. Members may be neighborly to each other, but it is difficult to imagine a strong common identity forming when the group is in flux. Identifying with a group requires the existence of a somewhat well-defined group, and as instability increases, the group's identity can become unclear.

Similarly, it may be difficult for members to understand one another, as no common language will evolve. If a core remains while the rest of the membership changes, the new and old members may have difficulty communicating effectively. The old members may be reluctant to repeat things they have said in the past, and the new members will not understand the group language that developed before they joined. Accurate communication will take more time and energy, so either comprehension or speaking opportunities will diminish.

Small democratic groups with unstable memberships may be able to confront these difficulties in a few ways. To address the problem of inclusiveness, the group will have to reach out to those who have left and try to understand why they departed. If these people were pushed out, the group may have to consider restructuring itself. Otherwise, the scope of the group's agenda may have to change in response to the changing needs and power of the membership.

As for commitment, the group may have to institutionalize itself more than other groups, safeguarding democratic norms and procedures that would otherwise be washed away by the changing tides of membership. The group can also require new members to undergo some period of training before joining the group, but if too demanding, this can turn away potential members.

Perhaps the group can maintain a common identity by looking beyond its current membership. For instance, if the group is a community-action planning committee, it may have five to fifteen members at any given time but identify itself with a relatively stable geographic area. Thus the membership identifies with something larger and more enduring than the group itself. In addition, group members can try to maintain a more personal group identity by engaging in ice-breaker activities at meetings.[11]

Similarly, the group members may communicate better if they speak in the vernacular of the larger community. The group can consciously avoid developing its own language, relying instead on an imperfect but common vocabulary and dialect. However, since the larger society is always the site for struggles among competing forms of discourse, the vernacular is likely to favor a particular speech community, such as the middle class.[12]

Time Pressure

Just as all groups have changing memberships, all groups face time pressures. Some groups regularly face severe time constraints, and most will, at one time or another, have to make a quick decision. Therefore, it is important to understand the problems this creates.

It is impossible to define severe time pressure in terms of hours or days. For groups accustomed to extended time lines, making a decision in one month may strain their capacities. For other groups a month is a luxury, with five minutes constituting a severe time constraint. The seriousness of a deadline depends not only on the absolute amount of time available but also on the procedures the group uses, the nature of the issue, and the group's experience with working under pressure.

When group time constraints are severe, members may exaggerate the need to end deliberation and delegate authority to an individual or ad hoc committee. If these delegates are responsible for reaching irrevocable decisions on behalf of the group, the group has temporarily yielded its final authority. When this must be done, it is important that delegates are given general parameters within which they must work.

It is also impossible to provide members with equal and adequate opportunities to speak when time is running short. If deliberation is rushed, members may have little chance to present their views, short of voting or responding to a call for consensus. Differences in speaking skills and styles are exacerbated, as the quicker and less reflective speakers will have greater speaking opportunities. The intense pressure to reach a decision may be felt most by those holding a minority opinion, or those who cannot easily articulate an opinion. This is especially true when members of a group majority become impatient with dissenters as a deadline approaches.[13]

The strain that time pressure places on group power and deliberation can usually be alleviated. Democratic groups can refrain from asking one or two members to take full responsibility for what is actually a group problem. Even if selected individuals have the group's confidence, they cannot discern the group's will by themselves. An alternative is to have the group establish a broadly defined policy and let a member or committee work out the details.

As for deliberation, groups may reduce meeting time by talking in subgroups beforehand. Groups under tight deadlines may not be able to do this, but they can at least take extra caution to avoid repeating one another's words. The group might aid this process by encouraging members to gesture quietly when they hear something with which they agree.

Finally, there is sometimes a solution to the time-pressure problem that groups overlook entirely. Some time constraints are imposed by forces outside the group, such as a foundation's deadline for drafting a grant proposal. Many deadlines, though, are determined by the group itself, and some of these are either arbitrary or reflect an overemphasis on speed. One of the virtues of Hermann Hesse's famous character Siddhartha was his ability "to wait."[14] Habitual impatience, as opposed to situational necessity, sometimes causes groups to set unnecessarily tight schedules, and such a habit is not conducive to democratic deliberation. To be resolved effectively, decisively, and democratically, some issues take more time than a group originally designates. Mifflin Co-op, for instance, set aside a great deal of time for discussing its tenure incentives policy, yet the group had to struggle to meet its original deadline. When it appeared that its first consensus might have been premature, the co-op found a way to extend deliberation.

Economic, Political, and Social Constraints

The final and most important situational constraint upon small group democracy is the ubiquitous influence of the political, economic, and cultural forces that transcend the group. *All* small groups are under these external constraints. Even the most sophisticated groups cannot entirely escape the power inherent in language and social norms, and political and economic power networks extend their tendrils to even the most isolated of social groups.[15]

Some groups, though, face particularly severe external constraints— ones that are painfully apparent whenever the group tries to reach and implement important decisions. For instance, groups that are actively involved in a competitive economic system may have more difficulty, because democratic values may have to compete with the pursuit of profits. The success of Mifflin Co-op shows that this is not an impossible situation, but it can prove difficult. Small democratic groups dependent on outside financial resources have the same problems, because their autonomy is constrained by people or organizations outside of the group.[16] Similarly, groups politically subordinate to a larger organization or a public body can have their agenda dictated to them by those in higher positions of authority. Even if the group has a great deal of power today, its authority is subject to removal tomorrow. This specter of powerlessness can distort group decisions in profound ways, causing group members to accept proposals that run counter to their own interests.

External forces may also make power unequal within the group. If one member sits on a board with authority over the group, this member may have an inordinate amount of influence. Even if group bylaws make member power officially equal, this external power imbalance results in a de facto inequality. Social stereotypes can also distort the distribution of power within the group by causing members to discriminate in favor of dominant social groups when making committee appointments or delegating tasks.[17]

Both overt and subtle power dynamics due to differences in class, ethnicity, culture, gender, etc., can also distort member relationships and deliberation.[18] For example, recent research on gender dynamics shows how sex stereotypes and socialization create patterns of individual and group behavior contrary to small group democracy.[19] Even among university students—a group one might expect to be less sexist than the overall population—studies have shown males to have greater confidence in their ability to persuade and more willingness to use controlling behaviors in mixed-sex groups.[20] In such groups, women adapt to men's nonverbal and verbal communicative styles more often than the reverse.[21] As Shirley Ardener argues, patriarchal social relations are designed to "mute" women in mixed-sex social situations. In this view, women may not actually be silent. On the contrary, "They may speak a great deal. The important issue is whether they are able to say all that they would wish to say, where and when they wish to say it. Must they, for instance, re-encode their thoughts to make them understood in the public domain?"[22] Even when females adapt to the "male" speaking style, other group members sometimes (but not always) continue to rate their speech less favorably than that of males.[23]

Charles Derber argues that patriarchy and other "stratification systems" tend to create "distinctions of social worth that are communicated, learned, and enforced in ordinary face-to-face processes."[24] Social conventions dictate that women remain nurturing and attentive, whereas men are socialized to be controlling and demanding of attention. The pressures exerted by conventions such as these go against democratic principles, such as the equality of speaking opportunities and mutual consideration.

The problems presented by external power relations can and need to be addressed. Groups whose agendas are directly controlled by external forces must start with what they have and work toward more autonomy over time. Strategies include breaking away from superiors and using persuasion to gain more power incrementally. Also, groups must confront inequalities among members that derive from external power imbalances. If dominant members are unwilling to relinquish their status, the group ought to seriously consider removing them. Otherwise, the group can consciously work on undoing the influence of the social and cultural inequalities that manifest themselves within the group.[25]

Notes

1. See Robert A. Dahl and Edward R. Tufte, *Size and Democracy* (Stanford, Calif.: Stanford University Press, 1973).

2. In a classic set of experiments, Solomon Asch graphically showed the power of conformity pressures in larger groups. He had undergraduate students say which of three lines on a card was longest; the student had to answer the question after all other members in the group—in collaboration with the experimenter—had given an incorrect answer. The participants in the study were more likely to give the wrong answer if there were more confederates answering incorrectly before them. "Opinions and Social Pressure," in Elliot Aronson, ed., *Readings about the Social Animal* (San Francisco: W. A. Freeman, 1962), 3–12.

3. I thank Paul Klinkman for providing information on the Clamshell Alliance. On the successes and failures of the alliance and its congress, see Gary L. Downey, "Ideology and the Clamshell Identity: Organizational Dilemmas in the Anti–Nuclear Power Movement," *Social Problems* 33 (1986): 357–73. Notice that despite its size, the alliance used consensus effectively. I helped facilitate an effective, large consensus group of Madison residents who had come together to protest the Gulf War. Approximately a hundred people came up with a wide variety of ideas for action, and small subgroups discussed each proposal. When the large group reconvened, the two most popular proposals were debated. Within a half hour, consensus was reached on a plan that effectively incorporated the two points of view. That evening the demonstration went according to plan, and the participants (most of whom had not attended the meeting) appeared satisfied with the way it was conducted.

4. Even Quakers have entered the electronic age by setting up computer bulletin boards for Friends and friends. On the proliferation of small newsletters, see Lynette Lamb, "Parallel Worlds," *Utne Reader* (November/December 1992): 111, 113–14. Michael Margolis, in *Viable Democracy* (London: MacMillan Press, 1979), suggests that an interactive computer-information network could be the centerpiece of a viable democratic system for the end of the twentieth century. Costs would be borne by users, making provisions for poorer citizens and cutting costs by using existing capital (e.g., cable television systems).

5. For a review of research on this issue see Robert Johansen, Jacques Vallee, and Kathleen Spangler, "Teleconferencing: Electronic Group Meetings," in Robert S. Cathcart and Larry A. Samovar, eds., *Small Group Communication*, 5th ed. (Dubuque, Iowa: William C. Brown Publishers, 1988), 140–54. John Levine and

Richard L. Moreland also discuss this topic briefly in "Progress in Small Group Research," *Annual Review of Psychology* 41 (1990): 585–634. For an optimistic view of computer-mediated communication's potential as a means of mitigating differences in status and expertise, see Vitaly J. Dubrovsky, Sara Kiesler, and Beheruz N. Sethna, "The Equalization Phenomenon: Status Effects in Computer-Mediated and Face-to-Face Decision-Making Groups," *Human-Computer Interaction* 6 (1991): 119–46.

6. On the nature of communication networks see Peter R. Monge, "The Network Level of Analysis," in Charles R. Berger and Steven H. Chaffee, eds., *Handbook of Communication Science* (Newbury Park, Calif.: Sage, 1987), 239–70.

7. I would like to thank the contributors to *Collection* for providing some of these insights.

8. Quote from Michael Schudson, "The Limits of Teledemocracy," *The American Prospect*, no. 11 (1992): 44.

9. On the importance of being face-to-face during meetings, see Mansbridge, *Beyond Adversary Democracy* (Chicago: University of Chicago Press, 1983), chap. 19. On the limits of noninteractive techniques, see Brant R. Burleson, Barbara J. Levine, and Wendy Samter, "Decision-Making Procedure and Decision Quality," *Human Communication Research* 10 (1984): 557–74.

10. On the importance of integrating new members see Starhawk, *Truth or Dare* (New York: Harper & Row, 1986); Eleanor F. Counselman, "Leadership in a Long-term Leaderless Women's Group," *Small Group Research* 22 (1991): 240–57.

11. The Madison Community Co-op board had a sizable member turnover every semester. To maintain bonds among members, "light and lively" activities were planned for the intermissions during board meetings. Activities included making up a story together, forming a human pretzel, and comparing hobbies and backgrounds. For books on group games, see pp.179-80 below.

12. As one example, see M. Huspek and K. E. Kendall, "On Withholding Political Voice: An Analysis of the Political Vocabulary of a 'Nonpolitical' Speech Community," *Quarterly Journal of Speech* 77 (1991): 1–19. For a review including this and other studies relevant to the issue of discourse, see John Gastil, "Undemocratic Discourse: A Review of Theory and Research on Political Discourse," *Discourse & Society* 3 (1992): 469–500.

13. A study by Arie W. Kruglanski and Donna M. Webster suggests the validity of these concerns. Groups under greater time pressure appear more likely to reject deviation and reward conformity. This problem may be exacerbated in very noisy group environments. "Group Members' Reactions to Opinion Deviates and Conformists at Varying Degrees of Proximity to Decision Deadline and of Environmental Noise," *Journal of Personality and Social Psychology* 61 (1991): 212–25.

14. Hermann Hesse, *Siddhartha* (New York: New Directions, 1951), 46.

15. For further discussion of these issues see Joyce Rothschild-Whitt, "Conditions for Democracy: Making Participatory Organizations Work," in John Case and Rosemary C. R. Taylor, eds., *Co-ops, Communes, and Collectives: Experiments in Social Change in the 1960s and 1970s* (New York: Pantheon Books, 1979), 215–44.

16. Structuration theory provides a rich conceptual framework for understanding power relationships. On the pervasiveness and character of power structures see Anthony Giddens, *Central Problems in Social Theory* (Berkeley: University of California Press, 1979), and *The Constitution of Society* (Berkeley: University of California Press, 1984); Ira Cohen, *Structuration Theory* (New York: St. Martin's Press, 1989). For an application of Giddens's terminology to small groups, see Marshall Scott Poole, Robert D. McPhee, and David R. Siebold, "Group Decision Making as a Structurational Process," *Quarterly Journal of Speech* 71 (1985): 74–102.

17. On the history of theory and research on stereotyping, see Arthur G. Miller, "Historical and Contemporary Perspectives on Stereotyping," in Arthur G. Miller, ed., *In the Eye of the Beholder: Contemporary Issues in Stereotyping* (New York: Praeger, 1982), 1–40. Cognitive psychology has created new conceptions of stereotyping and the potential for reversing stereotypical thinking patterns. See Patricia Devine, "Automatic and Controlled Processes in Prejudice: The Role of Stereotypes and Personal Beliefs," in A. R. Pratkanis, S. J. Breckler, and A. G. Greenwald, eds., *Attitude Structure and Function* (Hillsdale, N.J.: Erlbaum, 1989), 181–212; David J. Schneider, "Social Cognition," *Annual Review of Psychology* 42 (1991): 527–61.

18. On the influence of socioeconomic class see Mansbridge, *Beyond Adversary Democracy*, esp. 107–14, 199–208. On race see William Labov, "The Logic of Nonstandard English," in F. Williams, ed., *Language and Poverty: Perspectives on a Theme* (Chicago: Markham Publishing, 1970). On the impact of culture on political behavior see Richard M. Merelman, *Making Something of Ourselves: On Culture and Politics in the United States* (Berkeley: University of California Press, 1984), and *Partial Visions: Culture and Politics in Britain, Canada, and the United States* (Madison: University of Wisconsin Press, 1991). On the general influence of "cultural capital" see Pierre Bourdieu, *Distinction* (Cambridge, Mass.: Harvard University Press, 1984). For general reviews see Charles R. Berger, "Social Power and Interpersonal Communication," in Mark L. Knapp and Gerald R. Miller, eds., *Handbook of Interpersonal Communication* (Beverly Hills, Calif.: Sage, 1985), 439–99; Howard Giles and John M. Wiemann, "Language, Social Comparison, and Power," in Charles R. Berger and Steven H. Chaffee, eds., *Handbook of Communication Science* (Newbury Park, Calif.: Sage, 1987), 350–84.

19. On gender and democracy see Jane J. Mansbridge, "Feminism and Democracy," *The American Prospect*, no. 2 (1990), 126–39; Carole Pateman, "Feminism and Democracy," in Graeme Duncan, ed., *Democratic Theory and Practice* (Cambridge: Cambridge University Press, 1983), 204–17; Anne Phillips, *Engendering Democracy* (University Park, Pa.: Pennsylvania State University, 1991); Lynn M. Sanders, "Against Deliberation" (Paper presented at the annual meeting of the Midwest Political Science Association, Chicago, Ill., April 1991).

20. On the existence of gender differences in confidence at persuasive ability, see Patricia H. Andrews, "Gender Differences in Persuasive Communication and Attributions of Success and Failure," *Human Communication Research* 13 (1987): 372–85. On controlling behavior see Judi B. Miller, "Patterns of Control in Same-sex Conversations: Differences between Women and Men," *Women's Studies in Communication* 8 (1985): 62–69. On males' more domineering use of interruptions in group discussion, see Lynn Smith-Lovin and Charles Brody, "Interruptions in

Group Discussions: The Effects of Gender and Group Composition," *American Sociological Review* 54 (1989): 424–35. On men's greater likelihood to use autocratic leadership styles see Alice H. Eagley and Blair T. Johnson, "Gender and Leadership Style: A Meta-analysis," *Psychological Bulletin* 108 (1990): 233–56. For a very general and accessible treatment of the wide range of gender differences in conversational style, see Deborah Tannen, *You Just Don't Understand* (New York: Ballantine, 1990). It should be noted that many studies have *not* found communication differences based on gender. For example, see Cynthia S. Burgraf and Alan L. Sillars, "A Critical Examination of Sex Differences in Marital Communication," *Communication Monographs* 54 (1987): 276–94; Kathryn Dindia, "The Effects of Sex of Subject and Sex of Partner on Interruptions," *Human Communication Research* 13 (1987): 345–71.

It is important to move beyond the simple sex-difference approach to this subject. Researchers need to study the complex relationship between sex, socialization into gender roles, and adult differences in communication behavior. See Howard Giles and Richard L. Street, "Communicator Characteristics and Behavior," in Mark L. Knapp and Gerald R. Miller, eds., *Handbook of Interpersonal Communication* (Beverly Hills, Calif.: Sage, 1985): 212–16. Evidence suggests the importance of the mediating influence of socialization into gender roles with regard to group communication (Scott Seibert and Leopold Gruenfeld, "Masculinity, Femininity, and Behavior in Groups," *Small Group Research* 23 [1992]: 95–112), communication styles (Timothy D. Stephen and Teresa M. Harrison, "Gender, Sex-Role Identity, and Communication Style: A Q-sort Analysis of Behavioral Differences," *Communication Research Reports* 2 [1985]: 53–61), and cognition and behavior in general (Eleanor E. Maccoby and Carol N. Jacklin, *The Psychology of Sex Differences* (Stanford, Calif.: Stanford University Press, 1974).

21. Anthony Mulac et al., "Male/Female Gaze in Same-Sex and Mixed-Sex Dyads: Gender-Linked Differences in Mutual Influence," *Human Communication Research* 13 (1987): 323–43; Anthony Mulac et al., "Male/Female Language Differences and Effects in Same-Sex and Mixed-Sex Dyads: The Gender-Linked Language Effect," *Communication Monographs* 55 (1988): 315–35. See also James J. Bradac, M. O'Donnel, and Charles H. Tardy, "Another Stab at a Touchy Subject: Affective Meaning of Touch," *Women's Studies in Communication* 7 (1984): 38–50.

22. Shirley Ardener, "Introduction: The Nature of Women in Society," in Shirley Ardener, ed., *Defining Females* (London: Croom Helm, 1978), 21. See also Adam Jaworski, "How to Silence a Minority: The Case of Women," *International Journal of the Sociology of Language* 94 (1992): 27–41.

23. Studies finding biases toward males include Dore Butler and Florence Geis, "Nonverbal Affect Responses to Male and Female Leaders: Implications for Leadership Evaluations," *Journal of Personality and Social Psychology* 58 (1990): 48–59; Robert L. Duran and Rodney A. Carveth, "The Effects of Gender-Role Expectations upon Perceptions of Communicative Competence," *Communication Research Reports* 7 (1990): 25–33; Burgoon et al. (1986). More encouraging findings are reported by Craig Johnson and Larry Vinson, "'Damned If You Do, Damned If You Don't?': Status, Powerful Speech, and Evaluations of Female Witnesses," *Women's Studies in Communication* 10 (1987): 37–44. The latter study set up a mock budget-allocation process, and undergraduates gave female witnesses higher

credibility ratings and financial awards when they "spoke in a forceful manner" (pp. 41–42).

24. Charles Derber, *The Pursuit of Attention: Power and Individualism in Everyday Life* (Oxford: Oxford University Press, 1979). Giles and Street ("Communicator Characteristics and Behavior," 214–15) argue that communication differences between the genders tend to reflect women's lower social status or their different communication networks. Along similar lines, Nancy Henley draws a direct comparison among nonverbal style differences based on different stratification systems: *Body Politics* (Englewood Cliffs, N.J.: Prentice-Hall, 1977).

25. This is tantamount to the task of consciousness-raising groups. Catharine A. MacKinnon, *Toward a Feminist Theory of the State* (Cambridge, Mass.: Harvard University Press, 1989), chap. 5.

7

DEMOCRACY IN OUR DAILY LIVES

> There is a world of difference between accepting the democratic ideal
> for society at large and being willing to accept it as a guide for one's
> own everyday conduct.[1]
>
> —Bruno Lasker

Conversation

DEMOCRATIC PRINCIPLES HAVE direct implications for small group decision
making, but they also suggest guidelines for how we live day to day.
Conversations are a powerful part of social life, because it is often in
conversation that we decide how to view or "name" ourselves and our
world. A long and heartfelt talk with a spouse, sibling, or friend can
change a person forever, and many people can recall conversations that
became turning points in their lives. Even a talk between strangers on a
train can change the way they understand themselves and others.

This influence we have upon one another is a form of power, and in
democratic conversations, it is shared among participants. Equal power
manifests itself in the joint development of the conversation. No single
speaker dominates in shifting the conversation's topic or direction.

Democratic conversation has an open character. Although individual
conversations may involve only two or three participants, democratic
conversationalists seek to maintain an inclusive network of conversation
partners. Democratic conversationalists sometimes ask, who is not
present? Is anyone being ignored, and if so, why?[2]

Fully democratic conversations also embody the relational and
deliberative features of small group democracy. Partners respect and
appreciate one another, safeguard speaking and listening opportunities,
speak responsibly, and listen carefully. These idealized conversational

143

norms may sound familiar, because according to linguists, these rules define the conversational ideal in Western cultures.[3]

Unfortunately the norm is far from the ideal. In *The Pursuit of Attention*, Charles Derber shows how competitiveness, individualism, and narcissism predominate in many conversations in the United States:

> Everyone is in a competitive position in a conversation because the amount of attention received depends on the relative success of one's own initiatives to attract and hold the common focus. Commonly focused attention ... is limited and can become "scarce" if the amount any person seeks is greater than that available. Under conditions of unusual scarcity, the competitive features become more visible and pronounced.... However, in most settings the competition remains disguised because [participants] are expected to be more subtle and discreet.[4]

In three-fourths of the conversations Derber recorded, there was "significant inequality in the distribution of attention ... with one person described as clearly dominant in over fifty percent of the conversations." Sometimes a participant became virtually "invisible" by failing to obtain "even the minimum attention required to feel that his or her presence has been acknowledged and established."[5]

The opposite of the invisible participant is the "conversational narcissist." Whereas democratic conversationalists occasionally shift the conversation's topic, narcissists quickly shift the topic to themselves after dispensing with the requirements of politeness. Narcissists use supportive responses sparingly, and they sometimes use purposefully flawed timing to disrupt the flow of conversation. When they respond supportively, they typically use weak forms of support, such as background acknowledgments ("Mm-hmm," "Yeah"), instead of questions or statements that would better sustain the conversation's focus on the speaker and the speaker's topic.

Conversational narcissism may be more of a relational dynamic than a personality trait, with all people showing varying degrees of narcissism depending on the setting, circumstances, and conversational partners.[6] It is likely that everyone, whether intentionally or unwittingly, sometimes uses undemocratic conversational tactics.

Breaking the habit of conversational competition may be difficult, but it is far from impossible. The first and most important step is to become aware of one's own conversational behavior. As a personal example, I have always known that I have a tendency to talk at great length in certain situations, but I did not understand precisely when and why I did it. As I reflected on my past conversations, I realized that I become most competitive, unresponsive, and self-absorbed in conversations that have high social or political stakes and a relatively large number of participants. Now when I enter such a setting, I make an extra effort to remain calm, attentive, and self-restrained. Most of the time it works. I have even discovered that when I make a conscious effort to keep the conversation civil or respectful, other participants often follow suit. Compared to other social institutions, conversations are highly malleable, and earnest efforts to make them democratic can produce immediate and gratifying results.

Love and Relationships

Democratic ideals and politics have to be put into practice in the kitchen, the nursery and the bedroom.[7]

—Carole Pateman

Compared to conversations, intimate personal relationships involve explicit decisions. As Pateman suggests, couples make joint decisions about many issues, including cooking, child care, and sex. The foremost feature of a democratic partnership or marriage is an egalitarian power distribution. Decisions that have serious consequences for both partners are reached through consensus. If a decision requires great sacrifice by one partner (e.g., one has to move to follow the other's career), compensation, compromise, and balance are needed to maintain equality.

Aside from equal power relations, the hallmark of democratic relationships is *love*. Psychologist Erich Fromm revered human affection and caring as much as democracy, and his classic work, *The Art of Loving*, promotes a conception of love that is both romantic and democratic. For Fromm, love is expansive and inclusive. People who love only one person and remain indifferent to the rest have not love, "but a symbiotic attachment, or an enlarged egotism.... *Their love is, in fact, an egotism á deux*; they are two people who identify themselves with each other, and who solve the problem of separateness by enlarging the single individual into two."[8]

The partners in a fully democratic relationship do not withdraw from friends and family; instead, they allow their love to radiate to the others around them, strengthening their bonds to the larger world.

The other distinguishing feature of a democratic relationship is an artful balance between separate and shared identities. "Mature love," wrote Fromm, "is *union under the condition of preserving one's integrity*, one's individuality.... In love the paradox occurs that two beings become one and yet remain two."[9] Just as the members of a democratic group simultaneously affirm one another's individuality and mutuality, so do the partners in a democratic relationship cherish both their joint existence and their individual lives.

Existing relationships regularly deviate from this democratic ideal in every respect. In particular, long-term heterosexual partnerships have a tradition of male domination, exclusivity, and disrespect toward women.

Although numerous exceptions exist, husbands often regard their wives as less than equal partners when making important decisions, and a patriarchal legal structure has reinforced and legitimated this attitude. One of the most blatant examples is the historical absence of laws protecting wives from spousal rape. Even though there have been some legal advances in recent years, these changes are only partial, and underlying sexist attitudes too often remain unchanged. One need only listen to the words of Alaska Senator Paul Fischer, who insisted in 1985, "I don't know how you can have a sexual act and call it forcible rape in a marriage situation."[10]

As Fromm lamented, close relationships often lead to a withdrawal from larger social networks. Research on communication networks confirms this commonsense view.[11] An exception is that husbands have a tendency to seek political conversation partners outside of the marriage, because they devalue their spouse's political knowledge.[12] This move includes a person outside the relationship, but only at the cost of excluding the wife.

Patriarchal social norms in Western cultures discount women's competence not only as discussion partners but also as autonomous individuals capable of making their own decisions. As Pateman explains,

> Women have … been perceived as beings who, in their personal lives, always consent, and whose explicit refusal of consent can be disregarded and reinterpreted as agreement. This contradictory perception of women is a major reason why it is so difficult for a woman who has been raped to secure the conviction of her attacker(s). Public opinion, the police, and the courts are willing to identify enforced submission with consent.[13]

Pateman ties this denial of women's competence to a rejection of their individuality:

> Women find that their speech is persistently and systematically invalidated. Such invalidation would be incomprehensible if the two sexes actually shared the same status as "individuals." No person with a secure, recognized standing as an "individual" could be seen as someone who consistently said the opposite of what they meant and who, therefore, could justifiably have their words reinterpreted by others.[14]

All friendly and romantic relationships can involve unequal power, exclusivity, and disrespect for one or both partners' competence and individuality, but patriarchal cultural traditions exacerbate these problems in intimate relationships. As Fromm observed in 1956, "Love is by necessity a marginal phenomenon in present-day Western society."[15]

Nonetheless, most people can point to a handful of exceptional friends or neighbors who have forged democratic partnerships. These couples offer the hope that daily resistance to undemocratic habits and traditions can prove successful. These couples also show how constant personal struggle can benefit society by providing lessons and role models for others. As Richard Flacks writes,

> Every woman's assertion of a degree of autonomy, or of a recognition of her needs, or of a restructuring of the division of labor and the decision-making process in the household today represents not only a change in her personal condition but also in the social position and role definitions of all women. Every man's recognition of the legitimacy of such claims, every change individual men make in the exercise of their traditional dominance, similarly contributes to the social reconstitution of sexual power relations.[16]

Raising Children

When relationships involve both children and adults, new opportunities and challenges arise. The age requirements for voting and seeking elected office in the United States reflect the fact that children and adults tend to have markedly different levels of political maturity. The task for educators and parents is to learn how to raise children in a way that develops the attitudes and abilities necessary for full participation in democratic groups and large-scale political systems.

Democratic Schools

Many educational reformers have envisioned and created democratic classrooms and schools. Their view of democratic education incorporates all the features of small group democracy. Democratic schools give substantial power to students, make themselves inclusive, and instill a commitment to democratic values. A democratic education also develops children's autonomy, self-esteem, mutual respect, group identity, and friendliness, and it teaches children the skills and habits of deliberation and cooperative decision making. These ideas are discussed at length in the writings of educators and philosophers such as John Dewey and Polly Greenberg.[17]

The most challenging of these imperatives is the call for egalitarian power relations between students and faculty; this issue I wish to discuss briefly. Wholesale equalization of power is often unworkable, but some schools have chosen to use very egalitarian decision-making structures. One example is the Meeting School, whose experience may inspire others to explore the possibilities of democratic education.

At this Quaker boarding high school in New Hampshire, many important decisions are reached during weekly community gatherings. These three-hour meetings involve students and faculty (who also do the administrative work), and all participate as equals in a consensus method of decision making. During these meetings students and faculty have reached numerous decisions, ranging from the abolition of student curfews to the use of a cut Christmas tree. Although consensus provides a safeguard against hasty policy changes, students are given the power to shape the school rules that govern their daily lives.

Consensus and democracy do not always work to the satisfaction of the faculty and students at the Meeting School. Faculty can take pride in the fact that students have obtained greater power in recent years; however, these same students are reluctant to deal with many important issues. Faculty meetings, which retain final authority over hiring, firing, expulsion, and the annual budget, have had to address administrative and other concerns that the community might otherwise ignore. Student participation in the committees that draft policy proposals is less than ideal, and during community meetings students (and new faculty) have sometimes shown apathy, impatience, frustration, and an incomplete understanding of consensus.

The point of such a system, though, is to educate the students through direct participation in democratic decision making. Setbacks and errors due to inexperience are inevitable, and so long as they do not threaten the existence of the system itself, they can be as valuable for the students as they are frustrating. What counts is that students learn about the process and come to appreciate its virtues. According to two recent faculty members, the Meeting School appears to be succeeding in this regard.[18]

Democratic Families

Compared to education, the family has received relatively less attention in the literature on democracy. In the writings of some classical philosophers such as John Stewart Mill, one occasionally finds the claim that when "justly constituted," the family is the "real school of the virtues of freedom."[19] The implications of such a statement, however, are rarely drawn. More often, the family is ignored altogether or assumed consistent with democratic principles.

This inattention toward the family is unfortunate, since many family structures instill patently undemocratic dispositions in children. Because of its rarity and invaluable impact upon children, democratic parenting should not be devalued or taken for granted. Instead it should be viewed as a responsibility of citizenship, as highly regarded as other forms of civil service.[20]

Democratic relations between children and parents share many of the features of small group democracy.[21] The ultimate in family democracy, writes therapist Cameron W. Meredith, "is when the family begins to function as a democratic group and is truly a microcosm of our dream of a larger democratic society." An example is "a family council with regular meetings, rotating chairperson, and council minutes, but families need not be that structured to reach decisions democratically." The essential features of this example are equal power among participants and the inclusion of as many family members as is appropriate in a given situation.[22]

In all other respects, the task of democratic families parallels that of democratic educators. The family needs to provide a space in which children can become committed to the democratic process, develop healthy relationships with parents and peers, and learn how to speak and listen in a deliberative manner.[23]

It can be difficult for parents to pursue this ideal in their daily interactions with their children. Parents have to draw a delicate line between limiting children's choices and letting children make decisions for themselves. Some parents prohibit drug abuse or smoking, because these behaviors pose clear dangers to children's health. It is not as easy to establish and enforce rules about playing with war toys, overusing Nintendo, and watching too much television. In these cases it is not as clear that the cost of parental intervention—in terms of the child's reduced autonomy—outweighs the cost of the child's behavior. After all, many of today's parents laugh at the extreme restrictions previous generations of parents placed on romance, radios, and the reading of comics and other "unsuitable" books.

To resolve such dilemmas, some parents strike a middle ground by refusing to pay for war toys or video games, but allowing their children to spend their own money and use other children's toys. In effect the parents veto the use of family funds for these activities, while allowing their children the autonomy to engage in them through the use of their own personal resources—friends and allowances.

As in other democratic relationships, another problematic issue for families is the tension between individuality and mutuality. This is particularly true of patriarchal families, where the mother is the sole caretaker and gender roles are rigidly reinforced. In *The Reproduction of Motherhood*, Nancy Chodorow explains how the "sexual and familial division of labor" makes women "more involved in interpersonal, affective relationships than men" and "produces in daughters and sons a division of psychological capacities which leads them to reproduce this sexual and familial division of labor." Sacrificing their individual identities, daughters learn to overidentify with others, whereas sons develop an isolated sense of self at the cost of mutuality.[24]

The solution, Chodorow argues, is for fathers to fulfill a greater proportion of primary parenting responsibilities:

> Children could be dependent from the outset on people of both genders
> and establish an individuated sense of self in relation to both....This

would reduce men's needs to guard their masculinity and their control
of social and cultural spheres which treat and define women as secondary
and powerless, and would help women to develop the autonomy which
too much embeddedness in relationship has often taken from them.[25]

Shared parenting sows the seeds of a democratic adulthood by developing
a stronger sense of individuality in girls and mutuality in boys.

Parents also pass on to children their orientations toward political
discussion. In a study of married couples and their grade school children,
Steven Chaffee and his colleagues distinguished two ways in which
parents speak to their children. Some parents simply stress the need to
follow social and parental rules, whereas other parents openly discuss the
reasons behind these rules. The authors found that children from families
with the more deliberative orientation developed higher levels of political
knowledge and involvement; a deliberative child is more likely to become
a deliberative adult.[26]

Social Butterflies

People who, in the name of democracy, change the way they talk, relate
to one another, and raise their children are welcoming profound changes
into their lives. Such changes might seem insignificant, but these personal
acts are the building blocks of larger social habits and expectations. As
Richard Flacks explains in *Making History*, the minor victories we can win
in our everyday lives are all ripples in time: "Historical action is not
necessarily noted or recorded, nor is it always embodied in the kinds of
public happenings that are taught as history in schools. A historical act
may appear as exceedingly mundane behavior." Something as small as a
phone conversation, a lovers' quarrel, or a mother-daughter picnic "can
initiate a chain of actions and events that fundamentally reshape the lives
of millions."[27]

This view appears naive only if one stubbornly overlooks the ways in
which people influence one another every day. When Michael MacKuen
and Courtney Brown studied political conversations, they found that
people regularly change each other's minds and voting decisions. When
friends and acquaintances influence each other, there is an explosive
potential whereby Person A changes the votes of Persons B and C, then
Persons B and C change the votes of Persons D, E, F, and G, etc.[28] Just as
we change one another's votes, so do we influence the way we act in the
other parts of our lives.

Initially we might change our daily lives for purely personal reasons.
Even if unintended, these decisions have a profound effect upon the
ever-changing social world. The changes in our own lives affect people
close to us, and these friends and family members may, in turn, change the

lives of others. In the words of Czechoslovakian poet and president Vaclev Havel, "Everything in the world is so mysteriously and comprehensively interconnected that a slight, seemingly insignificant wave of a butterfly's wing ... can unleash a typhoon thousands of miles away."[29]

Notes

1. Bruno Lasker, *Democracy through Discussion* (New York: H. W. Wilson Co., 1949), 3.

2. In other instances there may be a need for exclusion, as is often the case when members of oppressed social groups desire conversation only with people in the same situation.

3. See Anthony Giddens, "Jurgen Habermas," in Quentin Skinner, ed., *The Return of Grand Theory in the Human Sciences* (Cambridge: Cambridge University Press, 1985), 121–39; H. Paul Grice, "Logic and Conversation," in P. Cole and J. L. Morgan, eds., *Syntax and Semantics 3: Speech Acts* (New York: Academic Press, 1975), 113–28; Jurgen Habermas, *Communication and the Evolution of Society* (Boston: Beacon Press, 1979 trans. T.A. McCarthy). John Wilson goes a step further by defining conversation as the condition of participants having equal speaking opportunities. Communication that violates this rule is not, by his definition, conversation. See *On the Boundaries of Conversation* (Oxford: Permagon Press, 1989).

4. Charles Derber, *The Pursuit of Attention: Power and Individualism in Everyday Life* (Oxford: Oxford University Press, 1979), 16–17.

5. Ibid., 17–19.

6. Ibid., 35. For recent research on conversational narcissism, see Anita L. Vangelisti, Mark L. Knapp, and John A. Daly, "Conversational Narcissism," *Communication Monographs* 57 (1990): 251–74. The distinction between narcissism as a trait versus a relational dynamic is conceptually similar to L. Edna Rogers-Millar and Frank E. Millar's distinction between the trait of domineeringness and the practice of dominance in relational communication. "Domineeringness and Dominance: A Transactional View," *Human Communication Research* 5 (1979): 238–46.

7. Carole Pateman, "Feminism and Democracy," in Graeme Duncan, ed., *Democratic Theory and Practice* (Cambridge: Cambridge University Press, 1983), 216.

8. Erich Fromm, *The Art of Loving* (New York: Harper & Row, 1956), 46, 55.

9. Ibid., 20, 21. So long as one relational partner views the other as something other than a competent and independent individual, the relationship will also lack truly mutualistic bonds. Mitchell Aboulafia makes this argument by applying the Hegelian master-slave dialectic to male-female relationships. True acknowledgment of one's independent existence can come only from another independent being; thus the master and the slave cannot receive recognition from one another until they reject their master-slave relation and become equals.

Similarly, male-female relationships are incomplete until prevailing patterns of male domination are rejected. "From Domination to Recognition," in Carol Gould, ed., *Beyond Domination* (Totowa, N.J.: Rowman & Allanheld, 1984), 175–85. Notice that this parallels Carol Gould's concept of "reciprocal recognition," discussed above in chapter 2.

10. Quoted in Susan Moller Okin, *Justice, Gender, and the Family* (New York: Basic Books, 1989), 42. On unequal power in marriage, see Carol Gould, "Private Rights and Public Virtues: Women, the Family, and Democracy," in Carol Gould, ed., *Beyond Domination* (Totowa, N.J.: Rowman & Allanheld, 1984), 3–18; Catharine A. MacKinnon, *Toward a Feminist Theory of the State* (Cambridge, Mass.: Harvard University Press, 1989); Okin, *Justice*; Pateman, "Feminism and Democracy."

11. M. P. Johnson and R. M. Milardo, "Network Interference in Pair Relationships: A Social Psychological Recasting of Slater's Theory of Social Regression," *Journal of Marriage and the Family* 46 (1984): 893–99.

12. Bettina Brickell, Robert Huckfeldt, and John Sprague, "Gender Effects on Political Discussion: The Political Networks of Men and Women" (Paper presented at the annual meeting of the Midwest Political Science Association, Chicago, Ill., April 1988).

13. Pateman, "Feminism and Democracy," 213.

14. Ibid.

15. Fromm, *The Art of Loving*, 132.

16. Richard Flacks, *Making History: A Radical Tradition in American Life* (New York: Columbia University Press, 1988), 240.

17. Classic writings by John Dewey on the subject include *Democracy and Education: An Introduction to the Philosophy of Education* (New York: Macmillan, 1964), and *Education Today* (New York: G. P. Putnam's & Sons, 1940), esp. chap. 5. Amy Gutman's recent book *Democratic Education* (Princeton, N.J.: Princeton University Press, 1987), is the most powerful theoretical work on the subject in recent years.

For a case study and advice to teachers and principals see Mary A. Hepburn, ed., *Democratic Education in Schools and Classrooms* (Washington, D.C.: National Council for the Social Studies, 1983). On democracy and elementary school education see Polly Greenberg, "Why Not Academic Preschool (Part 2): Autocracy or Democracy in the Classroom?" *Young Children* (March 1992): 54–64, and "Ideas That Work with Young Children," *Young Children* (July, 1992): 10–17; Emma E. Holmes, "Democracy in Elementary School Classes," *Social Education* (March 1991): 176–78; Shirley A. Kessler, "Alternative Perspectives on Early Childhood Education," *Early Childhood Research Quarterly* 6 (1991): 193–96. On democracy and adult education see Rick Arnold et al., *Educating for a Change* (Toronto: Doris Marshall Institute for Education and Action; Toronto: Between the Lines, 1991). On democracy and higher education see Bernard Murchland, ed., *Higher Education and the Practice of Democratic Politics: A Political Education Reader* (Dayton, Ohio: Kettering Foundation, 1991).

Unfortunately there is a paucity of systematic studies assessing the effects of different educational strategies on children's ability to develop the attributes needed for active democratic citizenship. Studies typically show how one's level of education correlates with political sophistication (e.g., Luskin). However, there is probably variation according to the type or quality of education children receive. In addition it is necessary to develop more elaborate methods for measuring citizenship; this is the aim of the "Measuring Citizenship" project underway at Rutgers University's Walt Whitman Center for the Culture and Politics of Democracy.

18. I thank Janet Hankins Gastil for discussing the Meeting School at length. She and George Gastil served on the faculty for three years. Her descriptions are current as of the academic year 1991–1992.

19. John Stuart Mill quoted in Pateman, "Feminism and Democracy," 211. On the treatment of the family in modern moral and political philosophy, see Okin, *Justice*, passim, esp. 8–10.

20. The idea for labeling democratic motherhood or parenting as a citizen responsibility, on par with other forms of public service, comes from Carole Pateman, "Political Obligation, Freedom and Feminism," *American Political Science Review* 86 (1992): 181–82; Anne Phillips, "Must Feminists Give Up on Liberal Democracy?" *Political Studies* 40, Special Issue (1992): 71.

21. One early attempt to develop a definition of democratic families is Mary Stewart Lyle's *Adult Education for Democracy in Family Life* (Ames, Iowa: Iowa State College Press, 1944). In the decades since, Adlerian therapists have taken an interest in the notion of the "democratic family." Unfortunately these scholars often define the term loosely and do not connect it to political theory (e.g., James W. Croake, "An Adlerian View of Life Style," *Journal of Clinical Psychology* 31 [1975]: 513–18). On the benefits of raising children democratically see Robert N. Bellah et al., *The Good Society* (New York: Alfred A. Knopf, 1991), 256–61; Martin Gold and Denise S. Yanof, "Mothers, Daughters, and Girlfriends," *Journal of Personality and Social Psychology* 49 (1985): 654–59. As with studies of democratic education, there is a need for more sophisticated research on the effects of different parenting strategies on the development of democratic dispositions and behaviors in children.

22. Cameron W. Meredith, "Democracy in the Family," *Individual Psychology: Journal of Adlerian Theory, Research and Practice* 42 (1986): 609.

23. During World War II, Lyle (*Adult Education for Democracy in Family Life*, 10) offered a similar understanding of the democratic family. In her study she defined democracy as "a quality of human relationships characterized by respect for individuality, by sharing in policy-making as well as in efforts to achieve the goals jointly determined, and by confidence in intelligence as the means of resolving conflicts and meeting situations successfully."

More recently, Richard M. Merelman argued that the real basis of sophisticated political thought is moral and cognitive development during childhood. The key factors necessary for the development of ideology are (1) maintaining a parental consensus on basic values within the family, and the child's identifying herself or himself with this consensus, and (2) giving the child responsibility, psychological discipline, and warmth, coupled with low frustration and anxiety. According to Merelman, these high standards are rarely met in our childhood, and that is why few citizens in the United States have sophisticated political ideologies; see "The

Development of Political Ideology: A Framework for the Analysis of Political Socialization," *American Political Science Review* 63 (1971): 1033–47.

24. Nancy J. Chodorow, *The Reproduction of Mothering: Psychoanalysis and the Sociology of Gender* (Berkeley: University of California Press, 1978), 7. Concerning negative effects on women of the maternal stereotype, see "The Fantasy of the Perfect Mother," cowritten with Susan Contratto, in Nancy J. Chodorow, *Feminism and Psychoanalytic Theory* (New Haven, Conn.: Yale University Press, 1989).

25. Chodorow, *The Reproduction of Mothering*, 218.

26. Steven H. Chaffee, Jack McCleud, and Daniel B. Wackman, "Family Communication Patterns and Adolescent Political Participation," in Jack Dennis, ed., *Socialization to Politics: A Reader* (New York: John Wiley & Sons, 1973), 349–64. These distinctions parallel the distinction between attitudes serving social-adjustive functions and those serving a value-expressive function. If parents influence which attitudinal functions undergird a child's adherence to democratic values, concept-oriented communication may aid the development of the more enduring and powerful commitment that comes with a value-expressive attitude. See John Gastil, "Why We Believe in Democracy: Testing Theories of Attitude Functions and Democracy," *Journal of Applied Social Psychology* 22 (1992): 423–50.

27. Richard Flacks, *Making History*, 3.

28. Michael MacKuen and Courtney Brown, "Political Context and Attitude Change," *American Political Science Review* 81 (1987): 471–90.

29. Vaclev Havel, "Politics and the World Itself," *Kettering Review* (Summer 1992): 13. The technical name for the butterfly effect is "sensitive dependence on initial conditions," and it appears to be a pervasive phenomenon in the physical world. See James Gleick, *Chaos: Making a New Science* (New York: Viking, 1987), 20–23.

8

SMALL GROUPS IN BIG WORLDS

> Were there a people of gods, their government would be democratic.[1]
>
> —Jean Jacques Rousseau

CREATING AN IDEAL large-scale democracy is impossible, but one can pursue the more modest goal of moving existing systems closer toward the democratic ideal. This is the task for advocates of democracy in the United States as much as in Africa and Eastern Europe.[2]

In this chapter I focus on the United States, because it is the political system with which I am most familiar. I do not mean to imply that it is closer to large-scale democracy than other systems, nor does it necessarily have the most potential to move in this direction.

Here, two directions are suggested for making national politics more democratic. The first strategy builds onto the existing political system in the United States, although its basic ideas could be applied elsewhere. The second proposal calls for a wholesale transformation of the political system, moving toward a more decentralized form of government. One strategy is more reformist and the other more radical, but both draw upon the principles and strengths of small group democracy.

Socioeconomic Reform and
a Fourth Branch of Government

On the historical time line, existing systems of representative government are new and undeveloped. As James Fishkin writes, "We have only a brief history of experimenting with the adaptations of democracy to the large-scale nation-state. There is plenty of room for innovations."[3] There is no shortage in proposed political reforms of the legislative, executive, and judicial branches of government in the United States and elsewhere. Campaign finance reforms, term limits, equal-time provisions, and many other proposals have merits, but there is a need to go further.[4]

The conception of small group democracy I have proposed emphasizes the need for all members of the demos to become directly and actively involved in the political process. Given the current mood and political sophistication of the electorate in the United States, it is essential that reforms within this country focus on developing the political spirit and capacities of the public. To move toward democracy, it is necessary to increase the quantity and quality of public participation and deliberation on national political issues.

The first step toward improved deliberation on a national scale involves serious socioeconomic reform. As Joshua Cohen and Joel Rogers insist, "Since the absence of material deprivation is a precondition for free and unconstrained deliberation, a basic level of material satisfaction ... would be required for all members of the political order." In addition to ensuring full employment, it is necessary to reduce "the labor time necessary to secure an acceptable level of material well-being for all." This, in turn, would "enhance the conditions of individual autonomy and social deliberation by increasing the availability of free time."[5]

These changes, in combination with electoral reform, would move the United States much closer to equal opportunities for participation in national politics. Equal access to elementary and adult education would further balance many inequalities in political skills and information. These reforms might even reduce the amount of political apathy; an increasing number of people, with more free time and political aptitude, would involve themselves in the political process.

With increases in the number of citizens able and willing to involve themselves in politics, it becomes possible to consider additional reforms aimed at stimulating public deliberation and further educating the citizenry. One possibility is grafting new political bodies onto existing political institutions.

I sketch the shape of this "fourth branch of government" in Figure 8.1, showing its structural relationships with the other branches of government. Public forums, a delegate house, a national meeting, and legislative juries would give citizens a direct experience in the political process and an opportunity to participate in meaningful deliberation. This experience could contribute to the development of more sophisticated public judgments on national issues, increased public involvement in all aspects of politics, a heightened sense of citizen self-confidence, and a more profound commitment to democratic norms.

Figure 8.1 The Fourth Branch of Government

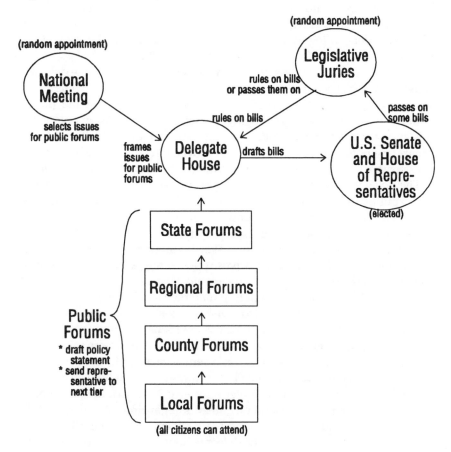

First, all citizens could participate in annual public forums. Participation would be voluntary but with direct or indirect incentives similar to those currently used for jury duty.[6] Forums would take place in every precinct in the nation, randomly dividing attenders into groups of fifty people each. Attenders would discuss two issues during forums, using briefing materials prepared by a subgroup of the previous year's participants (see below). These booklets would provide basic factual background and identify the full spectrum of policy proposals. Before closing, each forum would draft a policy-direction statement that reflects the judgment of the forum's participants.

A random drawing among volunteers would select a forum representative, confirmed by a simple majority of forum participants. (A vote of no confidence for the randomly chosen person would result in additional drawings until a suitable candidate was approved.) Representatives would then convene in groups of fifty, charged with the responsibility of integrating their different policy statements. Three additional tiers, integrated in a similar manner, would be more than adequate for representing over three hundred million citizens.[7]

The group of fifty citizens in the final tier would constitute the delegate house. The first task of the delegate house would be to draw up bills based on the integrated policy-direction statements developed in the public forums. Senators and congressional representatives could sign onto these bills and shepherd them through the legislative process. If the process of integrating policy-direction statements proved effective, these bills would have proven popular support, making them attractive to elected officials.[8]

The delegate house would also oversee preparations for the following year's public forums. A national meeting would draw a random sample of citizens from around the country, then meet for three days in ten thirty-person groups at a single site. The groups would identify the two most pressing national issues, then sketch rough frames for each one, identifying a set of policy alternatives representing a broad spectrum of political views. The delegate house would take responsibility for final revisions and approval of the briefing materials for the two issues.[9]

The delegate house would also consider legislation passed on to it by the legislative juries. With a one-third vote, the Senate or House could send a piece of passed legislation to a legislative jury. A one-time jury would then be formed consisting of a representative sample of two dozen citizens. The jury would convene via telecommunication links in a setting resembling a video-courtroom. Over a two-week period, the jury would listen to arguments and counterarguments regarding the pending bill, then deliberate and reach one of three decisions: veto the bill (with a four-fifths majority), send it to the delegate house for further debate (with a two-thirds majority), or accept it (with a failure of the two previous motions). The requirement of strong majorities would ensure that the jury serves as only a safeguard against exceptionally bad legislation.

Each part of the fourth branch is modeled after existing programs that have already had promising results. The public forums are based upon the Kettering Foundation's National Issues Forums (NIF). During the last ten years NIF has become one of the most widespread and rapidly growing civic education programs in the United States. NIF aims to develop the political sophistication and political activity of the public by placing citizens in face-to-face group discussions on current national issues.

The skeleton of NIF consists of moderator guides and issue books published by the Kettering Foundation, but the program takes life in the hands of local convenors, who integrate NIF with literacy classes, prison workshops, church programs, and community forums. Although the settings and participants vary widely from one site to another, NIF appears to have changed the political lives of many participants. Previous interviews and participant observations have produced numerous case studies of individuals who became more politically active, skilled, and hopeful after participating in NIF.[10]

The national meeting bears some resemblance to programs in Britain and the United States. In Britain, Granada Television periodically brings together a semirepresentative group of five hundred British citizens to discuss upcoming elections. After deliberating and consulting with party representatives and experts from different political organizations, the citizens travel to London, where, without rehearsal, they cross-examine the three major party leaders on national television.[11] In the United States, James Fishkin has proposed a more elaborate citizen convention that would scrutinize candidates in the presidential primaries. At the end of the convention, a "deliberative poll" would record the participants' views, providing a glimpse of how the public might vote if it had the time and resources necessary for full deliberation. In a recent article, Fishkin announced that plans are set to conduct the poll at the LBJ Library in Austin, Texas, for the 1996 presidential campaign.[12]

The legislative juries are inspired by the "policy juries" created by Minnesota's Jefferson Center for New Democratic Processes. These small groups of citizens have reached group judgments on issues such as medical ethics and the interplay between agriculture and the environment. The level of competence that jurors have shown is encouraging, given that, like jurors in the courtroom, their personal expertise does not always correspond to the policies before them. In 1993 a national citizen's jury is being assembled to make recommendations on federal policies.[13]

The success of these programs might suggest the potential effectiveness of the fourth branch. However, these programs are not all of comparable scale and institutional complexity, and they do not require nationwide involvement. Even if the fourth-branch proposal was adequately refined and funded, would it elicit widespread and sincere citizen participation? Would it gain more legitimacy and attractiveness than the jury duty system? As Anne Phillips cautions, the higher the demands a political procedure places upon citizens, the less widespread involvement will become. In other words, "The more participatory the politics, the less accountable [it is] to those who are passive or inert."[14]

This criticism is valid, but it can be addressed. The socioeconomic and educational reforms suggested above would mitigate the problem of unequal involvement. The occasional public forums, legislative juries, and national meeting are no more burdensome than jury duty; participants might view the programs as exciting, rather than inconvenient. Even with all personal expenses covered, the delegate house may appeal only to a minority of the population, but it is likely to prove far more representative of the general public than the House or Senate. After all, the fourth branch and the accompanying reforms are aimed at *improvement*, not perfection.

Decentralization

Some advocates of democracy would question these reforms and favor more fundamental political change—a move toward a decentralized political system. In this view the small democratic group is not an inspiring ideal for large-scale democracy; rather, small and medium-size groups are *the* appropriate model for democratic institutions. Decentralists argue that equal power, inclusiveness, commitment, democratic relationships, and genuine deliberation are realized only when a demos is a community of manageable size. C. George Benello goes so far as to argue that "democratic decision making *requires* face-to-face groups."[15]

Table 8.1   Centralized versus Decentralized Political Systems

Centralized Systems

FEDERALISM
Divisions: historical; corresponding to military conquests, economic exchanges, political redistricting, and negotiation
Levels: local, state, national, international
Power center: state and national
Politics: primarily representative (all levels); also direct (local, state) and indirect representative and ad hoc (international)

GLOBAL CITIZENSHIP
Divisions: historical
Levels: local, state, national, international
Power center: national and international
Politics: primarily direct (all levels); also representative (all levels)

Decentralized Systems

BIOREGIONALISM
Divisions: redrawn by residents; corresponding to ecosystems and cultures
Levels: local, regional, interregional
Power center: local, regional
Politics: primarily direct and representative (local and regional); also ad hoc (interregional)

To understand how a decentralized government might move society closer to the principles of small group democracy, it is necessary to compare highly centralized and decentralized systems. Table 8.1 contrasts these systems in terms of three questions: Through what process are political boundaries drawn or redrawn, and what criteria will be used to establish these divisions? How is decision-making power distributed among the different levels of government? Through what process do citizens participate in deliberation and decision making at the different levels of government?

The federalist system relies upon existing historical divisions among nations and regions. Although some activity takes place on local and international levels, power is centralized in nations and states. Elections at local, state, and federal levels send representatives to councils and assemblies, where most decisions are made. In addition some local and state governments permit direct forms of political participation, such as referenda, initiatives, and recall elections. International decisions are reached through assemblies of appointed representatives (e.g., the United

CONFEDERALISM
Divisions: historical localities subdivided by residents; corresponding to smaller existing communities
Levels: municipal, regional, interregional
Power center: municipal
Politics: primarily direct (municipal); also representative (regional) and ad hoc (regional, interregional)

COUNCIL DEMOCRACY
Divisions: historical
Levels: local, state, national, international
Power center: local and state
Politics: primarily indirect representative (state through international); also representative (local) and direct (local, state)

DEMARCHY
Divisions: redrawn entirely by citizens according to different public activities, as opposed to geography
Levels: local activity, regional activity
Power center: local and regional
Politics: primarily representative by lottery among volunteers (local, regional); also ad hoc (regional)

Nations, European Economic Community) and ad hoc negotiations and agreements (e.g., the General Agreement on Tariffs and Trade).[16]

An alternative centralized model, which I call global citizenship, relies upon existing divisions and governmental levels, but it *increases* the concentration of power by giving substantial authority to an international body. Under this scheme, the nature of political participation also changes, as citizens directly vote on many decisions at all levels. Taking advantage of innovations in telecommunication, the global citizen model uses computer networking and face-to-face videoconferencing to cross geographic boundaries. This system continues to rely upon weakened versions of traditional representative assemblies, and it creates an elected parliament at the international level.[17]

The four other systems in Figure 8.1 adhere to the decentralist principle: "decentralize all functions to their lowest possible level."[18] The bioregionalist approach begins by redrawing political boundaries to reflect existing ecosystems and cultural communities; this makes local and regional governance more meaningful and efficient. The sizes of locales and bioregions depend upon their unique features, and although political systems within these regions might also vary, bioregionalists emphasize the importance of direct democracy within local communities.[19]

Like bioregionalism, the confederalist system begins with a redrawing of political borders, focusing on the subdivision of counties and cities into smaller municipalities. Ten neighborhoods of 500 adults each constitute a municipality, and one hundred municipalities constitute a region or mini-nation of 500,000 people.[20] Most political activity takes place within municipalities, where citizens are directly involved in decision making and administration. Citizens within each municipality elect regional representatives, and interregional decisions are reached through ad hoc negotiations among these representatives and their appointees.[21]

Council democracy also bases itself upon local initiative. Such a system might use existing political boundaries, but it would redirect many political decisions to local councils. The council system might use local and state referenda and initiatives, but reliance upon a tiered system of representation is its distinctive feature. In a given locality, 10,000 citizens elect representatives to their town council. These local officials select a council member to represent them at the state council, then the state council sends a member to the national council, which selects a representative for the international council. If the state, national, and international councils consist of 100 members each, this four-tiered system can represent up to 10 billion people.[22]

Demarchy may be the most distinctive form of decentralized government, because it assumes a need to redistribute power both vertically and horizontally. In this view power is unnecessarily centralized at higher levels of government, but it is also overly centralized within each level of government. Power should be lowered to the most appropriate level and distributed among agencies concerned with different public activities at the same level of government. Thus the local transportation bureau would be independent of the local hospital board; no city council would control them. Demarchy's system of representation is also unique. The members of councils concerned with welfare, education, police, and other issues would all be selected through a lottery among volunteers. These lotteries would be designed to represent the interests of only those people directly affected by a given council's activities.[23]

As this comparison shows, centralized governments place far less emphasis on small group politics. The centralized systems use medium-size representative groups at all levels, but citizens make few, if any, decisions in face-to-face groups. The global citizen model gives individuals more direct influence, but the centralization of power makes it impossible for citizens to deliberate together on most issues.

By contrast, the bioregional and confederal systems give a great deal of power to small-scale citizen assemblies. These schemes also increase the potential for citizen deliberation during elections, because local and regional officials are elected by small communities or municipalities. The council model utilizes higher levels of government, but its tiered council system depends upon face-to-face relations and small group decision making among representatives. Demarchy also relies upon small representative councils, and the constituencies these councils represent are smaller, both because of more local and regional power and the specification of the people affected by each council's decisions.

In light of these advantages, decentralists argue that a radical restructuring of government is the most promising route toward democracy. This path is filled with uncertainties, since many of the ideas proposed by bioregionalists, demarchists, and others remain untested. Nonetheless some existing political systems suggest that decentralization is possible. Switzerland, for example, has incorporated elements of council democracy and confederalism into its political system; citizens play an active and often deliberative role in the political process through civil service, petitions, referenda, initiatives, and small-scale elections.[24] Switzerland and other countries like it have many problems and undemocratic features, but they show that there are alternatives to large-scale federalist governments.

From Here to There

The fourth branch and decentralization are shapes that a more democratic government might take. If either vision of the future is compelling, it is necessary to ask how to get from here to there. Envisioning a possible future makes its eventual existence more likely, but "good ideas" do not lead to democratic social change unless accompanied by a sound political strategy.[25]

A fully elaborated strategy is beyond the scope of this book, but I wish to make one point with regard to political action. Whether change will come through mainstream politics, third-party campaigns, union organizing, or community action, small democratic groups will play a vital role. As Sara Evans and Harry Boyte show in *Free Spaces*, democratic social movements in the United States have arisen from small voluntary groups with powerful democratic elements within them. Small interconnected groups contributed to the African American resistance to slavery, the civil rights struggle, working class protest, the suffragist and ERA movements, and the populist movement of the 1880s.[26] Participants in small voluntary groups

> discover in themselves and their traditions new resources, potentials, resonances. They repair capacities to work together for collective problem solving. They find out new political facts about the world. They build networks and seek contacts with other groups of the powerless to forge a more heterogeneous group identity. And this whole process in turn helps to clarify basic power relations in society. In sum, people deepen the meaning of what they are doing, from understanding politics merely as a protest against threat to coming to see the need for a struggle for new conceptions of rights and participation and power.[27]

When connected with participation in larger movements directed at fundamental social change, small group membership can transform not only individuals, but also society. In the United States today a renewed spirit of civic activism has created a wealth of opportunities for joining such groups in every part of the country.[28]

Small group democracies do not receive the attention given to national political systems, and for the foreseeable future, elites, the media, and the public will probably continue to ignore the actions of small, seemingly insignificant groups of citizens. Nonetheless, small group democracies can shape the course of history, because these microscopic societies forever change their members—the same individuals who constitute the larger social world.

Notes

1. Jean Jacques Rousseau, *The Social Contract and Discourses* (New York: E. P. Dutton & Co., 1950), 66.

2. For a very readable overview of the history of democracy and its prospects in the modern world, see Benjamin Barber and Patrick Watson, *The Struggle for Democracy* (Boston: Little, Brown, 1988); a PBS videotape series accompanies this book. For a general academic review see Robert A. Dahl, *Democracy and Its Critics* (New Haven, Conn.: Yale University Press, 1989). For academic case studies from around the globe, see Larry Diamond, ed., *The Democratic Revolution: Struggles for Freedom and Pluralism in the Developing World* (New York: Freedom House, 1992). There also exist many regional reviews, such as Samuel Decalo's appraisal of the potential for democratic change in Africa: "The Process, Prospects and Constraints of Democratization in Africa," *African Affairs* 91 (1992): 7–35. There are numerous writings on new democratic organizations: on the Greens see Andrew Dobson, *Green Political Thought* (London: Unwin Hyman, 1990) and Andrew Dobson, ed., *The Green Reader: Essays toward a Sustainable Society* (San Francisco: Mercury House, 1991); on the New Party in the United States see Sandy Pope and Joel Rogers, "Out with the Old Politics, in with the New Party," *The Nation* 255 (1992): 102–5.

3. James Fishkin, *Democracy and Deliberation* (New Haven, Conn.: Yale University Press, 1991), 25.

4. Critics of the American electoral system have made numerous recommendations. On improving the communication network between the public and elected or appointed officials, see F. Christopher Arterton, *Teledemocracy* (Newbury Park, Calif.: Sage, 1987); Alvin Toffler, *The Third Wave* (New York: William Morrow, 1980). On registration see Frances Fox Piven and Richard A. Cloward, *Why Americans Don't Vote* (New York: Pantheon, 1988). On public campaign financing and other reforms, see Benjamin Barber, *Strong Democracy* (Berkeley: University of California Press, 1984), chap. 10.

My belief in the importance of campaign finance reform was reinforced by my experience as codirector of the Janet Gastil for U.S. Congress Committee in 1992. I quickly learned that fund-raising was a central concern, because paid advertising was the primary means of reaching the voters. The opportunities for public deliberation were limited (no debates were televised on network television), and attendance at the few scheduled events was usually sparse. Gastil's opponent, Rep. Duncan Hunter (R-California), used a five-to-one spending advantage to wage a successful negative campaign through the mail, television, and radio.

5. Joshua Cohen and Joel Rogers, *On Democracy* (New York: Penguin Books, 1983), 157–58.

6. On selective incentives see Mancur Olson, *The Logic of Collective Action* (Cambridge, Mass.: Harvard University Press, 1965).

7. The tiered structure of the forums comes from a proposal presented by Mary Parker Follett, *Creative Experience* (New York: Longmans, Green, and Co., 1924). The representatives who go from one tier to the next would practice what Norberto Bobbio calls "representation by mandate," the "half-way house between representative and direct democracy" (*The Future of Democracy: A Defence of the Rules of the Game* [Oxford: Polity Press, 1987], 52). One problem for my system is the question of accountability. What would constitute an efficient and effective mechanism for recalling representatives who fail to fulfill the group's mandate?

8. The idea for a delegate house comes from Dahl's call for a minipopulus in *Democracy and Its Critics*, 340. See also Ernest Callenbach and Michael Phillips, *A Citizen Legislature* (Berkeley, Calif.: Banyan Tree Books, 1985).

9. The briefing materials are based upon the issue books that the Kettering Foundation prepares for the National Issues Forums (see n. 10, below). The materials I envision would have a wider range of choices and be less elaborate than the issue books. In my proposal, the public forums have only indirect power through the representatives sent to the delegate house. Toffler has suggested that citizen forums could be given tangible power in the form of a "bundle of votes." The results of a series of public forums would amount to, say, twenty votes in Congress, and the bundle could be given to the prevailing side in the debate or distributed in proportion to the percentages of participants with differing views. These votes would then figure into the final count when Congress voted on the issue. *The Third Wave*, 443–47.

10. On the purpose and success of the National Issues Forums, see John Dedrick, "The Results of National Issues Forums: A Review of Selected Documents, 1981–1991" (Kettering Foundation, 1991, manuscript); Noelle McAfee, Robert McKenzie, and David Mathews, *Hard Choices* (Dayton, Ohio: Kettering Foundation, 1991); David Mathews, *What Is Politics and Who Owns It?* (Dayton, Ohio: Kettering Foundation, 1992); Leonard P. Oliver, *Study Circles* (Washington, D.C.: Seven Locks Press, 1987), chap. 7. My current research is aimed at completing a large-scale study of the ways in which participation in National Issues Forums changes people's political lives. For more information on the National Issues Forums and related programs, readers can contact the Kettering Foundation at 200 Commons Road, Dayton, OH; 45459-2799, tel: (800) 221-3657. Another excellent source of information on public discussion programs is the Study Circles Resource Center, P.O. Box 203, Route 169, Pomfret, CT 06258; (203) 928-2616. On the modest successes of similar programs, such as the Alternatives for Washington project and Iowa's Health Vote '82 campaign, see Arterton, *Teledemocracy*.

11. Fishkin, *Democracy and Deliberation*, 95–96.

12. James Fishkin, "Talk of the Tube: How to Get Teledemocracy Right," *The American Prospect*, no. 11 (1992): 52; *Democracy and Deliberation*, chap. 8. Fishkin has stressed the differences between his own proposal for a National Issues Convention and other projects, such as CBS's "America on the Line" and the version of electronic democracy popularized by H. Ross Perot; see "Talk of the Tube" and "Beyond Teledemocracy: 'America on the Line,'" *The Responsive Community* 2, no. 3 (1992): 13–19. For further criticism of simplistic approaches to teledemocracy, see Arterton, *Teledemocracy*; Michael Schudson, "The Limits of Teledemocracy," *The American Prospect*, no. 11 (1992): 41–45. For another idea aimed at blending polls and public participation, see W. Phillips Davidson's proposal for forming a panel of pseudoelectors during presidential elections; "Simulating the Constitution, Or How to Upgrade Political Discussion in Presidential Election Years," *The Public Perspective* (July/August 1991): 30–32.

13. "Making the Voices of Ordinary Citizens Count," *USA Today* (Thursday, January 7, 1993): 15A. See also Fishkin, *Democracy and Deliberation*, 96–97. For more information contact the Jefferson Center for New Democratic Processes, 530

Plymouth Building, 12 South Sixth Street, Minneapolis, MN 55402. The idea of using lotteries in democratic political systems has received renewed interest in recent years. Barber (*Strong Democracy*, chap. 10) suggests its potential application to modern political systems. Bruce Ackerman finds that it favorably compares to majority rule in some instances; *Social Justice and the Liberal State* (New Haven, Conn.: Yale University Press, 1980), 285–89. The aforementioned proposal by Callenbach and Phillips (*A Citizen Legislature*) extends the idea by using random sampling for selecting members of Congress. John Burnheim takes the idea of random sampling even further, arguing that it can replace elections and referendums entirely: *Is Democracy Possible? The Alternative to Electoral Politics* (Berkeley: University of California Press, 1985), esp. 9–12, chap. 3.

14. Anne Phillips, *Engendering Democracy* (University Park, Pa.: Pennsylvania State University, 1991), 163.

15. C. George Benello, *From the Ground Up* (Boston: South End Press, 1992), 51. Similarly, Kirkpatrick Sale maintains that "the only true democracy ... is direct democracy"; *Human Scale* (New York: G. P. Putnam's Sons, 1980), 493. Richard W. Poston defines democracy as "a process by which free people in a free society are in communication with one another and together mold and control their own destiny *at the neighborhood or community level*"; *Democracy Is You: A Guide to Citizen Action* (New York: Harper & Bros., 1953), 8 (italics added).

16. Decentralists can learn from successes and failures of direct democracy in existing political systems. On referenda, initiatives, and recall elections, see Thomas E. Cronin, *Direct Democracy* (Cambridge, Mass.: Harvard University Press, 1989).

17. See, for example, the final chapter in Barber and Watson, *The Struggle for Democracy*; Toffler, *The Third Wave*, chap. 28. Regardless of any socioeconomic and technological changes in the coming century, it is difficult to see how global government can ensure *equal* participation and high-quality deliberation. In its defense, such a system addresses the need for international governance. Federal and decentralized systems must address the need for an overarching legal document or governing body that prevents tyranny and human rights violations within smaller nations or regions. All other systems, except council democracy, conduct international politics through ad hoc methods. On different models of international government see David Held, "Democracy: From City-states to a Cosmopolitan Order," *Political Studies* 40, Special Issue (1992): 10–39.

18. Benello, *From the Ground Up*, 51; see also Jane J. Mansbridge, "A Paradox of Size," in C. George Benello, *From the Ground Up* (Boston: South End Press, 1992), 161, 173, n. 3. It is important to portray accurately the empowerment that takes place under decentralization. Although an individual can have relatively more influence in a local decision, these decisions are less powerful; the power of a bill prohibiting censorship decreases as the scope of an assembly's jurisdiction grows smaller. See Robert A. Dahl and Edward R. Tufte, *Size and Democracy* (Stanford, Calif.: Stanford University Press, 1973). The decentralist simply argues that citizens are far more interested in censorship policy in their own communities; they are willing to relinquish their influence over other communities.

19. See Van Andruss, et al., eds., *Home! A Bioregional Reader* (Philadelphia: New Society Publishers, 1990); Kirkpatrick Sale, *Dwellers in the Land: The Bioregional Vision* (San Francisco: Sierra Club Books, 1985), chap. 7. I thank Christopher Plant for discussing bioregional visions of political decision making with me. Bioregionalists have focused more on the delineation of political boundaries than the decision-making processes within these. In fact, Sale's version of bioregionalism suggests that democratic principles might even be subordinate to bioregional ideals:

> Different cultures could be expected to have quite different views about what political forms could best accomplish their political goals.... It is quite possible that an extraordinary variety of political systems would evolve within bioregional constraints, and there is no reason to think that they would necessarily be compatible—or even, from someone else's point of view, *good*.

20. The numbers I use are from Edward Goldsmith, "Decentralization," in Andrew Dobson, ed., *The Green Reader: Essays toward a Sustainable Society* (San Francisco: Mercury House, 1991), 76; John Papworth, "The Best Government Comes in Small Packages," *Utne Reader* (January/February 1991): 58–59; Sale, *Human Scale* (New York: G. P. Putnam's Sons, 1980), chap. 7.

21. On confederalism in general, see Benjamin Barber, "Jihad vs. McWorld," *The Atlantic Monthly* (March 1992): 63; Murray Bookchin, "The Meaning of Confederalism," in Judith Plant and Christopher Plant, eds., *Putting Power in Its Place* (Philadelphia: New Society Publishers, 1992); Frank Bryan and John McClaughry, *The Vermont Papers: Recreating Democracy on a Human Scale* (Chelsea, Vt.: Chelsea Green, 1989); Sale, *Human Scale*; Toffler, *The Third Wave*, chap. 28. These authors dispel the myth that all decentralists advocate pure autarky; instead, they call for *semi*autonomous regions that cooperate in joint political and economic activities. Some go even further, arguing that it is both impractical and *immoral* to seek the creation of "pocket utopias." A prosperous community has an ethical obligation to maintain connections with other, less successful communities. See Kim Stanley Robinson, *Pacific Edge* (New York: Tom Doherty Associates, 1990).

22. This depiction of the council system is based upon C. B. Macpherson, *The Life and Times of Liberal Democracy* (Oxford: Oxford University Press, 1977), 108–12, and Benello, *From the Ground Up*, 50–53; see also Berit Lakey, *Strategy for a Living Revolution* (New York: Grossman, 1973), 162–63. For a tiered system designed to organize the economy through worker and consumer councils, see Michael Albert and Robin Hahnel, *Socialism Today and Tomorrow* (Boston: South End Press, 1981). In "A Paradox of Size," Mansbridge cautions that these systems can create too much psychological distance between citizens and higher councils. Also, higher councils would be unable to operate effectively by mandate; representatives would need considerable leeway to compromise and change their minds during council deliberation.

23. Burnheim, *Is Democracy Possible?*, esp. 106–24.

24. See George Woodcock, "Direct Democracy Thrives in Switzerland," *Utne Reader* (January/February 1991), 54. The case of Switzerland is useful as a contrast

to larger Western systems, but it is important to recognize the political problems that the country has had and continues to have; see Benjamin Barber, *The Death of Communal Liberty* (Princeton, N.J.: Princeton University Press, 1974); Carol L. Schmid, *Conflict and Consensus in Switzerland* (Berkeley: University of California Press, 1981). On small-scale polities, see Barber and Watson, *The Struggle for Democracy*. Barber's *The Death of Communal Liberty* offers a brief photographic contrast between direct and representative democracy that states his own preference for the former in rather stark terms (p. 275).

25. On the idea that articulating an alternative vision can increase the probability of its realization, see Pierre Bourdieu's discussion of heretical discourse in *Language and Symbolic Power*, John B. Thompson, ed., trans. Gino Raymond and Matthew Adamson (Cambridge, Mass.: Harvard University Press, 1991), chap. 5.

26. Sara M. Evans and Harry C. Boyte, *Free Spaces* (New York: Harper & Row, 1992). In their new introduction, the authors list some of the work that has drawn upon the concept of free spaces. For similar perspectives on the role of group activity in large-scale social change, see Virginia Sapiro, "The Women's Movement and the Creation of Gender Consciousness: Social Movements as Socialization Agents," in Orit Ichilov, ed., *Political Socialization, Citizenship Education, and Democracy* (New York: Teachers College, 1990), 266–80; Lawrence Goodwyn, "Organizing Democracy: The Limits of Theory and Practice," *democracy* 1 (1981): 25–40.

27. Harry Boyte, *Commonwealth* (New York: Free Press, 1989), 32.

28. The Institute for the Arts of Democracy, recently founded by Frances Moore Lappé and Paul Martin DuBois, is a source of information about such an approach to social change. Write to the Center for Living Democracy at RR#1, Black Fox Road, Brattleboro, Vt., 05301. For a directory of democratic workplaces see Len Krimerman and Frank Lindenfeld, *When Workers Decide: Workplace Democracy Takes Root in North America* (Philadelphia: New Society Publishers, 1991). For a directory of intentional communities and other alternative communities see Fellowship for Intentional Community and Communities Publications Cooperative, *Intentional Communities: A Guide to Cooperative Living* (Evansville, Ind: Fellowship for Intentional Community; Stelle, Ill: Communities Publications Cooperative, 1990); Corinne McLaughlin and Gordon Davidson, *Builders of the Dawn: Community Lifestyles in a Changing World* (Shutesbury, Mass.: Sirius Publishing, 1986).

SMALL GROUP EXERCISES

THESE DISCUSSION QUESTIONS and exercises are for groups seeking to understand themselves and become more democratic. They concern issues central to small group democracy: power, inclusiveness, commitment, competence, individuality and mutuality, congeniality, speaking opportunities and responsibilities, and listening.

Most of the questions and activities are geared toward groups of three to twenty people, but all can be adapted for larger groups: exercises and discussions can be streamlined, and large groups can do many of them by breaking into small groups. All of the exercises can be tailored to the unique purposes and features of the group.

Power

Discussion Questions

1. What is power? What are the different forms that power takes in the world and within our group?

2. What kind of power do we want our group to have? What do we hope to achieve by working together?

3. Do any external forces prevent us from realizing our goals? What can we do to change this situation?

4. How should we handle the power that we have? How should we distribute our group power among ourselves? If we want an equal distribution, *how* equal need it be?

5. Is our current distribution of power in synch with this ideal? If not, how did it become out of synch? What can we do to reach a better balance of power?

Group Activity

Group members rate themselves and the other members of the group on a 100-point scale according to how much power each person appears to have (100 signifies virtual omnipotence, whereas zero corresponds to powerlessness).[1]

If group members insist on viewing power as a zero-sum equation (i.e., when you gain power, I lose it), they can work with percentages. The combination of each group member's power score equals 100 percent. Otherwise, the group can rate group members independently; two or more group members could have over fifty points each.

When all group members have rated themselves and the rest of the group, scores can be compared. If the group is small, one person can quickly write the scores on the board in a matrix (rows for who did the ratings, columns for who's being rated). Comparisons could prove revealing. One person may be rated most or least powerful by all group members—or by all but themselves. Variations in ratings might reveal misunderstandings or complementary perspectives on power within the group. Group members might also find it useful to discuss what *kinds* of power they believe they and others possess.

Inclusiveness

Discussion Questions

1. When we formed our group, whose lives did we hope to change? What role do those people play in our decision-making process?

2. Has anyone besides current members expressed interest in joining the group? Why have they not joined?

3. Which people have left this group? Why did they leave?

4. How large can our group become?

5. Do we want anyone else to join our group or talk with group members on a regular basis? What can we do to encourage those people to join or maintain contact with our group?

6. Is there anything we do that might discourage people from joining us?

Group Activity

As a group, brainstorm to identify the different groups of people that your group affects when it makes and implements its decisions. On a chalkboard or flipchart, write a name or word for each group. Consolidate this list into a dozen or so groups, then mark each one according to the degree it is affected by your group's actions (1 = profoundly, 2 = significantly, 3 = marginally).

On another part of the chalkboard, draw three concentric circles. The inner circle represents full power within the group decision-making process. The second circle represents having influence upon the group, and the third circle symbolizes being disconnected from the group. Place each of the social groups you identified within one of these circles, according to their connection to the group.

A highly inclusive group would have ones in the inner circle, twos in the middle circle, and threes in the outer circle. There might even be twos in the inner circle and threes in the middle circle. A highly exclusive group would place none other than the group members themselves in the inner circle. Where does your group fall on this spectrum? Why?

Commitment to the Democratic Process

Discussion Questions

Talking about a commitment to democracy makes more sense after clarifying what exactly constitutes a democratic process. For this reason, the first two questions might help a group develop its own definition of small group democracy.

1. What does democracy mean to us? What would a fully democratic group look like?

2. What other groups have we been in or heard about? What features of these groups were democratic or undemocratic?

3. What are the different things we value in our group? What are our goals? How does democracy relate to our other goals? Do any take precedence over it?

4. What would each of us do if the group used a democratic process to reach a decision we strongly disliked? If this has happened before, what did we do?

5. Are our democratic principles embodied in our group's meetings? If not, how committed are we toward making our meetings more democratic?

6. Are our democratic principles embodied in our group's written procedures and bylaws? If not, what can we do to put our principles in writing?

Group Activity

Write on a chalkboard all of the words and phrases group members associate with democracy (e.g., "free speech," "equality"). Then cluster these ideas into categories and try to organize the clusters of terms coherently. Use these as a basis for defining the democratic process. (Groups might wish to focus on what democracy means in small groups.)

The list of terms and ideas may produce some contradictions. Clarify the meaning of the conflicting ideas (e.g., majority rule vs. consensus), making certain that the apparent tension between them is not superficial. Discuss any possibilities for integrating or reconciling the two opposing principles. The list should also produce some principles or procedures that all group members agree are a part of democracy. Clarify the degree to which the group agrees, building a definition of democracy all can accept.

Competence

Discussion Questions

1. What people do we think of as incapable of deciding what's in their own best interests? (If group members cannot think of any people, ask the group to consider conditions such as infancy, insanity, senility, and ignorance.)

2. In general, how much confidence do we have in one another? In what situations are we most willing to trust each other's judgment? When are we most likely to doubt one another's judgment?

3. Do we think we, as individuals, are the best judges of what's in our own personal interests? Under what circumstances would we prefer that someone else decide something for us?

4. Do we think we are the best judges of what's in the interest of our group? Under what circumstances would we prefer that someone outside the group make the decision for us?

5. What information or resources do we need in order to be competent judges of our own best interests? What do we need in order to be good judges of what decisions are in the group's best interests?

Group Activity

Each group member writes his or her name on a slip of paper and places it in a hat or other receptacle. Each member then writes an action, trivial or serious, that requires a decision (e.g., what school to attend, where to go to lunch, whether to marry, what movie to watch) and places these slips of paper into a separate container.

One by one each group member picks a name and an action and tries to make the decision for the other person. People should draw again if they draw their own names.

After each decision, the person deciding can say how it would feel to have made that decision for the other person. If people had to make the decision for someone else, what information would they need? Have they ever been put in a position where they played such a role?

People who had the decision made for them can also share their feelings. What would it feel like to have that other person make the decision for them? Have others in the past made such decisions for them?

Individuality and Mutuality

Discussion Questions

1. When we are together as a group, do we still maintain our identities as individuals?

2. When we are by ourselves, do we still sometimes view ourselves as part of the group?

3. At what times have we most clearly seen ourselves as individuals? When have we viewed our self-identity as independent of our association with the group?

4. At what times have we felt our strongest attachments to the group? When have we viewed our self-identity as connected to the group?

5. When is it most important to be treated as an individual? When would it be inappropriate for others to stress our group identity?

6. When is it most important to draw upon our identity as a group member? When would it be inappropriate to focus upon our separate, individual identities?

Group Activity

This exercise can be very revealing, and it may bring up strong emotions. On a piece of paper, write the name of each group member in a pattern that forms a circle. Make a photocopy of this circle of names for each group member, then have each draw straight lines connecting every pair of group members that has a strong bond. (In groups with less familiarity among members, draw lines for any moderately strong bonds, such as a budding friendship or regular friendly interaction.)

After drawing the lines, place arrowheads on them indicating which of these people seeks the other one out. There might be a one-way relation between two group members, or the relation may be reciprocal.

Compare members' different drawings, discussing any noteworthy similarities and differences in the patterns of lines and arrows. Discuss why some people have more or fewer lines connected to their name. Discuss why some group members have more arrows pointing toward them, and why some have more arrows pointing away from them.

Congeniality

Discussion Questions

1. Is it important to us that we create a comfortable or friendly group atmosphere?

2. What makes us feel comfortable in a group? What does it mean to be friendly or congenial with one another?

3. What do we do to make each other feel at ease? How do we show our affection for one another as group members?

4. In what ways do we express hostility toward one another? What do we do that might intimidate each other? When do we feel intimidated?

5. How can we show anger or frustration without making others feel defensive or hurt? Is it possible to be friendly while expressing "negative" emotions?

6. How do we treat the people we consider our friends? How is this different from how we treat each other? Why is it different?

Group Activity

For groups unaccustomed to sharing feelings openly, this exercise may make some members uncomfortable. Members each share with the others one group experience they have had that made them feel good (e.g., comfortable, happy) and one that made them feel bad (e.g., uncomfortable, angry, intimidated). It is preferable if these experiences occurred in the same group doing the exercise.

Speaking Opportunities

Discussion Questions

1. How does our group regulate speaking turns? (For example, "only one person can talk at a time," or "speak when called upon by the facilitator.") Do we follow these rules? Do these rules make us feel constrained, or do they make it easier for us to speak during meetings?

2. Do we all have ample opportunities to set our meeting agendas? Do we all get a chance to redefine the issues on the agenda, amending them or reframing them?

3. When we have bits of information, personal views, or arguments that we wish to share with the group, do we present them? If not, why not?

4. Do we all get a chance to vote during meetings? If we still disagree after a vote has been taken, is there a way we can reiterate our views?

5. What does it mean to "talk too much"? Do any of us do this? If so, what do we do when someone is doing this?

6. What does it mean to "talk too little"? Do any of us do this? If so, what do we do when someone is doing this?

7. How do we respond to silence during meetings? Does someone always take the floor quickly when there is a pause?

8. In what ways might a more reserved speaker join in a heated discussion? If it is difficult to do so at present, how can we ensure that a reticent speaker has access to the floor?

Group Activity

Sit in a circle with two chairs in the middle, facing each other. Going around the circle, place people in the middle in pairs until everyone has sat in the middle once. When a pair sits in the middle, both people begin talking and try to hold the floor as long as they can. Some pairs may wish to play in a no-holds-barred style, unrelentingly talking over one another for a minute. Others may try to gain and regain the floor using more subtle methods. After each pair returns to the circle, group members may wish to discuss the tactics used to hold the floor. Which of these are appropriate, and which are normally considered rude? How does the group enforce speaking norms? Should the group create new norms to make it easier for more reticent speakers to gain and hold the floor?

Next, bring a clock with a second hand into the room. A group member begins speaking to the group on a current issue. Each group member holds a notepad and listens attentively, then writes down the time at which they believe the speaker should stop talking. Everyone also writes what it was that made them believe it was time to stop talking. When the last person has written "stop now," compare the times and the reasons for wishing the speaker to stop.

After testing members' patience with speakers, the group can explore its feelings about silence. A group member makes a brief comment on a current issue, followed by total silence. Each group member writes when they think it is time for someone to speak. Group members also write what they did during the silence. Were they thinking? What distracted them? When did the silence become uncomfortable or cease to be productive?

Speaking Responsibilities

Discussion Questions

1. What kind of information can we justifiably withhold from one another?

2. If a decision requires specialized information that only one or two group members possess, should the group make the decision? In what

cases should the information be shared with others before making a decision? How detailed does this shared information need to be?

3. What effort do we make to ensure that our decisions are well informed? Do we conduct research whenever it is necessary? Do we check the accuracy of our assumptions before reaching a decision?

4. When we are trying to persuade other group members, what responsibilities do we have to them? What kinds of argument are unethical?

5. What role can emotion play in the persuasion process? Is it acceptable for a group to be swayed by emotions? When can a speaker appeal to the group's feelings? Is it okay to appeal to some emotions but not others (e.g., hope vs. fear)?

6. Is it okay for a speaker to make an argument based on weak evidence or unsound logic? What responsibility do speakers have to acknowledge any weaknesses they see in their own arguments?

Group Activity

Make a list of past decisions the group has reached and/or future issues the group may need to discuss. Identify the kinds of information that the group needed/would need to make informed decisions. Discuss how the group can ensure that it obtains the information it needs (e.g., we have a lawyer on retainer if we are sued, or one of us should learn more about noncompetitive children's games before we decide what activities to sponsor at the community fair).

Each group member shares with the others a time that they were moved by an argument, changing their beliefs or feelings on an issue. Identify what made the speaker effective, and consider when these speaking strategies might be unethical. Group members can also share a time they felt manipulated. What strategies made the speaker (or advertisement, etc.) manipulative or unethical?

Listening

Discussion Questions

1. When do we have trouble understanding one another? Do we speak too soft or too loud? Do others sometimes speak in words or styles that we cannot understand?

2. When do we have trouble expressing ourselves clearly?

3. Do we carefully consider what each other says? What speaking behaviors make it harder for us to listen to a person?

4. How do we show a speaker that we are listening? Do we nod or make eye contact? Do we ask for clarification or elaboration if we are unable to follow what a speaker is saying?

5. When we wish to speak, are we still able to listen to those who are presently speaking?

6. How do we feel when others listen to us? How does it affect us? How do we feel and react when we sense that others are not listening?

Group Activity

Every group member thinks of something that will be hard to express to the rest of the group (e.g., moving experiences they had by themselves or a technical concept from their workplace or classes). Members then take turns trying to express their idea or experience in a way others can comprehend. No one can interrupt the speaker. The group discusses what speakers did to try to make themselves clear.

Next, group members each think of something they would like others to hear about—an idea or an experience they have in mind. Members then take turns telling others about their idea or experience, without worrying so much about how best to express themselves. Listeners can interrupt the speaker only if they believe it is necessary to fully understand the speaker. This time the other members must make a concerted effort to listen and to let the speaker know they are listening. Discuss what it felt like to be heard and what signs made it clear that others were listening. Discuss anything that made it difficult to understand the speaker.

Other Group Exercises

Several books on group decision making provide helpful exercises. Here is a partial reading list for those who wish to try additional activities.

Brilhart, John K. *Effective Group Discussion*. 6th ed. Dubuque, Iowa: William C. Brown, 1989. *A small group communication textbook with discussion questions and exercises.*

Center for Conflict Resolution. *A Manual for Group Facilitators*. Madison, Wis.: Center for Conflict Resolution, 1977. *A guide for learning facilitation. Although it has few exercises, it can serve as the basis for discussion.*

————. *Building United Judgment*. Madison, Wis.: Center for Conflict Resolution, 1981. *An excellent manual for learning consensus.*

Coover, Virginia, Ellen Deacon, Charles Esser, and Christopher Moore. *Resource Manual for a Living Revolution*. Philadelphia: New Society Publishers, 1978. *This resource book on a wide variety of topics contains a* handful of great group process exercises, including methods for ensuring equal speaking opportunities.

Fluegelman, Andrew, ed. *The New Games Book*. New York: Headlands Press, 1976. *Includes many games for small and large groups of children and adults.*

Jensen, Arthur D., and Joseph C. Chilberg. *Small Group Communication*. Belmont, Calif.: Wadsworth, 1991. *A small group communication textbook with a special section to develop member skills in problem-solving groups.*

Johnson, David W., and Frank P. Johnson. *Joining Together: Group Theory and Group Skills*. 2d ed. Englewood Cliffs, N.J.: Prentice Hall, 1982. *A less academic group communication textbook with dozens of creative exercises.*

Rice, Wayne, and Mike Yaconelli. *Play It*. Grand Rapids, Mich.: Zondervan Publishing, 1986. *Group games for children and adults.*

Starhawk. *Truth or Dare*. New York: Harper & Row, 1986. *A spiritual and philosophical work, much of which focuses on group process.*

Notes

1. This is inspired by Jane Mansbridge's "power circle exercise" in *Beyond Adversary Democracy* (Chicago: University of Chicago Press, 1983), 183–84.

BIBLIOGRAPHY

Aboulafia, Mitchell. "From Domination to Recognition." In Carol Gould, ed., *Beyond Domination* Totowa, N.J.: Rowman & Allanheld, 1984.

Ackerman, Bruce. *Social Justice and the Liberal State.* New Haven, Conn.: Yale University Press, 1980.

Albert, Michael, and Robin Hahnel. *Socialism Today and Tomorrow.* Boston: South End Press, 1981.

Anderson, Charles W. *Pragmatic Liberalism.* Chicago: University of Chicago Press, 1990.

Anderson, Peter A. "Nonverbal Communication in the Small Group." In Robert S. Cathcart and Larry A. Samovar, eds., *Small Group Communication*, 5th ed., 333–50. Dubuque, Iowa: William C. Brown Publishers, 1988.

Andrews, Patricia H. "Gender Differences in Persuasive Communication and Attributions of Success and Failure." *Human Communication Research* 13 (1987), 372–85.

Andruss, Van, Christopher Plant, Judith Plant, and Eleanor Wright, eds. *Home! A Bioregional Reader.* Philadelphia: New Society Publishers, 1990.

Arblaster, Anthony. *Democracy.* Open University Press: Milton Keynes, 1987.

Ardener, Shirley. "Introduction: The Nature of Women in Society." In Shirley Ardener, ed., *Defining Females*, 9–48. London: Croom Helm, 1978.

Arnold, Rick, Bev Burke, Carl James, D'Arcy Martin, and Barb Thomas. *Educating for a Change.* Toronto: Doris Marshall Institute for Education and Action; Toronto: Between the Lines, 1991.

Arterton, F. Christopher. *Teledemocracy.* Newbury Park, Calif.: Sage, 1987.

Asch, Solomon E. "Opinions and Social Pressure." In Elliot Aronson, ed., *Readings about the Social Animal*, 3–12. San Francisco: W. A. Freeman, 1962.

Bachrach, Peter. *The Theory of Democratic Elitism: A Critique*. Boston: Little, Brown & Co., 1967.

Bachrach, Peter, and Aryeh Botwinick. *Power and Empowerment: A Radical Theory of Participatory Democracy*. Philadelphia: Temple University Press, 1992.

Baker, Andrea. "The Problem of Authority in Radical Movement Groups: A Case Study of a Lesbian-Feminist Organization." *Journal of Applied Behavioral Science* 18 (1982), 323–41.

Barber, Benjamin. *The Death of Communal Liberty*. Princeton, N.J.: Princeton University Press, 1974.

———. "Political Talk—and 'Strong Democracy,'" *Dissent* 31 (1984), 215–222.

———. *Strong Democracy*. Berkeley: University of California Press, 1984.

———. "Reply." *Dissent* 32 (1985), 385.

———. *The Conquest of Politics*. Princeton, N.J.: Princeton University Press, 1988.

———. "Jihad vs. McWorld." *The Atlantic* (March 1992), 53–55, 58–63.

———."Opinion Polls: Public Judgment or Private Prejudice." *The Responsive Community* 2, no. 2 (1992), 4–6.

Barber, Benjamin, and Patrick Watson. *The Struggle for Democracy*. Boston: Little, Brown, 1988.

Bass, Bernard M. *Bass & Stogdill's Handbook of Leadership*. New York: Free Press, 1990.

Batson, C. Daniel, Judy G. Batson, Cari A. Griffitt, and Sergio Barrientos. "Negative-State Relief and the Empathy-Altruism Hypothesis." *Journal of Personality and Social Psychology* 56 (1989), 922–33.

Batson, C. Daniel, Janine L. Dyck, J. Randall Brandt, Judy G. Batson, Anne L. Powell, M. Rosalie McMaster, and Cari Griffitt. "Five Studies Testing Two New Egoistic Alternatives to the Empathy-Altruism Hypothesis." *Journal of Personality and Social Psychology* 55 (1988), 52–77.

Beitz, Charles R. *Political Equality: An Essay in Democratic Theory*. Princeton, N.J.: Princeton University Press, 1989.

Bellah, Robert N., Richard Madsen, William M. Sullivan, Ann Swidler, and Steven M. Tipton. *Habits of the Heart: Individualism and Commitment in American Life*. New York: Harper & Row, 1985.

———. *The Good Society*. New York: Alfred A. Knopf, 1991.

Benello, C. George. *From the Ground Up*. Boston: South End Press, 1992.

Berger, Charles R. "Social Power and Interpersonal Communication." In Mark L. Knapp and Gerald R. Miller, eds. *Handbook of Interpersonal Communication*. 439–99. Beverly Hills, Calif.: Sage, 1985 .

Berman, Shelley. "Comparison of Dialogue and Debate." *Focus on Study Circles: The Newsletter of the Study Circles Resource Center* (Winter 1993), 9.

Binford, Michael. "The Democratic Political Personality: Functions of Attitudes and Styles of Reasoning." *Political Psychology* 4 (1983), 663–84.

Blumer, Jay G. "Communication and Democracy: The Crisis Beyond the Ferment Within." *Journal of Communication* 33 (1983), 166–73.

Bobbio, Norberto. *The Future of Democracy: A Defence of the Rules of the Game*. Oxford: Polity Press, 1987.

Bodden, Michael. "A Twenty-Year History of the Mifflin Street Community Co-op." Madison, Wis., 1990. Manuscript.

Bookchin, Murray. "The Meaning of Confederalism." In Judith Plant and Christopher Plant, eds., *Putting Power in Its Place*, 59–67. Philadelphia: New Society Publishers, 1992.

Bormann, Ernest G. "The Paradox and Promise of Small Group Research." *Speech Monographs* 37 (1970), 211–16.

———. "The Paradox and Promise of Small Group Research Revisited." *Central States Speech Journal* 31 (1980), 214–20.

———. "Symbolic Convergence Theory and Communication in Group Decision-Making." In Randy Y. Hirokawa and Marshall Scott Poole, eds., *Communication and Group Decision-Making*, 219–36. Beverly Hills, Calif.: Sage, 1986.

Boster, Franklin J. and Paul Mongeau. "Fear-Arousing Persuasive Messages." In R. N. Bostrom, ed., *Communication Yearbook* 8, 330–37. Beverly Hills, Calif.: Sage, 1984.

Boulding, Kenneth. "Perspectives on Violence." *Zygon* 18 (1983), 425–37.

———. *Three Faces of Power*. Newbury Park, Calif.: Sage, 1990.

Bourdieu, Pierre. *Distinction*. Cambridge, Mass.: Harvard University Press, 1984.

———. *Language and Symbolic Power*. Ed. John B. Thompson, trans. Gino Raymond and Matthew Adamson. Cambridge, Mass.: Harvard University Press, 1991.

Bowles, Samuel, and Herbert Gintis. *Democracy and Capitalism: Property, Community, and the Contradictions of Modern Social Thought*. New York: Basic Books, 1986.

Boyte, Harry C. *Commonwealth*. New York: Free Press, 1989.

Bradac, James J., M. O'Donnel, and Charles H. Tardy. "Another Stab at a Touchy Subject: Affective Meaning of Touch." *Women's Studies in Communication* 7 (1984), 38–50.

Brewer, John, and Albert Hunter. *Multimethod Research: A Synthesis of Styles.* Newbury Park, Calif.: Sage, 1989.

Briand, Michael. "Value, Policy, and the Indispensability of Politics." Kettering Foundation, Dayton, Ohio, 1991. Manuscript.

Brickell, Bettina, Robert Huckfeldt, and John Sprague. "Gender Effects on Political Discussion: The Political Networks of Men and Women." Paper presented at the annual meeting of the Midwest Political Science Association, Chicago, Ill., April 1988.

Brown, Penelope, and Stephen Levinson. "Universals in Language Usage: Politeness Phenomena." In Esther N. Goody, ed., *Questions and Politeness: Strategies in Social Interaction*, 56–289. Cambridge, Mass.: Cambridge University Press, 1978.

Bryan, Frank, and John McClaughry. *The Vermont Papers: Recreating Democracy on a Human Scale.* Chelsea, Vt.: Chelsea Green, 1989.

Buckhout, Robert, Steve Weg, and Vincent Reilly. "Jury Verdicts: Comparison of 6- vs. 12-Person Juries and Unanimous vs. Majority Decision Rule in a Murder Trial." *Bulletin of the Psychonomic Society* 10 (1977), 175–78.

Burgoon, Judee K. "Spatial Relationships in Small Groups." In Robert S. Cathcart and Larry A. Samovar, eds., *Small Group Communication*, 5th ed., 351–66. Dubuque, Iowa: William C. Brown Publishers, 1988.

Burgoon, Judee K., Deborah A. Coker, and Ray A. Coker. "Communicative Effects of Gaze Behavior: A Test of Two Contrasting Explanations." *Human Communication Research* 12 (1986), 495–524.

Burgraf, Cynthia S., and Alan L. Sillars. "A Critical Examination of Sex Differences in Marital Communication." *Communication Monographs* 54 (1987), 276–94.

Burleson, Brant R., Barbara J. Levine, and Wendy Samter. "Decision-Making Procedure and Decision Quality." *Human Communication Research* 10 (1984), 557–74.

Burnheim, John. *Is Democracy Possible? The Alternative to Electoral Politics.* Berkeley: University of California Press, 1985.

Butler, Dore, and Florence Geis. "Nonverbal Affect Responses to Male and Female Leaders: Implications for Leadership Evaluations." *Journal of Personality and Social Psychology* 58 (1990), 48–59.

Calhoun, Craig, ed. *Habermas and the Public Sphere.* Cambridge, Mass.: MIT Press, 1992.

Callenbach, Ernest, and Michael Phillips. *A Citizen Legislature.* Berkeley, Calif.: Banyan Tree Books, 1985.

Calvert, Gregory N. *Democracy from the Heart: Spiritual Values, Decentralism, and Democratic Idealism in the Movement of the 1960s.* Eugene, Ore.: Communitas Press, 1991.

Cappella, Joseph. "The Management of Conversations." In Mark L. Knapp and Gerald R. Miller, eds., *Handbook of Interpersonal Communication*, 393–438. Beverly Hills, Calif.: Sage, 1985.

Case, John, and Rosemary C. R. Taylor, eds. *Co-ops, Communes, and Collectives: Experiments in Social Change in the 1960s and 1970s.* New York: Pantheon Books, 1979.

Center for Conflict Resolution. *A Manual for Group Facilitators.* Madison, Wis.: Center for Conflict Resolution, 1977.

———. *Building United Judgment.* Madison, Wis.: Center for Conflict Resolution, 1981.

Chaffee, Steven H., Jack McCleud, and Daniel B. Wackman. "Family Communication Patterns and Adolescent Political Participation." In Jack Dennis, ed., *Socialization to Politics: A Reader*, 349–64. New York: John Wiley & Sons, 1973.

Chesebro, James W., John F. Cragan, and Patricia McCullough. "The Small Group Techniques of the Radical Revolutionary: A Synthetic Study of Consciousness Raising." *Speech Monographs* 40 (1973), 136–46.

Chodorow, Nancy J. *The Reproduction of Mothering: Psychoanalysis and the Sociology of Gender.* Berkeley, Calif.: University of California Press, 1978.

———. *Feminism and Psychoanalytic Theory.* New Haven, Conn.: Yale University Press, 1989.

Christiano, Thomas. "Freedom, Consensus, and Equality in Collective Decision Making." *Ethics* 101 (1990), 151–81.

Cialdini, Robert B. "Compliance Principles of Compliance Professionals: Psychologists of Necessity." In Mark P. Zanna, James M. Olson, and C. Peter Herman, eds.,, *Social Influence: The Ontario Symposium*, Vol. 5, 165–184. (Hillsdale, N.J.: Lawrence Erlbaum, 1987.

Clark, D. G. "Consensus or Stalemate?" *National Parliamentarian* 53, no. 1 (1992), 7.

Cleland, Trena M. "Living Democracy." *In Context*, no. 33 (1992), 34–36.

Cohen, Ira. *Structuration Theory.* New York: St. Martin's Press, 1989.

Cohen, Joshua. "The Economic Basis of Deliberative Democracy." *Social Philosophy & Policy* 6 (1988), 25–50.

———. "Deliberation and Democratic Legitimacy." In Alan Hamlin and Philip Pettit, eds., *The Good Polity*, 17–34. New York: Basil Blackwell, 1989.

———. Review of *Democracy and Its Critics*, by Robert A. Dahl. *Journal of Politics* 53 (1991), 221–25.

Cohen, Joshua, and Joel Rogers. *On Democracy.* New York: Penguin Books, 1983.

Coover, Virginia, Ellen Deacon, Charles Esser, and Christopher Moore. *Resource Manual for a Living Revolution*. Philadelphia: New Society Publishers, 1978.

Coser, Lewis. *The Functions of Social Conflict*. New York: Free Press, 1956.

Counselman, Eleanor F. "Leadership in a Long-term Leaderless Women's Group." *Small Group Research* 22 (1991), 240–57.

Croake, James W. "An Adlerian View of Life Style." *Journal of Clinical Psychology* 31 (1975), 513–18.

Cronin, Thomas E. *Direct Democracy*. Cambridge, Mass.: Harvard University Press, 1989.

Cummings, L. L., George P. Huber, and Eugene Arendt. "Effects of Size and Spatial Arrangements on Group Decision Making." *Academy of Management Journal* 17 (1974), 460–75.

Dahl, Robert A. *Democracy and Its Critics*. New Haven, Conn.: Yale University Press, 1989.

———. "A Rejoinder." *Journal of Politics* 53 (1991), 226–31.

Dahl, Robert A., and Edward R. Tufte. *Size and Democracy*. Stanford, Calif.: Stanford University Press, 1973.

Davidson, W. Phillips. "Simulating the Constitution, Or How to Upgrade Political Discussion in Presidential Election Years." *The Public Perspective* (July/August 1991), 30–32.

Davis, James H., Mark Stasson, Kaoru Ono, and Suzi Zimmerman. "Effects of Straw Polls on Group Decision Making: Sequential Voting Pattern, Timing and Local Majorities." *Journal of Personality and Social Psychology* 55 (1988), 918–26.

Davis, James H., Tatsuya Kameda, Craig Parks, Mark Stasson, and Suzi Zimmerman. "Some Social Mechanics of Group Decision Making: The Distribution of Opinion, Polling Sequence, and Implications for Consensus." *Journal of Personality and Social Psychology* 57 (1989), 1000–1012.

Decalo, Samuel. "The Process, Prospects and Constraints of Democratization in Africa." *African Affairs* 91 (1992), 7–35.

Dedrick, John. "The Results of National Issues Forums: A Review of Selected Documents, 1981–1991." Kettering Foundation, Dayton, Ohio, 1991. Manuscript.

Derber, Charles. *The Pursuit of Attention: Power and Individualism in Everyday Life*. Oxford: Oxford University Press, 1979.

Desjardins, Carolyn, and Carol O. Brown. "A New Look at Leadership Styles." *Phi Kappa Phi Journal* (Winter 1991), 18–20.

DeStephen, RoLayne S., and Randy Y. Hirokawa. "Small Group Consensus: Stability of Group Support of the Decision, Task Process, and Group Relationships." *Small Group Behavior* 19 (1988), 227–39.

Devine, Patricia. "Automatic and Controlled Processes in Prejudice: The Role of Stereotypes and Personal Beliefs." In A. R. Pratkanis, S. J. Breckler, and A. G. Greenwald, eds., *Attitude Structure and Function*, 181–212. Hillsdale, N.J.: Erlbaum, 1989.

Dewey, John. *How We Think*. New York: Heath & Co., 1910.

———*The Public and Its Problems*. Athens, Ohio: Swallow Press, 1927.

———*Education Today*. New York: G. P. Putnam's Sons, 1940.

———*Democracy and Education: An Introduction to the Philosophy of Education*. New York: Macmillan, 1964.

Diamond, Larry, ed. *The Democratic Revolution: Struggles for Freedom and Pluralism in the Developing World*. New York: Freedom House, 1992.

Dindia, Kathryn. "The Effects of Sex of Subject and Sex of Partner on Interruptions." *Human Communication Research* 13 (1987), 345–71.

Dobson, Andrew. *Green Political Thought*. London: Unwin Hyman, 1990.

———, ed. *The Green Reader: Essays toward a Sustainable Society*. San Francisco: Mercury House, 1991.

Downey, Gary L. "Ideology and the Clamshell Identity: Organizational Dilemmas in the Anti-Nuclear Power Movement." *Social Problems* 33 (1986), 357–73.

Dryzek, John S. *Discursive Democracy: Politics, Policy, and Political Science*. Cambridge: Cambridge University Press, 1990.

Dubrovsky, Vitaly J., Sara Kiesler, and Beheruz N. Sethna. "The Equalization Phenomenon: Status Effects in Computer-Mediated and Face-to-Face Decision-Making Groups." *Human-Computer Interaction* 6 (1991), 119–46.

Duncan, Graeme. "Introduction." In Graeme Duncan, ed., *Democratic Theory and Practice*, 3–17. Cambridge: Cambridge University Press, 1983.

Duran, Robert L., and Rodney A. Carveth. "The Effects of Gender-Role Expectations Upon Perceptions of Communicative Competence." *Communication Research Reports* 7 (1990), 25–33.

Eagley, Alice H., and Blair T. Johnson. "Gender and Leadership Style: A Meta-analysis." *Psychological Bulletin* 108 (1990), 233–56.

Eisler, Riane. *The Chalice and the Blade: Our History, Our Future*. San Francisco: Harper & Row, 1987.

Entman, Robert. *Democracy without Citizens*. Oxford: Oxford University Press, 1989.

Estes, Caroline. "Consensus Ingredients." In Fellowship for Intentional Community & Communities Publications Cooperative, eds., *Intentional Communities: A Guide to Cooperative Living*, 78–81. Evansville, Ind.: Fellowship for Intentional Community; Stelle, Ill.: Communities Publications Cooperative, 1990.

Evans, Sara M., and Harry C. Boyte. *Free Spaces*. New York: Harper & Row, 1992.

Evans, Charles R., and Kenneth L. Dion. "Group Cohesion and Performance: A Meta-analysis." *Small Group Research* 22 (1991), 175–86.

Falk, Gideon. "An Empirical Study Measuring Conflict in Problem-Solving Groups Which Are Assigned Different Decision Rules." *Human Relations* 35 (1982), 1123–38.

Falk, Gideon, and Shoshana Falk. "The Impact of Decision Rules on the Distribution of Power in Problem-Solving Teams with Unequal Power." *Group and Organization Studies* 6 (1981), 211–23.

Farwell, Hermon W. *The Majority Rules*, 2d ed. Pueblo, Colo.: High Publishers, 1988.

Field, Richard H. G., Peter C. Read, and Jordan J. Louviere. "The Effect of Situation Attributes on Decision Method Choice in the Vroom-Jago Model of Participation in Decision Making." *Leadership Quarterly* 1 (1990), 165–76.

Fishkin, James. *Democracy and Deliberation*. New Haven, Conn.: Yale University Press, 1991.

———. "Beyond Teledemocracy: 'America on the Line.'" *The Responsive Community* 2, no. 3 (1992), 13–19.

———. "Talk of the Tube: How to Get Teledemocracy Right." *The American Prospect*, no. 11 (1992), 46–52.

Fisk, Milton. *The State and Justice: An Essay in Political Theory*. Cambridge: Cambridge University Press, 1989.

Fiske, Susan T., and Shelley E. Taylor. *Social Cognition*. New York: Random House, 1984.

Flacks, Richard. *Making History: A Radical Tradition in American Life*. New York: Columbia University Press, 1988.

Fogg, Richard W. "Dealing with Conflict: A Repertoire of Creative, Peaceful Approaches." *Journal of Conflict Resolution* 29 (1985), 330–58.

Follett, Mary Parker. *Creative Experience*. New York: Longmans, Green, and Co., 1924.

Fott, David. "John Dewey and the Philosophical Foundations of Democracy." *Social Science Journal* 28 (1991), 29–44.

Freeman, Jo. "The Tyranny of Structurelessness." In Fellowship for Intentional Community & Communities Publications Cooperative, eds., *Intentional Communities: A Guide to Cooperative Living*, 76–77. Evansville, Ind.: Fellowship for Intentional Community; Stelle, Ill.: Communities Publications Cooperative, 1990.

Freire, Paulo. *Pedagogy of the Oppressed*. New York: Seabury Press, 1970.

Friedman, P. G. "The Limits of Consensus: Group Processes for Individual Development." In Gerald M. Phillips and Julia T. Wood, eds., *Emergent Issues in Human Decision Making*, 142–60. Carbondale, Ill.: Southern Illinois University Press, 1984.

Fromm, Erich. *The Art of Loving*. New York: Harper & Row, 1956.

Gaertner, Samuel L., Jeffrey Mann, Audrey Murrell, and John F. Dovidio. "Reducing Intergroup Bias: The Benefits of Recategorization." *Journal of Personality and Social Psychology* 57 (1989), 239–49.

Gandy, Oscar H. "The Political Economy of Communication Competence." In Vincent Mosco and Janet Wasko, eds., *The Political Economy of Information*, 108–124. Madison, Wis.: University of Wisconsin Press, 1988.

Gastil, John. "Generic Pronouns and Sexist Language: The Oxymoronic Character of Masculine Generics." *Sex Roles* 23 (1990), 629–43.

———. "A Definition of Small Group Democracy." *Small Group Research* 23 (1992), 278–301.

———. "Democratic Deliberation: A Redefinition of the Democratic Process and a Study of Staff Meetings at a Co-Operative Workplace." *Masters Abstracts* 30-04M (1992), 1114; University Microfilms No. 1348177.

———. "A Meta-Analytic Review of the Productivity and Satisfaction of Democratic and Autocratic Leadership." *Small Group Research* (in press).

———. "Undemocratic Discourse: A Review of Theory and Research on Political Discourse." *Discourse & Society* 3 (1992), 469–500.

———. "Why We Believe in Democracy: Testing Theories of Attitude Functions and Democracy." *Journal of Applied Social Psychology* 22 (1992), 423–50.

———. "Obstacles to Small Group Democracy." *Small Group Research* 24 (1993), 5–27.

———. "A Definition and Illustration of Democratic Leadership." *Human Relations*, in press.

Gastil, Raymond D. "Varieties of Democracy." Paper presented at the United States Agency for International Development's Perspectives on Democracy Conference, Nepal, India, 1992.

Gero, Anne. "Conflict Avoidance in Consensual Decision Processes." *Small Group Behavior* 16 (1985), 487–99.

Giddens, Anthony. *Central Problems in Social Theory*. Berkeley: University of California Press, 1979.

———. *The Constitution of Society*. Berkeley: University of California Press, 1984.

————. "Jurgen Habermas." In Quentin Skinner, ed., *The Return of Grand Theory in the Human Sciences*, 121–39. Cambridge: Cambridge University Press, 1985.

Giles, Howard, and Richard L. Street. "Communicator Characteristics and Behavior." In Mark L. Knapp and Gerald R. Miller, eds., *Handbook of Interpersonal Communication*, 205–62. Beverly Hills, Calif.: Sage, 1985.

Giles, Howard, and John M. Wiemann. "Language, Social Comparison, and Power." In Charles R. Berger and Steven H. Chaffee, eds., *Handbook of Communication Science*, 350–84. Newbury Park, Calif.: Sage, 1987.

Gleick, James. *Chaos: Making a New Science*, pp. 20–23. New York: Viking, 1987.

Gold, Martin, and Denise S. Yanof. "Mothers, Daughters, and Girlfriends." *Journal of Personality and Social Psychology* 49 (1985), 654–59.

Goldsmith, Edward. "Decentralization." In Andrew Dobson, ed., *The Green Reader: Essays toward a Sustainable Society*, 73–76. San Francisco: Mercury House, 1991.

Goodwyn, Lawrence. "Organizing Democracy: The Limits of Theory and Practice." *democracy* 1 (1981), 25–40.

Gould, Carol. "Private Rights and Public Virtues: Women, the Family, and Democracy." In Carol Gould, ed., *Beyond Domination*, 3–18. Totowa, N.J.: Rowman & Allanheld, 1984.

————. *Rethinking Democracy*. Cambridge: Cambridge University Press, 1988.

Gouran, Dennis S., and Randy Y. Hirokawa. "Counteractive Functions of Communication in Group Decision-Making." In Randy Y. Hirokawa and Marshall Scott Poole, eds., *Communication and Group Decision-Making*, 81–90. Beverly Hills, Calif.: Sage, 1986.

Gradstein, Mark. "Conditions for the Optimality of Simple Majority Decisions in Pairwise Choice Situations." *Theory and Decision* 21 (1986), 181–7.

Graebner, William. "The Small Group in Democratic Social Engineering, 1900–1950." *Journal of Social Issues* 42 (1986), 137–54.

Greenberg, Edward S. *Workplace Democracy: The Political Effects of Participation*. Ithaca, N.Y.: Cornell University Press, 1986.

Greenberg, Polly. "Why Not Academic Preschool (Part 2): Autocracy or Democracy in the Classroom?" *Young Children* (March 1992), 54–64.

————. "Ideas That Work with Young Children." *Young Children* (July 1992), 10–17.

Grice, H. Paul. "Logic and Conversation." In P. Cole and J. L. Morgan, eds., *Syntax and Semantics 3: Speech Acts*, 113–28. New York: Academic Press, 1975.

Gutman, Amy. *Democratic Education*. Princeton, N.J.: Princeton University Press, 1987.

Habermas, Jurgen. *Legitimation Crisis*. Trans. T. A. McCarthy. Boston: Beacon Press, 1975.

———. *Communication and the Evolution of Society*. Trans. T.A. McCarthy. Boston: Beacon Press, 1979.

———. *The Structural Transformation of the Public Sphere: An Inquiry into a Category of Bourgeois Society*. Trans. Thomas Burger with Frederick Lawrence. Cambridge: MIT Press, 1989.

Haiman, Franklyn S. *Group Leadership and Democratic Action*. Boston: Houghton-Mifflin, 1951.

Hartsock, Nancy C. *Money, Sex, and Power*. Boston: Northeastern University Press, 1983.

Havel, Vaclev. "Politics and the World Itself." *Kettering Review* (Summer 1992), 8–13.

Heifetz, Ronald A., and Riley M. Sinder. "Political Leadership: Managing the Public's Problem Solving." In Robert Reich, ed., *The Power of Public Ideas*, 179–203. Cambridge, Mass.: Ballinger, 1987.

Heisenberg, Mark. "A View from the Booth." *Utne Reader* (January/February 1993), 133–4.

Held, David. *Models of Democracy*. Oxford: Polity Press, 1986.

———."The Possibilities of Democracy." *Theory & Society* 20 (1991), 875–89.

———. "Democracy: From City-states to a Cosmopolitan Order." *Political Studies* 40, Special Issue (1992), 10–39.

Heller, Trudy, and Jon van Til. "Leadership and Followership: Some Summary Propositions." *Journal of Applied Behavioral Science* 18 (1982), 405–14.

Henley, Nancy. *Body Politics: Power, Sex, and Nonverbal Communication*. Englewood Cliffs, N.J.: Prentice-Hall, 1977.

Hepburn, Mary A., ed. *Democratic Education in Schools and Classrooms*. Washington, D.C.: National Council for the Social Studies, 1983.

Herman, Edward, and Noam Chomsky. *Manufacturing Consent*. New York: Pantheon, 1988.

Hesse, Hermann. *Siddhartha*. New York: New Directions, 1951.

Hewes, Dean E. "A Socio-Egocentric Model of Group Decision-Making." In Randy Y. Hirokawa and Marshall Scott Poole, eds., *Communication and Group Decision-Making*, 265–91. Beverly Hills, Calif.: Sage, 1986.

Hewes, Dean E., Michael Roloff, Sally Planalp, and David R. Seibold. "Interpersonal Communication Research: What Should We Know?" In Gerald M. Phillips and Julia T. Wood, eds., *Speech Communication: Essays to Commemorate the 75th Anniversary of the Speech Communication Association*, 130–80. Carbondale, Ill.: Southern Illinois University Press, 1990.

Hirokawa, Randy Y. "Does Consensus Really Result in Higher Quality Group Decisions?" In Gerald M. Phillips and Julia T. Wood, eds., *Emergent Issues in Human Decision Making*, 40–49. Carbondale, Ill.: Southern Illinois University Press, 1984.

———. "Group Communication and Decision-Making Performance: A Continued Test of the Functional Perspective." *Human Communication Research* 14 (1988), 487–515.

Hirokawa, Randy Y., and Marshall Scott Poole, eds., *Communication and Group Decision-Making*. Beverly Hills, Calif.: Sage, 1986.

Hirokawa, Randy Y., and Dirk R. Scheerhorn. "Communication in Faulty Group Decision-Making." In Randy Y. Hirokawa and Marshall Scott Poole, eds., *Communication and Group Decision-Making*, 63–80. Beverly Hills, Calif.: Sage, 1986.

Hirschman, Albert O. *Exit, Voice, and Loyalty*. Cambridge, Mass.: Harvard University Press, 1970.

Hoffman, John. *Marxism, Revolution, and Democracy*. Amsterdam: B. R. Gruner Publishing Co., 1983.

Holmes, Emma E. "Democracy in Elementary School Classes." *Social Education* 55 (1991), 176–8.

Huntington, Samuel. "The Democratic Distemper." *Public Interest* 41 (1975), 9–38.

———. *The Third Wave: Democratization in the Late Twentieth Century*. Norman, Okla.: University of Oklahoma Press, 1991.

Huspek, M., and K. E. Kendall. "On Withholding Political Voice: An Analysis of the Political Vocabulary of a 'Non-political' Speech Community." *Quarterly Journal of Speech* 77 (1991), 1–19.

Inkeles, Alex, ed. *On Measuring Democracy*. New Brunswick, N.J.: Transaction Press, 1991.

Iris, Madelyn A. "Threats to Autonomy in Guardianship Decision Making." *Generations* 14 (1990), 39–41.

Iyengar, Shanto. "Framing Responsibility for Political Issues: The Case of Poverty." *Political Behavior* 12 (1990), 19–40.

Janis, Irving L. *Groupthink*. Boston: Houghton Mifflin, 1982.

Jaworski, Adam. "How to Silence a Minority: The Case of Women." *International Journal of the Sociology of Language* 94 (1992), 27–41.

Jensen, Arthur D., and Joseph C. Chilberg. *Small Group Communication.* Belmont, Calif.: Wadsworth, 1991.

Johansen, Robert, Jacques Vallee, and Kathleen Spangler. "Teleconferencing: Electronic Group Meetings." In Robert S. Cathcart and Larry A. Samovar, eds., *Small Group Communication.* 5th ed., 140–54. Dubuque, Iowa: William C. Brown Publishers, 1988.

Johnson, Craig, and Larry Vinson. "'Damned If You Do, Damned If You Don't?': Status, Powerful Speech, and Evaluations of Female Witnesses." *Women's Studies in Communication* 10 (1987), 37–44.

Johnson, M. P., and R. M. Milardo. "Network Interference in Pair Relationships: A Social Psychological Recasting of Slater's Theory of Social Regression." *Journal of Marriage and the Family* 46 (1984), 893–9.

Kaplan, Martin F., and Charles E. Miller. "Group Decision Making and Normative versus Informational Influence: Effects of Type of Issue and Assigned Decision Rule." *Journal of Personality and Social Psychology* 53 (1987), 306–13.

Kelly, L., and C. Begnal. "Group Members' Orientations toward Decision Processes." In Gerald M. Phillips and Julia T. Wood, eds., *Emergent Issues in Human Decision Making,* 63–79. Carbondale, Ill.: Southern Illinois University Press, 1984.

Kerr, Norbert L., Robert S. Atkin, Garold Stasser, David Meek, Robert W. Holt, and James H. Davis. "Guilt Beyond a Reasonable Doubt: Effects of Concept Definition and Assigned Decision Rule on the Judgments of Mock Jurors." *Journal of Personality and Social Psychology* 34 (1976), 282–294.

Kessler, Shirley A. "Alternative Perspectives on Early Childhood Education." *Early Childhood Research Quarterly* 6 (1991), 183–97.

King, Andrew. *Power and Communication.* Prospect Heights, Ill.: Waveland Press, 1987.

Kohn, Alfie. *No Contest.* New York: Houghton Mifflin, 1986.

Kraig, Robert A. "The Hitler Problem in Rhetorical Theory: A Speculative Inquiry." University of Wisconsin-Madison, 1992. Manuscript.

Kramer, Daniel C. *Participatory Democracy: Developing Ideals of the Political Left.* Cambridge, Mass.: Schenkman, 1972.

Krimerman, Len, and Frank Lindenfeld. *When Workers Decide: Workplace Democracy Takes Root in North America.* Philadelphia: New Society Publishers, 1991.

Kruglanski, Arie W., and Donna M. Webster. "Group Members' Reactions to Opinion Deviates and Conformists at Varying Degrees of Proximity to Decision Deadline and of Environmental Noise." *Journal of Personality and Social Psychology* 61 (1991), 212–25.

Kumar, Krishna, ed. *Democracy and Nonviolence.* New Delhi: Gandhi Peace Foundation, 1968.

Kutner, Bernard. "Elements and Problems of Democratic Leadership." In Alvin W. Gouldner, ed., *Studies in Leadership,* 459–67. New York: Harper & Row, 1950.

Labov, Teresa. "Ideological Themes in Reports of Interracial Conflict." In Allen D. Grimshaw, ed., *Conflict Talk,* 139–59. Cambridge: Cambridge University Press, 1990.

Labov, William. "The Logic of Nonstandard English." In F. Williams, ed., *Language and Poverty: Perspectives on a Theme.* Chicago: Markham Publishing, 1970.

Lakey, Berit. *Strategy for a Living Revolution.* New York: Grossman, 1973.

Lakoff, Robin T. "The Logic of Politeness; Or Minding Your p's and q's." In C. Colum et al., eds., *Papers from the Ninth Regional Meeting of the Chicago Linguistic Society,* 292–305. Chicago: Chicago Linguistic Society, 1973.

Lamb, Lynette. "Parallel Worlds." *Utne Reader* (November/December 1992), 111, 113–14.

Lane, Robert. *Political Ideology.* New York: Free Press, 1962.

Lappé, Frances Moore, and Paul Martin DuBois. "Power in a Living Democracy." *Creation Spirituality* (September/October 1992), 23–25, 42.

Lasker, Bruno. *Democracy through Discussion.* New York: H. W. Wilson Co., 1949.

Lee, Judith A. B., ed. *Group Work with the Poor and Oppressed.* New York: Haworth Press, 1989.

Levin, Michael. *The Spectre of Democracy: The Rise of Modern Democracy as Seen by Its Critics.* New York: New York University Press, 1992.

Levine, John M., and Richard L. Moreland. "Progress in Small Group Research." *Annual Review of Psychology* 41 (1990), 585–634.

Lijphart, Arend. *Democracy in Plural Societies: A Comparative Exploration.* New Haven, Conn.: Yale University Press, 1977.

———. *Democracies: Patterns of Majoritarian and Consensus Governments in Twenty-one Countries.* New Haven, Conn.: Yale University Press, 1984.

Lim, Tae-Seop, and John W. Bowers. "Face-work: Solidarity, Approbation, and Tact." *Human Communication Research* 17 (1991), 415–50.

Lipset, Seymour M., Martin Trow, and James Coleman. *Union Democracy.* Garden City, N.Y.: Anchor, 1956.

Littlejohn, Stephen W. *Theories of Human Communication,* 3d ed. Belmont, Calif.: Wadsworth, 1989.

Locke, John. *Two Treatises of Government*. Cambridge: Cambridge University Press, 1960.

Love, James P. "Democratizing the Data Banks: Getting Government Online." *The American Prospect*, no. 9 (1992), 48–50.

Lull, James, and Joseph Cappella. "Slicing the Attitude Pie: A New Approach to Attitude Measurement." *Communication Quarterly* 29 (1981), 67–80.

Lummis, Charles Douglas. "The Radicalism of Democracy." *democracy* 2 (1982), 9–16.

Lyle, Mary Stewart. *Adult Education for Democracy in Family Life*. Ames, Iowa: Iowa State College Press, 1944.

Maccoby, Eleanor E., and Carol N. Jacklin. *The Psychology of Sex Differences*. Stanford, Calif.: Stanford University Press, 1974.

Mackie, Diane M., and Leila T. Worth. "Processing Deficits and the Mediation of Positive Affect in Persuasion." *Journal of Personality and Social Psychology* 57 (1989), 27–40.

MacKinnon, Catharine A. *Toward a Feminist Theory of the State*. Cambridge, Mass.: Harvard University Press, 1989.

MacKuen, Michael, and Courtney Brown. "Political Context and Attitude Change." *American Political Science Review* 81 (1987), 471–90.

Macpherson, C. B. *The Life and Times of Liberal Democracy*. Oxford: Oxford University Press, 1977.

Manin, Bernard. "On Legitimacy and Political Deliberation." Trans. Elly Stein and Jane Mansbridge. *Political Theory* 15 (1987), 338–68.

Mann, Leon, Charlotte Tan, Crisetta MacLeod-Morgan, and Anne Dixon. "Developmental Changes in Application of Majority Rule in Group Decisions." *British Journal of Developmental Psychology* 2 (1984), 275–81.

Mannix, Elizabeth, Leigh L. Thompson, and Max H. Bazerman. "Negotiation in Small Groups." *Journal of Applied Psychology* 74 (1989), 508–17.

Mansbridge, Jane J. "Time, Emotion, and Inequality: Three Problems of Participatory Groups." *Journal of Applied Behavioral Science* 9 (1973), 351–68.

———. *Beyond Adversary Democracy*. Chicago: University of Chicago Press, 1983.

———. Review of *Strong Democracy*, by Benjamin Barber. *American Political Science Review* 81 (1987), 1341–2.

———. *Beyond Self-Interest*. Chicago: University of Chicago Press, 1990.

———. "Feminism and Democracy." *The American Prospect*, no. 2 (1990), 126–39.

———. "A Paradox of Size." In C. George Benello, *From the Ground Up*, 159–76. Boston: South End Press, 1992.

Manz, Charles C., and Henry P. Sims. *Superleadership*. New York: Prentice Hall, 1989.

Marable, Manning. *The Crisis of Color and Democracy: Essays on Race, Class, and Power*. Monroe, Maine: Common Courage Press, 1992.

March, James G. "Preferences, Power, and Democracy." In Ian Shapiro and Grant Reeher, eds., *Power, Inequality, and Democratic Politics*, 50–66. Boulder, Colo.: Westview Press, 1988.

Margolis, Michael. *Viable Democracy*. London: MacMillan Press, 1979.

Mathews, David. *What Is Politics and Who Owns It?* Dayton, Ohio: Kettering Foundation, 1992.

McAfee, Noelle, Robert McKenzie, and David Mathews. *Hard Choices*. Dayton, Ohio: Kettering Foundation, 1991.

McCarthy, T. A. "A Theory of Communicative Competence." *Philosophy of the Social Sciences* 3 (1973), 135–56.

McCroskey, James C., and Virginia P. Richmond. "Communication Apprehension and Small Group Communication." In Robert S. Cathcart and Larry A. Samovar, eds., *Small Group Communication*, 5th ed., 405–20. Dubuque, Iowa: William C. Brown Publishers, 1988.

McLaughlin, Corinne, and Gordon Davidson. *Builders of the Dawn: Community Lifestyles in a Changing World*. Shutesbury, Mass.: Sirius Publishing, 1986.

McKenzie, Robert H. "Learning to Deliberate and Choose." *Public Leadership Education* 4 (1991), 11–12.

Meredith, Cameron W. "Democracy in the Family." *Individual Psychology: The Journal of Adlerian Theory, Research and Practice* 42 (1986), 602–10.

Merelman, Richard M. "The Development of Political Ideology: A Framework for the Analysis of Political Socialization." *American Political Science Review* 63 (1971), 1033–47.

———. *Making Something of Ourselves: On Culture and Politics in the United States*. Berkeley: University of California Press, 1984.

———. *Partial Visions: Culture and Politics in Britain, Canada, and the United States*. Madison: University of Wisconsin Press, 1991.

Michaelsen, Larry K., Warren E. Watson, and Robert H. Black. "A Realistic Test of Individual versus Group Consensus Decision Making." *Journal of Applied Psychology* 74 (1989), 834–9.

Mill, John S. *Utilitarianism and Other Writings*. New York: Meridian, 1962.

Miller, Arthur G. "Historical and Contemporary Perspectives on Stereotyping." In Arthur G. Miller, ed., *In the Eye of the Beholder: Contemporary Issues in Stereotyping*, 1–40. New York: Praeger, 1982.

Miller, Charles E. "Group Decision Making under Majority and Unanimity Decision Rules." *Social Psychology Quarterly* 48 (1985), 51–61.

Miller, David. "Deliberative Democracy and Social Choice." *Political Studies* 40, Special Issue (1992), 54–67.

Miller, Gerald R. "On Being Persuaded: Some Basic Distinctions." In Michael Roloff and Gerald R. Miller, eds., *Persuasion*, 1–28. Beverly Hills, Calif.: Sage, 1980.

———. "Persuasion." In Charles R. Berger and Steven H. Chaffee, eds., *Handbook of Communication Science*, 446–83. Newbury Park, Calif.: Sage, 1987.

Miller, James. *Democracy Is in the Streets: From Port Huron to the Siege of Chicago*. New York: Simon & Schuster, 1987.

Miller, Judi B. "Patterns of Control in Same-sex Conversations: Differences between Women and Men." *Women's Studies in Communication* 8 (1985), 62–69.

Miller, Katherine I., and Peter R. Monge. "Participation, Satisfaction, and Productivity: A Meta-analytic Review." *Academy of Management Journal* 29 (1986), 727–53.

Miller, Nicholas R. "Pluralism and Social Choice." *American Political Science Review* 77 (1983), 734-47.

Monge, Peter R. "The Network Level of Analysis." In Charles R. Berger and Steven H. Chaffee, eds., *Handbook of Communication Science*, 239–70. Newbury Park, Calif.: Sage, 1987.

Morgan, Robin. "Chai Ling Talks with Robin Morgan." *Ms.* (September/October 1990), 12–16.

Morrison, Roy. *We Build the Road as We Travel*. Philadelphia: New Society Publishers, 1991.

Mortensen, C. David. "Communication, Conflict, and Culture." *Communication Theory* 1 (1991), 273–93.

Mulac, Anthony, L. B. Studley, John M. Wiemann, and James J. Bradac. "Male/Female Gaze in Same-sex and Mixed-sex Dyads: Gender-linked Differences in Mutual Influence." *Human Communication Research* 13 (1987), 323–43.

Mulac, Anthony, John M. Weimann, Sally J. Widenmann, and Toni W. Gibson. "Male/Female Language Differences and Effects in Same-sex and Mixed-sex Dyads: The Gender-linked Language Effect." *Communication Monographs* 55 (1988), 315–35.

Mumby, Dennis K. "The Political Function of Narrative in Organizations." *Communication Monographs* 54 (1987), 113–27.

Murchland, Bernard, ed. *Higher Education and the Practice of Democratic Politics: A Political Education Reader.* Dayton, Ohio: Kettering Foundation, 1991.

Nemeth, Charlan. "Interactions Between Jurors as a Function of Majority vs. Unanimity Decision Rules." *Journal of Applied Social Psychology* 7 (1977), 38–56.

Nozick, Robert. *Anarchy, State, and Utopia.* New York: Basic Books, 1974.

Offe, Claus, and Ulrich K. Preuss. "Democratic Institutions and Moral Resources." In David Held, ed., *Political Theory Today,* 143–71. Stanford, Calif.: Stanford University Press, 1991.

Okin, Susan Moller. *Justice, Gender, and the Family.* New York: Basic Books, 1989.

Oliver, Leonard P. *Study Circles.* Washington, D.C.: Seven Locks Press, 1987.

Olson, Mancur. *The Logic of Collective Action.* Cambridge, Mass.: Harvard University Press, 1971.

Orwell, George. "Politics and the English Language." In George Orwell, *The Orwell Reader,* 355–66. New York: Harcourt, Brace, 1956.

Osborn, Michael, and Suzanne Osborn. *Alliance for a Better Public Voice.* Dayton, Ohio: NIF Institute, 1991.

Papworth, John. "The Best Government Comes in Small Packages." *Utne Reader* (January/February 1991), 58–59.

Park, Won-Woo. "A Review of Research on Groupthink." *Journal of Behavioral Decision Making* 3 (1990), 229–45.

Parks, Malcolm R. "Interpersonal Communication and the Quest for Personal Competence." In Mark L. Knapp and Gerald R. Miller, eds., *Handbook of Interpersonal Communication,* 171–201. Beverly Hills, Calif.: Sage, 1985.

Pateman, Carole. *Participation and Democratic Theory.* Cambridge: Cambridge University Press, 1970.

———. "Feminism and Democracy." In Graeme Duncan, ed., *Democratic Theory and Practice,* 204–17. Cambridge: Cambridge University Press, 1983.

———. *The Disorder of Women.* Cambridge: Polity Press, 1989.

———. "Political Obligation, Freedom and Feminism." *American Political Science Review* 86 (1992), 179–82.

Pateman, Trevor. *Language, Truth and Politics.* Nottingham: Russell Press, 1975.

Patton, Michael Q. *Qualitative Evaluation Methods.* Beverly Hills, Calif.: Sage, 1980.

Peters, John D. "Democracy and American Mass Communication Theory: Dewey, Lippman, Lazarsfeld." *Communication* 11 (1989), 199–220.

Phillips, Anne. *Engendering Democracy.* University Park, Pa.: Pennsylvania State University, 1991.

———. "Must Feminists Give Up on Liberal Democracy?" *Political Studies* 40, Special Issue (1992), 68–82.

Piven, Frances Fox, and Richard A. Cloward. *Why Americans Don't Vote.* New York: Pantheon, 1988.

Pitkin, Hanna F., and Sara M. Shumer. "On Participation." *democracy* 2 (1982), 43–54.

Platt, J. "What Can Case Studies Do?" In R. G. Burgess, ed., *Studies in Qualitative Methodology,* Vol. 1, 1–24. Greenwich, Conn.: JAI Press, 1988.

Pollard, Francis E., Beatrice E. Pollard, and Robert S. W. Pollard. *Democracy and the Quaker Method.* London: Ballinsdale, 1949.

Poole, Marshall Scott, Robert D. McPhee, and David R. Siebold. "Group Decision Making as a Structurational Process." *Quarterly Journal of Speech* 71 (1985), 74–102.

Pope, Sandy, and Joel Rogers. "Out with the Old Politics, in with the New Party." *The Nation,* no. 255 (1992), 102–5.

Poston, Richard W. *Democracy Is You: A Guide to Citizen Action.* New York: Harper & Bros., 1953.

Protess, David, and Maxwell McCombs, eds., *Agenda Setting: Readings on Media, Public Opinion, and Policymaking.* Hillsdale, N.J.: Lawrence Erlbaum Associates, 1992.

Raboy, Marc, and Peter A. Bruck, eds., *Communication for and Against Democracy.* New York: Black Rose Books, 1989.

Radcliff, Benjamin. "Majority Rule and Impossibility Theorems." *Social Science Quarterly* 73 (1992), 511–22.

Rae, Douglas W. "The Limits of Consensual Decision." *American Political Science Review* 69 (1975), 1270–94.

———. "Knowing Power: A Working Paper." In Ian Shapiro and Grant Reeher, eds., *Power, Inequality, and Democratic Politics,* 17–49. Boulder, Colo.: Westview Press, 1988.

Rawlins, W. K. "Consensus in Decision-Making Groups: A Conceptual History." In Gerald M. Phillips and Julia T. Wood, eds., *Emergent Issues in Human Decision Making,* 19–39. Carbondale, Ill.: Southern Illinois University Press, 1984.

Rawls, John. *A Theory of Justice.* Cambridge, Mass.: Harvard University Press, 1971.

Reich, Robert B. *The Power of Public Ideas*. Cambridge, Mass.: Ballinger, 1988.

Robert, Henry M. *Robert's Rules of Order Newly Revised*. Glenview, Ill.: Scott, Foresman, 1990.

Robinson, Kim S. *The Wild Shore*. New York: Ace Science Fiction Books, 1984.

———. *Pacific Edge*. New York: Tom Doherty Associates, 1990.

Rogers-Millar, L. Edna, and Frank E. Millar. "Domineeringness and Dominance: A Transactional View." *Human Communication Research* 5 (1979), 238–46.

Roseman, Ira, Robert P. Abelson, and Michael F. Ewing. "Emotion and Political Cognition: Emotional Appeals in Political Communication." In Richard R. Lau and David O. Sears, eds., *Political Cognition*, 279–94. Hillsdale, N.J.: Lawrence Erlbaum, 1986.

Rosenberg, Shawn W., Dana Ward, and Stephen Chilton. *Political Reasoning and Cognition*. Durham, N.C.: Duke University Press, 1988.

Rossel, Robert D. "Word Play: Metaphor and Humor in the Small Group." *Small Group Behavior* 12 (1981), 116–36.

Rothschild-Whitt, Joyce. "Conditions for Democracy: Making Participatory Organizations Work." In John Case and Rosemary C. R. Taylor, eds., *Co-ops, Communes, and Collectives: Experiments in Social Change in the 1960s and 1970s*, 215–44. New York: Pantheon Books, 1979.

Rousseau, Jean Jacques. *The Social Contract and Discourses*. New York: E. P. Dutton, 1950.

Rucinski, Dianne E. "The Centrality of Reciprocity to Communication and Democracy." *Critical Studies in Mass Communication* 8 (1991), 184–94.

Ryn, Claes G. *Democracy and the Ethical Life: A Philosophy of Politics and Community*, 2d ed. Washington, D.C.: Catholic University of America Press, 1990.

Sale, Kirkpatrick. *Human Scale*. New York: G. P. Putnam's Sons, 1980.

———. *Dwellers in the Land: The Bioregional Vision*. San Francisco: Sierra Club Books, 1985.

Sandel, Michael J., ed. *Liberalism and Its Critics*. New York: New York University Press, 1984.

Sanders, Lynn M. "Against Deliberation." Paper presented at the annual meeting of the Midwest Political Science Association, Chicago, Ill., April 1991.

Sapiro, Virginia. "The Women's Movement and the Creation of Gender Consciousness: Social Movements as Socialization Agents." In Orit

Ichilov, ed., *Political Socialization, Citizenship Education, and Democracy*, 266–80. New York: Teachers College, 1990.

Sashkin, Marshall. "Participative Management Is an Ethical Imperative." *Organizational Dynamics* 12, no. 4 (1984), 5–22.

Schmid, Carol L. *Conflict and Consensus in Switzerland.* Berkeley: University of California Press, 1981.

Schneider, David J. "Social Cognition." *Annual Review of Psychology* 42 (1991), 527–61.

Schudson, Michael. "The Limits of Teledemocracy." *The American Prospect*, no. 11 (1992), 41–45.

Schwartz, Barry. *The Battle for Human Nature.* New York: W. W. Norton, 1986.

Schwartzman, Helen. *The Meeting: Gatherings in Organizations and Communities.* New York: Plenum, 1989.

Scott, James C. *Domination and the Arts of Resistance: Hidden Transcripts.* New Haven, Conn.: Yale University Press, 1990.

Scott, Robert L. "Rhetoric and Silence." *Western Speech* 36 (1972), 146–58.

Seibert, Scott, and Leopold Gruenfeld. "Masculinity, Femininity, and Behavior in Groups." *Small Group Research* 23 (1992), 95–112.

Sheeran, Michael J. *Beyond Majority Rule.* Philadelphia: Philadelphia Yearly Meeting, 1983.

Simmons, A. John. *Moral Principles and Political Obligations.* Princeton, N.J.: Princeton University Press, 1979.

Simmons, John, and William Mares. *Working Together.* New York: Alfred A. Knopf, 1983.

Skinner, Quentin. "The Empirical Theorists of Democracy and Their Critics: A Plague on Both Their Houses." *Political Theory* 1 (1973), 287–306.

Slater, Philip, and Warren G. Bennis. "Democracy Is Inevitable." *Harvard Business Review* 68, no. 5 (1990), 167–76.

Smith, Kenwyn K., and David N. Berg. "A Paradoxical Conception of Group Dynamics." *Human Relations* 40 (1987), 633–58.

Smith-Lovin, Lynn, and Charles Brody. "Interruptions in Group Discussions: The Effects of Gender and Group Composition." *American Sociological Review* 54 (1989), 424–35.

Starhawk. *Truth or Dare.* New York: Harper & Row, 1986.

Stasser, Garold, and William Titus. "Pooling of Unshared Information in Group Decision Making: Biased Information Sampling During Discussion." *Journal of Personality and Social Psychology* 48 (1985), 1467–78.

Steinem, Gloria. *Revolution from Within.* Boston: Little, Brown, 1992.

Stephen, Timothy D., and Teresa M. Harrison. "Gender, Sex-Role Identity, and Communication Style: A Q-sort Analysis of Behavioral Differences." *Communication Research Reports* 2 (1985), 53–61.

Straffin, Philip D., Jr. "Majority Rule and General Decision Rules." *Theory and Decision* 8 (1977), 351–60.

Strauss, George. "Worker Participation in Management: An International Perspective." *Research in Organizational Behavior* 4 (1982), 173–265.

Sturgis, Alice. *Standard Code of Parliamentary Procedure*, 3d ed. New York: McGraw-Hill, 1988.

Sundancer, Elaine. *Celery Wine: The Story of a Country Commune*. Yellow Springs, Ohio: Community Publications Cooperative, 1973.

Tannen, Deborah. *You Just Don't Understand*. New York: Ballantine, 1990.

Thompson, Leigh L., Elizabeth Mannix, and Max H. Bazerman. "Group Negotiation: Effects of Decision Rule, Agenda, and Aspiration." *Journal of Personality and Social Psychology* 54 (1988), 86–95.

Tjosvold, Dean, and Richard H. G. Field. "Effects of Social Context on Consensus and Majority Vote Decision Making." *Academy of Management Journal* 26 (1983), 500–506.

Toffler, Alvin. *The Third Wave*. New York: William Morrow, 1980.

Toqueville, Alexis de. *Democracy in America*. Phillips Bradley, ed. New York: Vintage, 1969.

Ueland, Brenda. "Tell Me More: On the Fine Art of Listening." *Utne Reader* (November/December 1992), 104–9.

van Dijk, Teun A. "Structures of Discourse and Structures of Power." In J. A. Anderson, ed., *Communication Yearbook* 12, 18–59. Newbury Park, Calif.: Sage, 1989.

Vangelisti, Anita L., Mark L. Knapp, and John A. Daly. "Conversational Narcissism." *Communication Monographs* 57 (1990), 251–74.

Verba, Sidney. *Small Groups and Political Behavior*. Princeton, N.J.: Princeton University Press, 1961.

Verba, Sidney, and Gary R. Orren. *Equality in America*. Cambridge, Mass.: Harvard University Press, 1985.

Vroom, Victor H., and Arthur G. Jago. *The New Leadership*. Englewood Cliffs, N.J.: Prentice Hall, 1988.

Walzer, Michael. *Radical Principles: Reflections of an Unreconstructed Democrat*. New York: Basic Books, 1980.

———. *Spheres of Justice: A Defense of Pluralism and Equality*. New York: Basic Books, 1983.

Warren, Mark. "Democratic Theory and Self-Transformation." *American Political Science Review* 86 (1992), 8–23.

Watson, Warren, Larry K. Michaelsen, and Walt Sharp. "Member Competence, Group Interaction, and Group Decision Making: A Longitudinal Study." *Journal of Applied Psychology* 76 (1991), 803–9.

Watzlawick, Paul, Janet Beavin, and Don Jackson. *Pragmatics of Human Communication: A Study of Interactional Patterns, Pathologies, and Paradoxes*. New York: Norton, 1967.

Whyte, William F., and Kathleen K. Whyte. *Making Mondragon: The Growth and Dynamics of the Worker Cooperative Complex*. Ithaca, N.Y.: ILR Press, 1988.

Wilson, John. *On the Boundaries of Conversation*. Oxford: Permagon Press, 1989.

———. *Politically Speaking*. Cambridge, Mass.: Basil Blackwell, 1990.

Wiseman, John A. *Democracy in Black Africa: Survival and Renewal*. New York: Paragon House, 1990.

Wodak, Ruth. "1968: The Power of Political Jargon—A 'Club-2' Discussion." In Ruth Wodak, ed., *Language, Power, and Ideology*, 137–63. Amsterdam: John Benjamins, 1989.

Wolin, Sheldon S. "What Revolutionary Action Means Today." *democracy* 2 (1982), 17–28.

Wood, Julia T. "Alternative Methods of Group Decision Making." In Robert S. Cathcart and Larry A. Samovar, eds., *Small Group Communication*, 5th ed., 185–91. Dubuque, Iowa: William C. Brown Publishers, 1988.

Woodcock, George. "Direct Democracy Thrives in Switzerland." *Utne Reader* (January/February 1991), 54.

Xenos, Nicholas. "Democracy as Method: Joseph A. Schumpeter." *democracy* 1 (1981), 110–23.

Yankelovich, Daniel. *Coming to Public Judgment*. New York: Syracuse University Press, 1991.

Yin, Robert K. *Case Study Research*. Beverly Hills, Calif.: Sage, 1989.

INDEX